SPADA
AN ANTHOLOGY OF SWORDSMANSHIP
IN MEMORY OF EWART OAKESHOTT

Chivalry Bookshelf

SPADA
ANTHOLOGY OF SWORDSMANSHIP
IN MEMORY OF EWART OAKESHOTT

Authors
Clements, John (1965-)
Hand, Stephen (1964-)
Hick, Steve (1949-)
Martinez, Ramon
Mele, Gregory (1970-)
Mitchell, Russel (1971-)
Oakeshott, Ewart (1916-2002)
Price, Brian R. (1964-)
Wagner, Paul (1967-)
Wilson, William E. (1956-)

Published in the United States by
The Chivalry Bookshelf
Union City, California, 94587
tel. 866.268.1495 (US)
fax 978.418.4774
http://www.chivalrybookshelf.com

Chivalry Bookshelf

SPADA

CONTENTS

THIS ANTHOLOGY IS DEDICATED TO

EWART OAKESHOTT
(1916-2002)

Whose work in this field has inspired
countless enthusiasts, scholars, reenactors
and whose character clearly marks him
as a chivalric exemplar

FROM THE EDITOR

Stephen Hand

When I took over the editorship of SPADA one of the things that gave me great joy as well as great trepidation was the knowledge that I would be editing a submission from Ewart Oakeshott. For several decades Ewart Oakeshott has stood alone as the world's foremost expert on medieval swords. At the tender age of 14, I bought a copy of *The Sword in the Age of Chivalry*. It sits in a proud place on my bookshelf, black thumbed pages testimony to the swords I made while consulting it. If not for Ewart Oakeshott I would know a lot less about swords and I might not be here.

In the course of working on SPADA I had to phone Ewart and talk to him about his article. I only spoke to him once, but those few minutes confirmed the mental picture I had built over twenty five years of reading his books. It was a picture of a kind, peaceful man, a scholar and a gentleman. I value that short time I spent with Ewart, even when he stopped me in mid sentence and said "I'm very old and very deaf and you'll have to shout". Far from diminishing the man, it made him more human. It somehow made his achievements the greater for being the work of a man, not of some mythical creature possessed of superhuman powers.

Ewart Oakeshott possessed no superhuman powers. He died on Monday, September 30th 2002.

Ewart Oakeshott was an icon. It is hard when an icon dies. Ewart Oakeshott represented more than just a man, although that is what he was. People have referred to him as a father, as a mentor, as a shining light. He was all these things. The loss of Ewart Oakeshott lessens us all, because his presence made us all greater. But all that was Ewart Oakeshott is not gone. His writings remain, including perhaps his last work. *Studying Arms within the Wider Circumference of History: a Personal Approach* was already the lead article in SPADA. It is a whimsical piece, dealing not with facts and figures, treatises and techniques, but with the sword as a powerful and enduring symbol in western culture and literature. Just as most of the papers in SPADA deal with the inhuman side of the sword, its use as a utilitarian instrument of killing, so Ewart's article deals with the human side of the sword, as a symbol of just power. How ironic, to be reminded of our humanity by a man sadly no longer with us.

The other thing that remains of Ewart Oakeshott is his example to us all, an example of scholarly and gentlemanly behaviour.

"And thou so much distinguished, he was wise
And in his bearing modest as a maid.
He never yet a boorish thing had said
In all his life to any, come what might;
He was a true, a perfect gentle-knight"

Goodbye Ewart, the community will miss you.

From the community's loss, let us return to this volume, which I sincerely hope will be viewed as being to the community's gain. When SPADA was announced in Houston in May 2000, who'd have thought we would wait two years for the first issue? The journal has had a bumpy beginning, but I'm confident that the final product has been worth the wait.

The first editor of SPADA was SSI Associate Director J. Mark Bertrand. Within months of SPADA's announcement, Mr. Bertrand's academic and professional commitments made it impossible for him to spearhead the project, and the torch passed to SSI's Director Greg Mele. Greg's accident in late 2000 cost us six months (it cost Greg considerably more) as the rest of us involved with SPADA dithered about, not knowing how to proceed or even whether to do so in Greg's absence. Eventually, when Greg was well enough to do business, the mantle of editor was passed to me. Then we began the slow process of writing papers and having them peer reviewed.

From the beginning SPADA was intended to showcase the very best research that this talented community could offer. The process of achieving that involves peer review, with hard questions being asked and sometimes research being rejected. In every case, what were, by and large, excellent papers to begin with, were vastly improved by being read (and periodically savaged) by knowledgeable people in the community. Not all of the submissions survived the process. It's not nice, but I don't think that anyone reading the papers that were included could possibly doubt that peer review has resulted in research of a professional standard.

One thing that struck me as I read each submission is the tremendous leap in research quality made by this community in such a short time. Papers that would have been cutting edge in 1999 are barely adequate in 2002. This improvement in research skill is a credit to each and every student and scholar of historical swordsmanship who strives for that snippet of knowledge that will increase their understanding of Fiore or Talhoffer or Capo Ferro. Everyone in this community feeds off each other. People feed off each other's ideas, their enthusiasm, new revelations and considered rejections of old ideas. Not one paper in this volume could have been written without consultation with others in the community,which is entirely as it should be.

One of the more controversial decisions I made as editor was to allow each author to use his own national version of English in his paper. With so many different languages being quoted, including English from several different centuries, it seemed wrong to enforce one of the various national spellings. (I will also admit to a personal reason for doing this. I'm constitutionally incapable of spelling the word defence -from which we derive fencing- with an s.)

Having spoken of the delays, let me give credit to the fine people without whom SPADA would have not been possible. First and foremost are the fantastic peer review team of Steve Hick and Maestro Ramon Martinez. Each of the papers in SPADA was initially reviewed by either myself, Steve or the Maestro. If we considered the paper to be suitable then we recruited other reviewers to give their own thoughts.

Steve Hick is in many ways the grandfather of historical fencing, because it was his on-line transcription of George Silver that first attracted many of us to the historical fencing manuals. Steve is still the source of more information about the whereabouts of more texts than anyone I know. Not only does he look like Santa, but periodically he brings the community a present of a new treatise. Steve reviewed more papers than anyone else working on SPADA and always offered constructive and useful criticism. When we think of the historical fencing *community*, nobody epitomizes it more than Steve Hick.

Maestro Ramon Martinez makes the most difficult fencing manoeuvres seem effortless, and is justly famous for his reconstruction of *La Destreza*, the Spanish style of rapier fencing. Less well known are Maestro Martinez's extraordinary attention to detail in research, and his meticulous wording of anything he writes. Maestro Martinez is also part of an extraordinary team with his immensely talented wife, Maestro Jeannette Acosta-Martinez. When I sent a paper to the Martinez's, I invariably received two reviews back, both with insightful comments.

Steve, Ramon and I sent the papers that we had reviewed out to secondary reviewers who again generously gave of their time and expertise to comment, and often to help rewrite these papers. Those not already mentioned were (in alphabetical order), Sydney Anglo, Jörg Bellinghausen, Terry Brown, Stefan Dieke, John Dodd, Valerie Eads, Matt Easton, David Edge, Sean Hayes, Ian Johnson, Pete Kautz , Tom Leoni, Rob Lovett, Andrea Lupo Sinclair, Greg Mele, Russ Mitchell, Mark Rector, Wayne Robinson, Roger Siggs, Ray Smith, Chris Thompson, Milo Thurston, Christian Tobler and William Wilson.

Special mention goes to the unfailing generosity of members of the young Western Martial Arts community to the authors of the papers in SPADA. Those who wrote papers on general subjects know that these would have been impossible without the assistance of specialists on particular masters who generously provided translations, examples of techniques and explanations of peculiar aspects of their speciality.

Finally Brian and Ann Price and the rest of the team at Chivalry Bookshelf are to be congratulated for the superb job they've done with layout and printing.

SPADA includes more than just papers. There are reports on the major conferences held since the formation of SSI, a report on the Capo Ferro translation project, an SSI sponsored translation of one of the key fencing treatises on that most popular weapon, the rapier and a report on the SSI itself.

The papers are loosely arranged in chronological order and with more general papers followed by more specific ones. Therefore SPADA begins with a general paper about medieval parrying and ends with a specific one about 18th century Highland swordsmanship.

It is my opinion that SPADA represents the finest collection of research on the history of swordsmanship ever done. I believe that there are papers which will interest every historical fencing enthusiast, whatever his area of specialty. It has been my immense privilege to work with the other authors. I sincerely hope that some of our thrill of discovery rubs off on you and that we manage to make you just a little bit more enthusiastic about the amazing systems of personal combat practiced by our ancestors.

Stephen Hand
Sydney, Australia
October 2002

FROM THE DIRECTOR
Gregory Mele

As the Director of Swordplay Symposium International (SSI), it is my particular pleasure to see this first volume of *SPADA* come to fruition. The quest to bring *SPADA* to print largely mirrors the history of SSI itself.

The 1990s saw a rapid growth of interest in the survival and revival of historical European martial arts. One of the earliest (and best) resources for these martial artists and researchers was *Hammerterz Forum*, a short, quarterly print journal published by J. Christoph Amberger. Much of the first serious research into European martial arts to be published in English since the late Victorian era appeared in the *Forum*, and many of the figures responsible for the current "Renaissance" of interest in the Western traditions first became acquainted with each other through its pages.

By 1999 *Hammerterz Forum*'s publication schedule had become erratic, at nearly the same time that attention to its subject matter had begun to accelerate. I felt that there was a suitable interest for an annual journal dedicated to the serious study of historical European swordsmanship (basically, the 13th – 19th centuries). The latter I defined by borrowing openly and enthusiastically from Carl Thimm's *A Complete Bibliography of Fencing & Dueling* (1886):

> The subject of Fence embraces all works relating to the art of offence and defence with all weapons held in the hands, for the science of arms should include the use of all non-ballistic weapons, from foil to bayonet, and from dagger to battleaxe (p. x)

I approached a number of my colleagues: Mark Bertrand, Jörg Bellinghausen, John Clements, David Cvet, Stephen Hick, and Mark Rector, and proposed the idea of developing just such a journal – *SPADA*. The response was extremely positive, but Mark Bertrand had his own announcement. He had been thinking of developing an association comprised of the principal western martial artists, academic researchers, swordsmiths and armourers, where they could meet to exchange ideas, knowledge and resources, with the ultimate goal of developing and supporting the fledgling "Western Martial Arts" community. After some

further discussion, we decided to merge the two ideas, with *SPADA* becoming the official journal for the new *Swordplay Symposium International*. In addition to the publication of *SPADA*, SSI would serve as a common meeting ground for academics, artisans, and practitioners interested in the research and revival of historical European swordsmanship. To help facilitate this, SSI would conduct a bi-annual Symposium in which members and guests might present papers, give demonstrations, and share insights, discoveries, theories and information amongst colleagues and fellows in a spirit of friendship and respect.

I took the role of director, with Mark Bertrand and Mark Rector serving as my Associate Directors. We invited Terry Brown to be the Associate Director for Europe. Invitations were issued to prospective advisors, and the organization slowly took shape. Once it was clear that SSI was a go, we began planning our first actual Symposium, which the Historical Armed Combat Association hosted in May 2000.

With our first symposium an unqualified success, we turned our attention to SSI's next project, the publication of *SPADA*. It was clear that I could not head the organization and successfully serve as the journal's editor, so with a heavy heart I turned editorial duties over to Mark Bertrand. Mark issued a call for papers, and began making production and distribution plans for what we hoped would be a 90-page journal. All seemed to be on track…

In September of 2000 I suffered a severe fall that hospitalized me for just under three months, and left me in intensive physical rehabilitation for over an additional year. While I was recuperating, Mr. Bertrand's own combination of academic, professional and personal commitments first made his role as *SPADA*'s editor, and ultimately his entire roll in the organization, impossible. Having one of the founders of such a young organization sidelined was bad; having two unable to actively continue was catastrophic. The entire organization, let alone the journal, ground abruptly to a halt.

Then in Spring of 2001, three of SSI's advisors, Stephen Hand, Steve Hick, and Ramon Martinez decided to press on with the journal; Mr. Hand reissued the call for papers, and began establishing a process of peer review. Since *SPADA* was clearly going to be at least six to nine months late, the decision was made that, if enough high-quality submissions were made, the journal's size should increase to 120 pages. As the papers began to file in, the quality proved to be first rate, but as such they were also both long and heavily illustrated. Our contributors were over achievers, and while this could only help the quality of the final project, we had several new challenges, principle of which was the increased costs associated with the larger size and graphic-heavy content. The journal had outgrown its budget. Spring became summer and summer slipped into fall…

Since the project had grown beyond anyone's expectations, a single, managing editor was again needed, and Stephen Hand formally took on this role. By this point I had recuperated to the point of being able to again focus some attention on the organization, and while he saw that each article went through peer review (and to my growing horror, accepted *more* submissions), I sought ways to finance *SPADA* without reducing the quality or content we had agreed upon. Fall became winter, and winter bloomed into spring…

The problem was at last solved that summer when *Chivalry Bookshelf* agreed to act as *SPADA's* publisher, and the decision was made to let the journal become a book-sized anthology. We had now answered all of our critical challenges in terms of size, production quality, cost and distribution.

Meanwhile, much has changed and grown in the nearly three years since SSI first convened. At the time SSI was created, there were no major events in the Western Martial Arts community. There are now three annual workshops in the United States, each drawing an international attendance, an annual Australian gathering, and several pan-European events. Where there were only a handful of organizations spread out through North America and the UK, with a scattering of other salles and academies in Italy and Australia, this list has now grown both within those nations and without, including France, Germany, Poland and Sweden. Where there were no more than three titles on the history and/or practice of historical European swordsmanship in May of 2000, there are now at least nine more, including translations and reprints of key 15th – 18th century texts, with more to come.

Despite these sweeping changes, I feel that the need and basic format for SSI remains sound: a place to present papers, new interpretations, to give demonstrations and advance the growth of the community in an open environment. SSI's advisors and Directors have been at the forefront of those developments, authoring the vast majority of these new printed titles, as well as three different videos to their credit, and with more work on the way. The organization remains a web presence at www.swordplaysympsoium.org and will continue to develop this site as a gateway to exploring the Western martial tradition. As of this writing, planning is also underway for the next Symposium, which will be held in Europe in 2003.

First and foremost, however, our organization is an academic one, and the journal sits at the heart of that aspect of our mission. Nearly four years after I first conceived of the idea, having gone through three different formats, multiple editors and a seemingly limitless series of challenges, *SPADA* has come to fruition, and at two and a half its originally projected size brings together over twelve articles and nine authors from around the world to create an anthology unlike anything that has gone before. Credit for all of this is due first and foremost to the anthology's editor, Stephen Hand, who tirelessly labored to see this project through, secondly to Steve Hick and Ramon Martinez, who helped keep this project alive in those early months after my injury, and who have acted as proof-readers and peer-reviewers on much of its contents. Finally, to SSI's advisors, who remained resolutely supportive of not only this project, but of SSI and its goals throughout the long hiatus.

Meanwhile, Mr. Hand informs me that he has already received the first five articles for **SPADA** II…

Gregory D. Mele
Director
Swordplay Symposium International

WMA COMMUNITY EVENTS

2000 - 2002

Swordplay Symposium International 2000

By J. Mark Bertrand, Gregory Mele, Brian Price, and Mark Rector

Opening Remarks

Greg Mele opened the conference with a short statement outlining his hope for the weekend that SSI Members and Advisors representing different approaches to the study of European swordsmanship would be able to come together successfully to trade insights and experiences, build bridges and establish friendships, and that everybody in attendance would be enriched in the process. The full text of the opening remarks appears in Appendix A. John Clements followed Mr. Mele with a brief statement welcoming the attendees. He read messages of support for the Symposium from esteemed sword historian and SSI Advisor Ewart Oakshott; David Edge, Curator of the Wallace Collection, London; and John Waller and Keith Ducklin of the Royal Armouries in Leeds, UK. The inaugural conference of Swordplay Symposium International was held over Memorial Day weekend, May 27, 28, 29, 2000, at the Clarion Inn Hotel, Houston, Texas. The event was organized by the SSI Directors in conjunction with the Historical Armed Combat Association (HACA), and most of the key logistical work was coordinated by Christian and Natasha Darcé of Purpleheart Armoury.

SSI Director Greg Mele and Associate Directors J. Mark Bertrand and Mark Rector were joined by the following SSI Advisors: John Clements (HACA Director, Houston, TX), David Cvet (Academy of European Medieval Martial Arts, Toronto, Ontario), Stephen Hand (Stoccata School of Defence, Sydney, Australia), Steve Hick (Falls Church, VA), Maestro Paul Macdonald (Dawn Duelist Society, Macdonald Armouries, Edinburgh, Scotland), Maestro Ramon Martinez (Martinez Academy of Arms, New York, NY), Brian Price (Schola St. George, Union City, CA), Hank Reinhardt (HACA founder, Conyers, GA), and Maestro Andrea Lupo Sinclair (FISAS, Milan, Italy); who supported the event by preparing workshops, practicums, demonstrations, sparring sessions and lectures. In addition, 36 students of the sword from a variety of martial arts, historical reenactment, or theatrical combat backgrounds attended as participants.

The Symposium was designed to be both scholastic and practical, formal and interactive. Many of the attendees have commented favorably on the mix of historical, philosophical and practical material, the high quality of the instruction and presentations, and the interaction between Advisors, vendors, scholars and students.

DAY ONE
Keynote Address

J. Mark Bertrand delivered the keynote address by SSI Advisor Dr. Sydney Anglo, the leading academic scholar in the field of European Martial Arts. Mr. Bertrand read an excerpt from chapter four of Dr. Anglo's forthcoming book, The Martial Arts of Renaissance Europe (Yale University Press, 2000). The excerpt focused on the task of la communicativa, the manner in which Renaissance masters of defense attempted to communicate their practice on the printed page — an appropriate subject, considering the various approaches to interpreting these writings on display at SSI 2000.

Schwerteniemen & Entering Techniques
John Clements, HACA/SSI

Mr. Clements presented a fascinating demonstration of entering techniques designed for use with the longsword, taken mostly from dei Liberi and Talhoffer. Schwerteniemen (literally "sword taking") are highly sophisticated binds and disarms, derived from the Ringkunst, or unarmed grappling arts, of the medieval masters-at-arms.

Sidesword to Rapier
Maestro Andrea Lupo Sinclair, FISAS/SSI

Despite the delay of the arrival of his weapons from London, Maestro Andrea Lupo Sinclair conducted a superb class in the development of fencing with the sidesword, or spada di lato, the precursor of the rapier and the weapon actually described in the treatises of Marozzo, di Grassi and Saviolo. Maestro Lupo Sinclair led the class through the basics of the proper stance and hand positions, emphasizing the importance of moving the feet in concert with the sword and the use of contracting and expanding motions of the body. The Maestro explored the ideas of fluid, circular movements, the eight lines of attack and defense, and taught that voids must be made at right angles to the line of attack. The class continued with drills for various thrusts, parries, disarms and false edge, or falso filo attacks. A few words of wisdom from the Maestro: "Always attack ready to parry; always parry ready to attack." "Never enter your opponent's distance unless you know how to get out." "Strike your blows with the body, not just the arm." It was a highlight of the Symposium to receive instruction in the historical Italian methods of the side sword in the accents of the peninsula from such an accomplished, charming and thoughtful Maestro di armi.

Dom Duarte's Regementio
Steve Hick, SSI

Critics of the medieval masters have always questioned the provenance of their work. How widespread where their teachings? Do they reflect the art as practiced by knights and professional warriors, or merely the athletic pursuits of urban guildsmen and early bourgeois duelists? In an effort to answer these questions, Steve Hick spent 12 years searching for the Regementio para aprender a jogar as armas of Dom Duarte, "The Eloquent", the 11th King of Portugal (1433-1438). Dom Duarte was the son of D. João I, King of Portugal; grandson of John of Gaunt; great-grandson of King Edward III of England; cousin to King Henry IV of England; and related through marriage to the ruling houses of Burgundy and Aragon. Prior to and during his reign, Dom Duarte produced many articles and writs in which he attempted to convey his knowledge and insights to his subjects in the many areas his interests led him, including training in the martial arts. Mr. Hick covered the general details of his 12 year quest for Duarte's fencing treatise, including searches through 19 th Century bibliographies, explorations of American and Portuguese libraries, and conferences with Portuguese government officials. In the end, the manuscript was found in plain sight, and proved to be a total of only 15 fifteen lines long! However, the Regementio, when taken alongside Duarte's notes on fighting from horseback in his Bem Cavalgar, still offers important insights into the training of knightly combatants in the 15th Century, including:

· Training with wooden and blunted weapons
· Cross training
· The same identification of 8 angles of attack found in German and Italian sources
· The use of Italian loan words, suggesting a cross-pollination of ideas and methodologies through out the Mediterranean

The first issue of SPADA will feature an expanded edition of Mr. Hick's paper, including the full translation of the Regementio para aprender a jogar as armas.

"What Happens When They're Sharp?" Test Cutting Demo
Hank Reinhardt, SSI

Following the lunch break, Hank Reinhardt and Mr. Clements demonstrated the devastating effects of cutting weapons, using cardboard tubes (which are similar to the sheaves of bamboo used by Asian martial artists for cutting practice), riveted mail, a phonebook and a Windlass Steelcrafts replica of a 15th Century barbute. The mail and plate held up exceedingly well, highlighting the effectiveness of armour. The other materials, however, were subjected to a devastating series of slices and cuts. Observers remarked upon the ease with which Mr. Reinhardt approached cutting. It seemed an almost effortless act with him. When he invited participants to have a try, however, they discovered just how difficult cutting correctly with a sword could be.

Other than the obvious fun to be had in cutting things apart with sharp swords, the session graphically demonstrated the effects of cutting blades on armour and flesh, and emphasized that cutting practice could be used to help validate technique..

Practical Saviolo
Stephen Hand, Stoccata School of Defence/SSI

Stephen Hand is the world's foremost expert on the teachings of Vincentio Saviolo, and has devoted much of the past several years in interpreting Saviolo's treatise, His Practice, 1595, the first rapier fencing book written in English. Mr. Hand led an exciting hands-on class that examined and clarified Saviolo's techniques. Working step-by-step, the participants were allowed to experience at first hand the deadly efficacy of more than a dozen actions from this 16th Century Italian master. In addition, Mr. Hand led the class through the basic stances and hand positions; explained and demonstrated the paramount importance of footwork to Saviolo's method; and demonstrated the concepts of cavatione, sincture, and counter-attacks in stesso tempo.

International Competition Initiatives
Brian Price, Schola St. George/International Medieval Alliance/SSI

Until recently, most competitive medieval-based swordsmanship has been in the hands of the reenactment and living history community, who have a variety of objectives, and employ varying degrees of realism. With the growth of an international community studying the historical fencing treatises, the interest in competition and tournaments is a foregone conclusion. Focusing on pre-16th Century swordsmanship, Brian Price delivered a paper entitled Tournament Formats & Combat Systems: Internationalization in Medieval Martial Arts, which attempted to present an overview of the entire community of swordsmanship practitioners and tournament sponsors. Mr. Price compared martial artists to Chaucerian characters – people from different backgrounds, employing different methods, pursuing different paths. However, underlying everything they do is a strong sense of fraternity and universally valid truths.

In this paper, Mr. Price categorized the organizations interested in historical swordsmanship, and briefly analyzed their methods, purposes and goals:

Living History – concerned with historical correctness and "living archaeology". Groups are small and insular; research is focused.
Combat Societies – focused on fighting; many have lower standards of authenticity and attract people who join simply for recreation.
Tournament/Knightly – focused on reenactment and combat; go for the glory of feats of arms.
Scholars – focused on the role of combat as it is rooted in cultural and social history.
Historical Fencing Schools and traditional fencing

salles – focused on authentic martial arts, weapons and study methods. These schools usually have one leader, and use historical treatises to reconstruct the art of medieval and Renaissance combat. Some traditional salles have a living tradition to early modern swordsmanship, and use this connection as the basis for their own reconstruction of earlier styles.

Mr. Price also analyzed extant combat systems used by these organizations, and proposed next step directions for those who were interested in the establishment of an international tournament circuit for medieval martial arts. The new AEMMA combat system and tournament format, to be used at the 2nd Annual Western Martial Arts Workshop in Toronto in October, 2000, was particularly highlighted. Mr. Price also presented a pre-release version of the rules proposals he was making to the International Medieval Alliance.

SSI Executive Session
The Directors and Advisors went into Executive Session while the attendees engaged in open fencing. A variety of topics were discussed, and decisions were made to pursue the production of SPADA, the SSI annual journal; to assemble and implement a communication and marketing plan; to become actively involved in the translation of historical fencing texts; and to establish a legislative watchdog committee to monitor international governmental actions affecting swords and swordsmanship.

Open Fencing
SSI Members were able to cross swords with rapiers, wasters, HACA padded weapon simulators, and steel blunts. Christian Darcé (HACA) and Jared Kirby (New Dawn Duellist Society) oversaw the fencing, which consisted primarily of informal, hold-the-field encounters.

DAY TWO
SSI Advisor Panel Discussion on Training Equipment
On Sunday morning the Advisors gathered to field questions and hold an open discussion on fencing equipment. Several weapons vendors joined the panel, including Scott Wilson of Darkwood Armory, Christian Fletcher of Christian Fletcher Medieval Military, and Christian Darcé of Purpleheart Armoury. The discussion revolved around the difficulty in finding affordable, high quality gear that was appropriate for use in practice and fencing. The discussion focused on practice weapons for later Renaissance swordsmanship, with a brief discussion on armour. There was general agreement that practice weapons should share the handling characteristics of real weapons as much as possible. We also discussed the fact that there are examples of actual historical practice weapons that could be used as models for modern equipment, such as the practice longswords on display last summer at the Metropolitan Museum of Art in New York City. It was further suggested that students should posses a blunt steel practice weapon

for drilling and fencing and a sharp reproduction weapon for solo and cutting work.

Mr. Clements, Mr. Hand, Maestro Lupo Sinclair and Maestro Martinez strongly advocated the use of steel reproduction weapons for their authenticity. Maestro Martinez described the ideal practice rapier: its length should be historically correct, with a proper hilt; the blade should be of a flattened rectangular cross-section, rather than a diamond cross-section, to diffuse the force of cuts; the blade should have a long, thick ricasso, as can be seen in illustrations of practice weapons in historical treatises; and the blade should be accurately weighted and rather stiffer than more flexible, to facilitate actions on the blade. Maestro Martinez further stated that at present, there is no completely satisfactory practice rapier in production anywhere.

There was a general feeling that consumers could provide more feedback to the swordsmiths and retailers. Mr. Reinhardt suggested that Windlass Steel is capable of making the best weapons available, but they lack the demand and there is currently no profit in making accurate practice weapons. Until the armourers perceive a profitable market for accurate practice weapons, they are not likely to manufacture them. It was suggested, however, that small "back yard" forges might be an option for obtaining affordable, purpose-built practice weapons. There was a brief discussion on protective gear, in which it was suggested that more protection to the body is no substitute for control in execution. Often, when people layer on more protective gear, they strike with more force and less control, and are unable to feel the force of a blow until it is sufficient to injure them. Offered for the examination of those present were a pair of prototype practice rapiers commissioned by HACA, and the new all-steel fencing helmet from Christian Fletcher Medieval Military. Though there was interest among the participants for some kind of SSI "seal of approval" on equipment, this action was set aside in favor of a more informal process to examine and review new products, working with both small and large-scale cutlers, armourers and manufacturers to steadily improve the range of practice equipment available. There was neither interest nor advocacy of a single unified code of standards for equipment.

Longsword of Filippo Vadi
Paul Macdonald, DDS/Macdonald Armouries/SSI Maestro Paul Macdonald of the Dawn Duelist Society and Macdonald Armouries of Edinburgh, Scotland, taught a course on the longsword methods of Filippo Vadi's Ars Gladiatoria, a 15th Century treatise that is one of the earliest surviving Italian fencing texts, and which draws heavily on Fiore dei Liberi's earlier work, Flos Duellatorum (1409).

Maestro Macdonald began with an examination of the mindset of the combatant, as depicted in dei Liberi's illustration of the cutting diagram, or segno, which Maestro

Macdonald had reproduced on a silk banner. Four animals surround the segno, representing different aspects of the warrior's mindset: the leopard (celerity), wolf (prudence), lion (bravery), and elephant (a strong foundation). These animals represent the qualities of a good swordsman, and Maestro Macdonald traced the evolution of these concepts from dei Liberi, through Vadi, and onto George Silver (1599) and the late 17th Century Scots smallsword instructor, Sir William Hope. This exposition was first rate, though the medieval animals were a bit difficult to identify (Maestro Macdonald helped by explaining it was a " Fifteenth Century" leopard, wolf, lion or elephant). The hands-on portion of the class focused on the three low guards of Vadi's system, and the natural counter attacks and defenses from these guards at both the gioco largo (long distance), and the gioco stretto (close distance). This portion of the class supported the interconnection between swordsmanship and grappling techniques, which had been established in Mr. Clements' class the day before.

The Spear - Swordsman's Nightmare
John Clements, HACA/SSI
The medieval and Renaissance swordsman trained in a variety of arms, with the expectation that he would have to face dissimilar weapons in both civilian and military encounters. Mr. Clements taught a class on the use of the long spear (9'), against the longsword and single short sword. Mr. Clements' thesis was that if a longswordsman and a spearman met in single combat, and were equally skilled, the outcome would generally favor the spearman. The thesis was well supported by demonstrations, with Mr. Clements trading back and forth with his partners in the role of swordsman and spearman, as the basic tactical parameters of a longsword/spear encounter were laid out. The demo focused principally on the use of distance and time to control the engagement, and a variety of techniques for both the spearman and the swordsman to use to obtain superiority.

La Verdadera Destreza
Maestro Ramon Martinez, Martinez Academy of Arms/AHF/SSI
Maestro Ramon Martinez and his wife, Provost (now Maestro) Jeanette Acosta-Martinez, taught an extremely interesting course that demonstrated the elegance and efficacy of the Spanish style. Confronted with the beauty of the Verdadera Destreza, many die-hard medievalists became enamored with a post-1500 weapon style for the first time. Maestro Martinez discoursed briefly on the background of the Spanish school and debunked some of the modern myths that have arisen around it. The Maestro discussed several concepts, including tacto, similar to the French sentiment de fer, and the importance of the "mystic circle" as a mental construct that operates in three dimensions, rather than as a physical object drawn on the floor. Maestro Martinez led the class in drills on specific techniques, including stance, footwork, distance, angulation, engagement, disengagement, "derailing the attack", cuts, counterattacks, and the use of the dagger. Maestro

Martinez condensed several months of material into a few hours, in a class that held the attendees spellbound.

Arts of Mars
Gene Tausk, SSI
Gene Tausk presented a paper on the martial culture of Ancient Rome. Beginning with a brief overview of the equipment and training of the Roman legionnaire, Mr. Tausk illustrated the role of the soldier, and the focus on unit skills and tactics. He then turned to the subject of gladiators and their schools.

The gladiatorial training schools (lunistae), were fully equipped facilities with fight masters (doctorae), masseuses, armourers, physical trainers and mortitians. Surviving mosaics display a variety of choke holds, kicks, and other grappling techniques; combined with a wide variety of knife, sword, trident and flexible weapon skills; and examples of the Romans' detailed anatomical knowledge. Imperial Rome had no police force, only personal bodyguards. There is evidence to suggest that the lunistae may have trained both professional bodyguards and normal civilians wanting to learn self-defense.

HACA Contact Sparring Demo
John Clements, HACA/SSI
Mr. Clements and members of HACA performed a demonstration of the HACA Contact Sparring System, using padded weapon simulators, wooden wasters, and blunt steel weapons. The HACA system is internally consistent; it uses all three types of training weapons, taking advantage of their individual strengths, in conjunction with cutting practice with sharps, in order to build competent swordsmen.

"Will the Real George Silver Please Stand Up?" — George Silver Roundtable
Stephen Hand, Stoccata School of Defence/SSI
George Silver's Brief Instructions Upon My Paradoxes of Defence, written at the turn of the 17th Century, but unpublished until 1899, has become increasingly better known to modern students of the sword. It is recognized as a monumental practical work on the use of the cutting sword, either alone or with dagger or buckler. Brief Instructions also provides techniques for a variety of two-handed weapons and their use against dissimilar arms. However, while many students read and train from Silver, finding two devotees who agree on what he actually says is another matter entirely. We seem incapable of agreeing on Silver's most basic techniques.

Stephen Hand led this round-table discussion by offering his own presentation of Silver's method as the basis for analysis and debate. The discussion began with Silver's basic concepts: the true and false times, and the "four grounds of true fighting" (judgment, distance, time and place). The discussion moved into Silver's guards or wards, with Mr. Hand reading from the text and then demonstrating his interpretation with the assistance of

Mr. Mele. The Open, True Guardant, Bastard Guardant, and Variable wards were all covered, as well as possible alternate interpretations or variants, based on Silver's text. Maestro Lupo Sinclair contributed a demonstration of several of the similar guards of Achille Marozzo, which led to a brief. comparison of the tactical considerations of the two 16ᵗʰ Century masters.

Throughout the round table, Mr. Hand stressed that students need to be extremely literal when studying a given master's work, and avoid seeing what they want to see, or finding answers to their questions from what they think they already know. Otherwise, there is a danger in using techniques that may or may not be martially effective, but do not reflect the true teachings of the historical masters.

Work For Cutlers - Or a Merrie Dialogue Between Sword, Rapier, & Dagger
Mark Rector, Chicago Swordplay Guild/SSI

In 1615, two years after James I's edict for the suppression of the duel was published, the Fellows of Cambridge University were treated to a light entertainment entitled Worke for Cutlers, or a Merrie Dialogue between Sword, Rapier and Dagger. It is a rollicking discourse in which Sword and Rapier face off, with Dagger attempting to keep the peace. Full of puns and wordplay and not-so-oblique references to Guy Fawkes and his "Gunpowder Plot," the characters wrangle over which weapon is better, whether the rapier is a suit-able arm for a soldier, and what to make of those interlopers, "Bow, Bill and Gunne." In the end, Dagger puts Sword and Rapier in their proper place and persuades them to shake hands and be friends. Worke for Cutlers was discovered in the Harleian Miscellany of the British Museum by Mr. A. Forbes Sieveking in the early days of the 20ᵗʰ Century, when several English gentlemen of note were devoting serious study to the revival of historical European swordsmanship. The play was performed at least twice in a program of Elizabethan music and swordplay. The first performance was, fittingly, at Trinity Hall, Cambridge, in 1903. Captain Alfred Hutton, the author of Cold Steel and The Sword and the Centuries, and Mr. T.H. Toynbee, "one of those remarkable members of the London Rifles Brigade," demonstrated the broad sword & buckler, dagger v. unarmed man, case of rapiers, and rapier & dagger. The second performance was in 1904 for the Royal Historical Society, and featured Captain Cyril Matthey, who revived George Silver's treatises on English swordplay, and Mr. Toynbee in a demonstration of "broad sword & buckler v. broadsword & dagger, as taught by Mr. George Silver in his Paradoxes of Defense; case of rapiers according to Vincentio Saviolo; and rapier & dagger." In both performances, Mr. Sieveking appeared in Worke for Cutlers in the role of Dagger. Ignored for the better part of a century, Worke for Cutlers was recently rediscovered once again by Milo Thurston of the Linacre School of Defence, Oxford, at a time when historical swordsmanship is undergoing another renaissance. It was performed at SSI with the lovely and talented Ms. Ann Candler Harlan as

Rapier, the doughty Mr. Steve Fenley as Sword, and Mr. Rector as Dagger, under the direction of Mr. Rector, with the assistance of Ms. Linda McCollum. The heavy-handed fencing puns and sexual double entendre were perfectly suited to the SSI audience. At one point, in true Elizabethan fashion, Mr. Rector updated his line, "I know it to be true," by ad libbing "I read it on the Internet." The room exploded with howls of laughter. After nearly 400 years, Worke for Cutlers finally found its audience.

Dusak Techniques and Practice
Maestro Paul Macdonald, DDS/Macdonald Armouries/SSI

Maestro Macdonald taught a class on the Dusak, a 16ᵗʰ Century practice weapon, imported from Bohemia, that began to appear in German fencing halls at the same time that the Messer (the single-edged "long knife" of the German bourgeois) was falling into disuse. Assisted by Jared Kirby of the NDDS, Maestro Macdonald demonstrated the basic principles of the Dusak, and instructed the class in the low, broad stance with the left arm held behind the back; pivoting footwork; cuts; guards: including the Wechsel ("Changing", corresponding roughly to the Iron Door), Mittelhut ("Middle Guard"), Bogen.("Bow"), Eber ("Boar"), Stier ("Steer"), Oberhut ("High Guard"), and Zornhut ('Guard of Wrath'); supported blocks; deflections; grips; and hand parries.

Chivalry and the Study of Swordsmanship
Brian Price, Schola St. George/IMA/SSI

Mr. Price led a combination lecture and roundtable focused on the evolution of the concept of "chivalry" from the medieval period to today. This discussion demonstrated the link between chivalric philosophy and the study of swordsmanship, and highlighted how these components could be approached in a modern context. Attendees examined the history of knighthood and the chivalric ideal, and three main social elements that helped shape it in the 12ᵗʰ through 15ᵗʰ Centuries: the warrior aristocracy Chivalry was created for, the Church, and the Cult of Courtly Love.

The discussion continued with an examination of how these elements evolved into the romanticized Victorian model, and what their possible ramifications are today. Chivalry attempted to channel the use of prowess – swordsmanship – along constructive lines, essentially trying to answer the question of what to do with the power that is created through the study and profession of arms. Mr. Price drew a similar parallel to today's martial artist, particularly the student of antique weapons, and how a study of the ethical ideas and personal responsibility inherent in the chivalric model could be a positive addition to the modern Western martial arts curriculum.

DAY THREE
Longsword vs. Sword and Dagger
John Clements, HACA/SSI
In a class that could have gone on far longer than the brief time allotted to it, Mr. Clements led a large group of participants through an exploration of techniques for fighting with the longsword against the sword and dagger. Everybody was armed with wooden wasters or blunt steel. Sword and dagger combatants were paired with longsword combatants. In the first part of the class we examined sword
and dagger counter-attacks to longsword attacks. We reversed the practice in the second part of the class, allowing the longsword combatants to discover counters to sword and dagger attacks.

Open Fencing and SSI Executive Session
While the SSI Directors and Advisors went into Executive Session, the SSI Members enjoyed a final opportunity to participate in friendly combat. Fencers engaged each other with rapier, longsword, backsword, sword & buckler, and pole-arms in challenging, fun-filled fights that lasted well past the allotted time.

Conclusion
SSI 2000 was an unqualified success. There were occasional differences of opinion, differences of opinion, but much more consensus. Everybody came together with an appropriate spirit of openness to celebrate swordsmanship, to make new friends, to "add a face to an email", and to explore different approaches to the study of historical swordplay.

Appendix A:
SSI Inaugural Introduction, May 27, 2000.

When we set out to establish Swordplay Symposium International, I realized we needed to define just what we meant by swordplay. I decided to openly and enthusiastically borrow from the opening preface of Carl Thimm's A Complete Bibliography of Fencing & Dueling (1896): The subject of Fence embraces all works relating to the art of offence and defence with all weapons held in the hands, for the science of arms should include the use of all non-ballistic weapons, from foil to bayonet, and from dagger to battleaxe.

Indulge me a moment, then, while I speak of Art and Song. To my knowledge, the Iberian poet Federico Garcia Lorca had no interest in swords or fencing. Rather, he was driven by his passion for the old, native Andalusian music, cante jondo, or Deep Song. Yet, Lorca speaks to the frustration felt by every modern student of the Western martial tradition when he wrote in his essay, "Deep Song": It does not seem possible that the deepest, most moving songs of our mysterious soul should be maligned as debauched and dirty.

For modern swordsmen, the ancient song is that of the sword, the rapier and the buckler, and it has been replaced so thoroughly by the click of flexible, whip-like foils and the buzz of electronic scoring apparatus, that the public associates the word "fencing" with nothing else. Perhaps this is better than the images invoked by the names "rapier," "sword," or "battleaxe," which have been relegated to stage, screen and Renaissance Festivals for decades. Today we have a paradox in which most Westerners can quickly and easily draw a rough image in their mind when told that someone is a student of karate, kung fu, Aikido, or another Eastern Martial Art, yet they will often stare blankly, if not incredulously, at the very idea of a Western Martial Art. What happened?

The proverbial finger can be pointed in a variety of directions, but largely two factors outweigh the others. The first was a growing interest in the idea of Darwinian evolution, particularly in the sense of evolution as a progressive "improvement" towards some perfect ideal. The Middle Ages must have been a brutish, violent era, with "rough and untutored" brawling. The development of the Noble Art and Science of fencing could only be possible in the warm glow of the Renaissance. Likewise, the sword fighting of the Renaissance could hardly be as sophisticated or developed as the fencing of the Enlightenment; which in turn, could hardly match the perfection of the fin de siecle salles d'armes, in which, "it is hard to imagine that there are any wonders in the world left to discover."

This sort of naïve arrogance was not unique to fencing historians. Unfortunately, in the case of fencing, these ideas were taking root at the same time the sword itself had lost nearly all relevance on the battlefield, and the duel was virtually obsolete. In the following decades, particularly after World War I had erased the sword's military relevance forever, the focus became increasingly in the modern, evolving sport of fencing, and the "Darwinian" model of fencing history became entrenched. The Art and Science of Fencing no longer , embraced all works relating to the art of offence and defence with all weapons held in the hands, but rather had become something else…art for art's sake. So much so that, in his Introduction to The Works of George Silver (1899), Cyril G.R. Matthey complained that: I suggest that sword fighting is not taught and that it should be. Fencing should be encouraged to the utmost, but fighting should be regarded as a distinct subject and of much greater importance in the majority of cases.

Matthey was no stranger to fencing or historical martial arts. Rather, he was part of a remarkable group of Victorian fencing enthusiasts that included Egerton Castle, Gustav Hergsell, Alfred Hutton, Francesco Novati, T.H. Toynbee and Carl Thimm, who set out to rescue the ancient art from obscurity, and preserve it for future generations. Hergsell translated and published three of Talhoffer's six manuals in 1887, and Novati published a facsimile edition of dei Liberi in 1902. Egerton Castle's monumental Schools and Masters of Fence was published in 1885, and has remained the standard text on the history of 16th - 19th Century fencing for over a hundred years. In the early days of the 20th Century, Castle, Hutton, Matthey and Thimm actually displayed the use of these weapons in a series of exhibitions at Trinity Hall, Cambridge, the Royal Historical Society, and for the Prince of Wales. Matthey published The Works of George Silver, while Hutton published Old Swordplay, a small book aimed at teaching short lessons in everything from the two-handed sword and sword and buckler of Marozzo, through the smallsword of Domenico Angelo.

History is a harsh mistress, however, and the Victorian era died in the trenches of the Somme. The efforts of Castle, Hutton and Hergsell were swept away in the brutality of two World Wars, and their discoveries mostly forgotten. By 1932, even the brilliant Italian Maestro, Luigi Barbasetti, himself a tutor to the Austrian army, simply could not break free of the old preconceptions. In the history of fencing at the end of his Art of the Foil, Barbasetti showed

he was familiar with two of the earliest known sword masters, Liechtenauer and dei Liberi, and even included plates for the latter's book. He could say little more about their style than that it resembled a combination of strong, heavy blows and "a kind of pancration and Japanese wrestling," and finally concluded that due to the brutality and barbarity of the period: It is easy to understand how this state of affairs prevented the practical development of fencing during the Middle Ages.

But Castle and Hutton have not been altogether forgotten. Their books have gone in and out of print, and through them a tenuous thread to the past remained. The late 14th Century master, Fiore dei Liberi, showed uncanny foresight, when he wrote in his Flos Duellatorum of 1409: Although I didn't want to write this book, I realized that it was important for the survival of the art of fighting. Bibliographies like Thimm's have provided the clues to finding other four and five hundred year old treatises on the art of the sword.

Today, with the virtue of phones, faxes, and the Internet, students of the sword worldwide have been able to find and communicate with each other to exchange manuals, leads, and concepts. Indeed, the Symposium you are now attending was largely initiated and organized through electronic means, and has brought instructors from across North America, Europe and Australia together to share their knowledge and insights. The Noble Art and Science may now have more interest and potential adherents than it has enjoyed in over a century. Therefore, rather than pull our beards and lament at what was lost, I encourage all of you to celebrate what is found - our heritage. We are not doing something new, but rather, continuing the efforts of those who have gone before to restore what is old.

I began with Lorca, and I shall end with him. When he presented his essay on cante jondo at the Centro Artistico, he began by trying to surmise why he and its other adherents were so impassioned to preserve the old music. His words will serve us well, here today: We are trying to do something worthy and patriotic. This is a labor of preservation, friendship, and love.

2nd Annual International Western Martial Arts Workshop
By David Cvet

On the weekend of October 13, 14, 15, 2000, in Toronto, the 2nd Annual International Western Martial Arts Workshop (WMA) was held, hosted by the Academy of European Medieval Martial Arts (AEMMA) at the facilities of the Medieval Times at Exhibition Place. There were 130 attendees at this 3 day event, coming from the UK, Scotland, Italy, Belgium, Spain and the USA and Canada. Four of the five representatives of the International Master at Arms Federation (IMAF) were present at this workshop delivering workshop sessions in each of their areas of expertise.

Friday's workshop encompassed a number of lectures and presentations, including the current developments of Dr.Singman's I.33 manuscript research project. Secondly, Brian Price delivered a lecture entitled "Chivalry and the Modern Practice of Medieval Martial Arts". Each of the masters from IMAF provided a 30-minute "state of the union" address regarding the state of western martial arts in their particular countries, including Terry Brown for the UK. This was followed by physical workshops and then followed by a late historical tournament, administered under the rules and guidelines of the Association of Historical Fencing (AHF). Christian Darce won the late historical tournament.

Saturday had dual-streaming workshops, each workshop focused on different weapons types and periods. This was followed by, what was perceived as the highlight of the weekend workshop, the armoured tournament. This was judged by Maestro Ramon Martinez, Maestro Andrea Lupo-Sinclair, Maestro Paul Macdonald and Marian Zakrzewski.

Mr. Brian Price took the role of field judge for the tournament (within the list). The rules of the tournament were based on the rules as defined by King Rene. These were posted on the AEMMA web site. 17 participants engaged in heavy armoured tournament, often described as brutal and exhilarating. The tournament was definitely a crowd pleaser. Anton Cvet won the armoured tournament.

Sunday's workshop included Liberi knife techniques, Spanish rapier, dusak to name a few. The overall energy and interest in the workshop was very high. Everyone reported to have a wonderful and educational time. Everyone also indicated that they are looking forward and planning for the next workshop to be hosted by the Martinez Academy of Arms, in New York city next October.

Other notable events, included the invitation to Marian Zakrzewski to participate in the IMAF designated as maestro. Secondly, the IMAF invited William Wilson to the IMAF as maestro in training, with the expectation of full maestro designation in approximately one year. Lastly, IMAF had also designated David Cvet as their first "Acknowledged Instructor" or AI for longsword training. Congratulations to all three gentlemen.

AEMMA wishes to thank David Cvet, who had put in an incredible amount of time, energy and resources to pull the WMA 2000 workshop off, and to the students of AEMMA for their efforts during the weekend workshop to ensure that things ran smoothly without incidents. Also, for Brian McIlmoyle, who took on the role of master of ceremonies and glued the entire workshop together during the weekend.

Western Martial Arts Workshop 2001
By Stephen Hand

WMAW2001 was held in New York barely a month after the tragic events of September 11th. In the light of the terrorist attacks there was some doubt as to whether the event should go ahead, but unanimously the instructors decided that it should.

The workshop was hosted by the Association for Historical Fencing (AHF) on October 12th to 14th. Under trying circumstances the Chairman of the organizing committee, Fawzi Al-Nawal did a splendid job, as did his team. The venue, the neo Gothic Riverside Church in upper Manhattan was truly beautiful.

As with any of these events the key to success was having good teachers and enthusiastic students. Although September 11th seems to have scared off some of the prospective students it did nothing to dampen the enthusiasm of those who did make the journey to Manhattan.

WMAW2001 ran two types of class, 1 ½ hour presentations and three hour master classes, more in depth classes with the more sought after instructors. But the first workshop was the opposite of the Master Classes. The International Master at Arms Federation (IMAF) gave a series of presentations on basic elements of fencing with each of the seven main weapons that they teach. With so many people denied access to good teaching, such workshops are worth their weight in gold.

Simply to list the classes would exhaust the space allotted for this report and to single out individual classes would unfairly slight those not mentioned. Every class was discussed favourably by those who attended it. The greatest difficulty of the weekend was to choose between two and sometimes three excellent classes which were running simultaneously. Congratulations are in order to all the instructors, Jeannette Acosta Martinez, Christoph Amberger, Cosimo Bruno, Bob Charron, David Cvet, Stephen Hand, Craig and Ian Johnson, James Loriega, Paul McDonald, Ramon Martinez, Ken Pfrenger, Lorenzo Ravazzani, Christian Tobler, Brad Waller and alphabetically last, but certainly not least, William Wilson.

With classes running from as early as 8.30AM to as late as 10PM each day, it's surprising that anyone had any energy left to put what they'd learned into practice. As well as the almost continuous free bouting that took place between participants, there were two tournaments. The armoured tournament was low on numbers, but hard fought. One of the highlights for the crowd was when the seemingly invincible David Cvet was felled by a perfectly executed wrestling move straight from Fiore Dei Liberi. With a low number of participants the prize of a dagger was awarded to Ken Mondschein for displaying the best fighting spirit.

The rapier tournament had a large number of entrants and was as hard fought as its armoured counterpart. With a single elimination, four rounds were fought. Some bouts lasted just seconds while others saw a conversation of blades that went on for several minutes. In the final bout Stephen Hand was victorious over John O'Meara, though with the closeness of some of the earlier bouts, luck played as big a part in this result as skill. Throughout these tournaments, a huge good will was in evidence, with many of the combatants embracing after the completion of their bouts.

The fellow feeling generated during the weekend started with a superb evening for the instructors at the home of Maestri Ramon and Jeannette Martinez, who proved the most gracious hosts. It continued through the classes and tournaments to late night get togethers on each night of the workshop. As with so many of these events, with such a short time to see people from different states, countries and even continents, the first casualty is sleep.

In what seemed like a heartbeat the workshop was over. Before it ended, the International Master at Arms Federation announced the admission of Brian McIlmoyle and Bob Charron as Acknowledged Instructors and Stephen Hand as a Masters Candidate. And then it was time to part. It seems incomprehensible that lifelong friendships can be forged between people who meet once or twice a year, but they are. Events like WMAW2001 create a sense of brotherhood only felt by people who share a passion. The passion of the attendees for the western martial arts was fueled at WMAW2001 by perhaps the best event of its nature held to date. The next event, in Chicago in 2002 is surely not to be missed.

Western Martial Arts Workshop 2002
By Brian R. Price

Simply Superb. Nicole Allen, Greg Mele and the rest of the Chicago Swordplay Guild have outdone themselves to sponsor what was without question one of the finest WMA events thus far. Beginning with the choice of site — the Episcpoal retreat at the Dekovan foundation in Racine, Wisconsin — and carrying through the myriad of classes, presentations, free fencing, tournaments and many opportunities for downright silly fun, one could not but have a splendid time.

But the truly great thing about these events is not of course the venue — nor even is it the fighting/fencing/whatever-you-want-to-call-it — it's the people. And there too the event excelled, bringing people and fostering new connections to further build out this splendid community we're building upon the shoulders of some really fine people. Whether it was snatching a few moments with old friends like Aaron Toman, Joe Radding or Christian Tobler — or getting to know some really fine new ones such as Peter Johnsson (whom I think is perhaps the world's finest medieval swordsmith working today), the event was a whirlwind of people-fighting-training-people — and I doubt anyone can say that they found things wanting.

Before the event commenced the outstanding direction by Nicole Allen and the rest of the Chicago Swordplay Guild helped to realize an ambitious vision built upon the roots of the event set up by Greg Mele and Pete Kautz before WMAW 1999, and upon the experiences of SSI / Houston and WMAW 2000 (Toronto), WMAW 2001 (New York) and the two Livermore events — one in 2001 and the other this year in 2002. From the beautifully crafted look and feel of the website, graphics and shirts (thanks to the equally decorative and intelligent CSG Scholar Ashley Bishop) to the pre-event polling and database support provided by Dave Peck and John O'Meara and a few others, the pre-event communication exceeds anything that has been done so far and will be very hard to top.

By selecting the Dekovan site several things were accomplished. First, the site created the ambiance that helps everyone to stay in a mindset that is cooperative and evocative of the elegance we seek by studying the sword. Second, by renting Taylor Hall — with 60 beds — not only could the instructors be housed without cost to them but also the social fabric of the event could be extended well beyond the usual 10 or 11pm closing time for the main halls — indeed, I found myself up chatting and philosophizing until 4 or 5 every night, unwilling to give up a minute of contact — they are just too precious.

With respect to the classes themselves, I cannot say that I've seen better. In my usual mode I took only a few, unwilling to over-write material from too much data. I did, however, take Bob Charron's crossed swords class, and it was the cleanest presentation of his material I've yet, seen; maybe the cleanest in the Medieval side of the WMA community. My compliments to Bob for his ability to build one sub-technique upon another and to handle a class of 50 or so while adhering to his lesson plan and conveying enough to build a solid core from which students could build.

I also took the first half of Stephen Hand's I.33 class. This was also wonderful, for Stephen has done what few have accomplished for any of the medieval masters — he has distilled the principals of the system and in working through only the first four plates of the manuscript has distilled the keys needed to develop a sword-and-buckler technique in harmony with the rest of the manuscript. Unfortunately I had to leave early, as I had reached the point where only more drill could set the elements of necessary footwork in place, but it was enough to begin and I think we'll see more I.33 at Livermore; not only with Stephen, but with Paul Wagner as well.

As I watched other classes, it became clear that the quality of presentations continues to grow. With instructors with the caliber of Ramon & Jeanette Acosta-Martinez, Cosimo Bruno, Dave Cvet, Jeffrey Forgeng, Stephen Hand, Craig Johnson, Steaphen Fick, Sean Hayes, Ian Johnson, Paul MacDonald, Ken Pfrenger, Andrea Lupo Sinclair, Milo Thurston, Brad Waller, Bill Wilson, Tom Leoni and Pete Kautz, how could one lose?

My own "Ponderous, Cruel & Mortal" class was a bit more chaotic than I'd like, with just under 50 students for a class originally projected for 24. But the students were patient and afterwards expressed great enthusiasm, and we did get to spend two and a half wonderful hours building some basic skills with the azza doing coups, tours de bras, thrusts, displacements, and some elementary grapples and levering attacks. I hope that at least a few of you will go on to harness up and practice the axst further, since there was some real talent displayed amongst the student core. For myself, future classes in hache will focus on specific elements; say, "Displacements with the Hache" or, in the case of Livermore 2003, "Streitaxst (poleaxe) plays from Talhoffer 1467". The survey will remain, but it needs to be cut down still further, something I think all of the medieval instructors have discovered at one time or another. For those of you who took the class, suggestions are more than warmly welcomed. Oh, and a GREAT thanks to Steve Hick, my "Ben" for the class, who was great — except that he cannot be thrown. The man proved to me here and as my partner in the I.33 class to be an "elephant" on ball-bearings; his graceful footwork should not be possible for a man of his size — but there it is.

Other than in classes, I had the opportunity to cross swords with my old friend Christian Tobler, always a distinct pleasure. I have to say that this is perhaps some of the event experiences that I always cherish the most, that intimate connection upon the field under the stress of an exchange, drawing one another to ever-higher levels of prowess and understanding.

Of Vendors & Swordsmiths

On the professional front, it was a very great pleasure to meet Peter Johnsson, whose work reproducing stunningly accurate and "alive" medieval swords is I believe I have already said — the best in the world today. Peter's attention to detail was matched by an unbelievable willingness to give of his knowledge and to make it interesting as he proved in his talk, but also to do so with the utmost in sincerity and humility, a fine expression of the chivalric ideals we all espouse. It will be a great pleasure working with Pete in the future.

There were a bunch of fine vendors present, too, including Tinker, Gus Trim, Craig Johnson from Arms & Armor, Hal Siegel from Therion Arms, Christian D'Arcy from Purple-Heart Armouries, Paul MacDonald, Brian Wilson of Darkwood Armoury and the folks from Albion Arms. It was great to talk with all of you, though of course there wasn't nearly enough time to spend. Or money.

But the vendor list was very great and of a very high caliber; our own Chivalry Bookshelf booth did well, and I would offer my thanks to the community for this. As we continue to bring out titles, we deeply appreciate the support from the community and will try to do our best to keep them coming. SPADA, Arte of Defense, Jousts & Touarnaments, Chivalrous Conqueror, Highland Broadsword and Fillipo Vadi are all now in production!

The Medieval Tournament

This year, to support Greg as the main entrepreneur for the tournament, we worked together on the rules. We were determined to advance the blossfechten tournament alongside the armoured one, and with great success this was done at WMAW for the first time. The combatants, armed in a gambeson, steel helmet and gauntlets fought with the impact-absorbing CSG weapons, and this was generally successful. Many of the CSG folks in particular displayed an excellent grasp of medieval technique, the prizes going to Ashley Bishop (overall) and to Jain Schuster (Technical). Dave, Keith and Jesse also did very, very well; all of the CSG combatants were a credit to the CSG in general and to their trainer, Greg Mele, in particular. Keep it up!

My thanks to Ian Johnson, Keith Jennings and Dave Peck, Bob Charron, Nicholas Cioran, Christian Tobler and to Steaphen Fick for acting with me as defenders for the blossfechten. This crew did a fantasic job at bringing out the best in our challengers — and I think we generally succeeded in our job here. A finer group of defenders I could not ask for. Thank you also to Nicole for her fine work with the lists, to Greg for his good work as judge, for Aaron Toman and Charles Davis for their marshalling, and to the four arming sergeants who kept the pace close on a very tight time budget.

At Livermore, we will have the blossfechten tournament alongside the rapier one, this time using the aluminum weapons (with some form of mesh face defense) or the CSG-style weapons with the standard grilles.

The armoured list was perhaps less well refined, to be expected when many of the combatants could not thrust. I believe that the biggest challenge to the WMA community currently lies not in getting combatants to step off-line and to attempt to execute techniques — here Livermore and WMAW 2002 showed remarkable improvement over the same events in 2001 — but rather in equipping the majority of armoured combatants to allow them to use thrusting in harness.

To be sure, most medieval feats of arms employed "counted blows," not "counted thrusts-to-the-armpit," indicating a disconnect between the objectives of medieval tournament sponsors and WMAW sponsors. We see this strongly reflected in the difference between tournaments sponsored by the Tournaments Companies such as the Company of Saint George or the Company of Saint Michael and those sponsored by WMA schools such as the CSG or the Schola Saint George. What we in the WMA community seek is not for combatants to give and receive blows, but rather to execute the techniques recorded in the fechtbücher. This is not a small task, as many of the techniques are meant for anything but friendly combat — the term compano aside — though the principles of the medieval masters can and should be applied.

If we begin to see competent halfswording, stepping off-line, counter attacks in single time, techniques from both the German and Italian traditions from binden or en croisade, regardless of whether or not we use grappling — then I'll be very pleased. Ultimately, I think we'll describe combats without grappling as à plaisance, while those than employ it will be à plaisance sans encumbrance.

All in all, some fine engagements with much learning on both sides — and some fine deeds of prowess to record. I was very pleased with all of my opponents, especially Kel, Jain, and Ashley. I look forward not only to meeting them again, but to engaging with those I've not met before, such as Anton, David, Jesse, Colin, and Steaphen. Well met!

Brian R. PriceSchola / Company of Saint George

Report on the Second Annual FISAS Meeting
by Michael Su

Taking place over the weekend of the second of December, 2000, in the town of Castellanza (about 30 miles west of Milan), the Second International Meeting for Antique, Historical, and Classical Fencing also served as the annual meeting for FISAS students. FISAS founder Maestro d'Arme Andrea Lupo Sinclair was joined by IMAF members Maestro Ramon Martínez, Maestro Jeannette Acosta-Martínez, Maestro Paul McDonald, Maestro Mario Magni, and ENBF founders Maestro Italo Manusardi and Maestro Lorenzo Ravazzani. Invitations were extended to BFHS member Robert Brooks, Mr. Stefan Dieke from Germany, and AHF members Ken Mondschein and myself. Though the meeting itself took place from the early hours of Saturday, December 2, to the late hours of Sunday, December 3, the aura of empathy first reared its head Friday evening when Maestro Andrea Lupo-Sinclair and Ms. Manuela Lecchi invited the foreign visitors to dinner at their home. Hearing and speaking exclusively about fencing, we set the stage for the following day.

On Saturday, Maestro Jeannette Acosta-Martínez took the lead with her intensive seminar on early French smallsword (following Monsieur L'Abbat's treatise). Maestro Ramon Martínez followed with a seminar on the Spanish school of Fencing, *La Verdadera Destreza*, using the single rapier and the rapier and dagger. Maestro Andrea Lupo-Sinclair continued the series with his seminar on the Italian dueling sword (*striscia italiana*) before Maestro Paul McDonald took his turn with the medieval German weapon, the dussack. Finally, Maestro Italo Manusardi and Maestro Lorenzo Ravazzani concluded the day's work with their seminars on the mixed and Italian schools of *grand baton*. On this first day, all classes were held in an intimate but spacious room accommodating about 30 students. Visitors passed in and out, but the students had a mere 15 minutes' pause before the next seminar. Students worked with each other while the masters walked through the room, giving instructions and corrections. At moments, the language barrier slowed down the rate at which a master's knowledge could be disseminated. Nevertheless, the fundamental understanding and appreciation for fencing preserved us. (That, and international body language, of course.)

The annual FISAS dinner gala took place later that evening at the Barbarossa Restaurant in the neighboring town of Legnano.

Undeterred by the late hour at which the previous night ended, the next day's sun shone on over sixty FISAS students at the Castellanza sport stadium. The increased capacity of the stadium also brought in many more spectators. On this day, Maestro Mario Magni took point with his class on the longsword. Teaching in the manner of an otherwise regular class, Maestro Magni started off with stretching exercises, and continued with carefully orchestrated footwork and blade actions. Maestro Andrea Lupo-Sinclair stepped up the pace with his class on the *spada da lato* of the 16th century. The morning ended with a class salute led by Maestro Andrea Lupo consisting of over sixty people forming a very large circle.

After lunch, the venue floor was open to all students and masters. Those interested in similar weapons and styles congregated before approaching the respective masters for further elaboration and demonstration. Everyone who was not a spectator could be found deep in the sea of people. Walking through the crowd one could hear conversations in Italian, English, French, and even Spanish being tossed about, while rapiers, swords, and smallswords made their way around. For a short hour and a half the action on the floor did not stop. Knowing this was our last opportunity for questions and explanations, the pace increased to a crescendo before the session was regretfully concluded. Thereafter, students and masters alike became spectators. For this last phase, the FISAS member school *Milites Castri Salinae* from the region of Venice demonstrated their *Moresca d'Arme* military dance of the 14th century. Continuing the demonstrations were the various FISAS member schools, each having chosen to exhibit distinct weapons and styles. After students of all the various schools had finished, the masters took to the floor with demonstration lessons and bouts.

By this time in the afternoon the stadium was full of people. Roughly as many spectators turned up as students, bringing the total number of persons to over one hundred twenty. After the fencing finished, the meeting itself was concluded by the presentation of certificates of participation to every single student.

It was an unforgettable weekend, not only because of the events of the meeting itself, but also because of the air of understanding and, ultimately, communication that came about which allowed all of us thereafter to breathe our fencing more easily. I should like to further extend my gratitude for the hospitality of FISAS, and in particular, that of Maestro Andrea Lupo-Sinclair, Manuela Lecchi, and Provost Alberto Giannone and Marco Carenzio.

The Lansing Swordfighting and Martial Arts Convention May 12th-14th 2000
By John Lennox and Jared Kirby

In October of 1999, John Lennox and Jared Kirby attended a swordfighting convention in Chicago. Having had such a wonderful experience at the Chicago Swordplay Group's convention, John Lennox decided to create one at Lansing Community College in Michigan, where he works. Jared immediately became his co-coordinator, and the Lansing Swordfighting and Martial Arts Convention was born.

John found the money, and Jared provided the instructors. John was able to bring in some instructors via grants from LCC, and obtained free rooms for the instructors from the Radisson Hotel in Lansing. Jared put together his list. When the two were done with their work, one of the largest conventions in North America, with some of the most respected instructors was the result.

It was a weekend that saw Western martial artists meeting with their Eastern brethren along with stage combatants in two and a half days of comraderie and learning. It was an educational experience for the students, instructors and staff, yet the 50-60 people that came together for this event made sure that there was no short supply of fun.

The weekend started on Friday night with a meet and greet session. The instructors were introduced and gave a short synopsis of their classes. The students asked lots of questions so that they could decide what classes to take.

The instructors present were:

KEN PFRENGER- Ohio, teaching Irish Stick play, and Celtic Wrestling; STEPHEN HAND- Australia, teaching the single rapier techniques of Vincentio Saviolo and the single sword of George Silver; DWIGHT C. McLEMORE- Virginia, teaching Bowie Knife; TIM RUZICKI- Oregon, teaching wrestling according to the German master Petter; JARED KIRBY- New York, teaching the German master's Meyer's Dusack; BRETT ECKHART- Michigan, teaching quarterstaff techniques; J.J. PIDO- Illinois, teaching Filipino Martial Arts, and Escrima Sticks; JOHN S. LENNOX- Michigan, teaching katana; MARK RECTOR- Illinois, teaching the offensive use of the dagger in rapier and dagger fighting; MIKE MAY- New York, teaching Capoeira; MAESTRO PAUL MACDONALD- Scotland, teaching dei Liberi/Vadi longsword techniques, smallsword and the German duelling shield; PETER KAUTZ- New York, teaching Marozzo's unarmed vs. knife technique; STEFAN DIEKE- Germany, teaching German rapier from the pages of Meyer's manual; WILLIAM WILSON- Arizona, teaching sword and buckler wards of Marozzo.

With this many instructors, there were so many classes offered in the three day period that there was little time for rest. Despite this, everyone had a great time. When the classes were over, many people gathered again to relax with a glass of beer and reflect on the joys of the weekend.

With the success of this convention, the Lansing International Swordfighting and Martial Arts Convention continues in August of 2001 with many of the same instructors, and many new ones. The 2000 Lansing Swordfighting and Martial Arts Convention set the stage to create an annual major workshop in Northwestern America that we hope will last for years to come.

The Lansing Swordfighting and Martial Arts Convention August, 2001
By John Lennox

In August of 2001, the second annual Lansing International Swordfighting and Martial Arts Convention took place, and was again a huge success. It was held again at Lansing Community College in Michigan and hosted by the Art of Combat and The New Dawn Duellists Society. Once again, the Radisson Hotel sponsored the event by providing free rooms for the instructors.

The instructors present were:
KEN PFRENGER- Ohio, teaching Irish Stick play and Paschen Wrestling; TIM RUZICKI- Oregon teaching Pugilism; JARED KIRBY- New York, teaching an old German training weapon, the Dusack, and Fabris Rapier & Cloak; J.J. PIDO- Illinois, teaching American Free Style Martial Arts, and Escrima Sticks; JOHN S. LENNOX- Michigan, teaching Katana and Hutton Saber; MAESTRO PAUL MACDONALD- Scotland, teaching Italian Longsword and Single Stick; WILLIAM WILSON- Arizona, teaching sword and buckler wards of Marozzo, and Fabris Rapier. MAESTRO SEAN HAYES teaching Italian Duelling Sword; GUY WINDSOR teaching Italian Longsword; MAESTRO ANDREA LUPO SINCLAIR teaching Italian Sidesword and Italian Rapier; MAESTRO JEANNETTE ACOSTA-MARTINEZ teaching French Smallsword; and MAESTRO

RAMON MARTINEZ teaching Spanish Rapier.

The total attendance was around 40 participants. The class schedule was structured with two classes running simultaneously which made for some very tough decisions, but a lot of fun. This workshop offered more class opportunity than last year's convention, which is a trend we hope to continue in 2002. Both the new participants and old enjoyed the infamous Lansing statue and we were proud to offer a short, but informative class from Yoda, the Jedi master.

The success of the Lansing Swordfighting and Martial Arts Convention 2000, and 2001 has solidified the base for continuing this major workshop in Northwestern America. The Art of Combat and The New Dawn Duellists Society are proud to host this event that has been a powerful way of spreading the passion and knowledge of this craft to others. Plans are being made to stretch the convention to 4 or 5 days and the target date is set for Aug. 1st to the 5th. All of the instructors are eager to return, and we are working on bringing back instructors from the first workshop, as well as some new ones. To find out more information please visit the Art of Combat web page at http://artofcombat.org/public/thespis/index.htm.

The Australian Historical Fencing Convention 2000

by Stephen Hand

On July 22nd and 23rd 2000 50 individuals from five Australian historical fencing groups came together in Sydney for the 2nd Australian Historical Fencing Convention. The event was hosted by The Stoccata School of Defence in Sydney. Also in attendance were the Australian College of Arms (ACA), based in Albury, Finesse from Canberra, HACA from the Gold Coast and Prima Spada who operate in Brisbane.

The convention took the typical form of lectures, workshops and free fencing. Scott McDonald of the ACA demonstrated rapier and cloak techniques from Di Grassi's manual of 1594. Keith Beattie of Prima Spada talked about the concepts of timing used by different masters. Paul Wagner of Stoccata gave demonstrations of English quarterstaff and also sword and buckler according to MSS. I.33, the world's oldest fencing manual. HACA's Craig Gemeiner gave two enjoyable classes on grappling in swordplay.

On a different note, Julian Clark of Finesse discussed how an accurate understanding of late 16th century fencing is critical to understanding Shakespeare's plays, most of which contain fencing scenes. Stephen Hand of Stoccata presented a demonstration of La Destreza, Spanish rapier fencing and gave a class on the rapier fencing of Vincentio Saviolo, the first Italian fencing master to teach in England. Discussions were also held on Historical Fencing around the world and the future of Historical Fencing in Australia.

All the presentations were well researched and very well received. In the free fencing sessions, held in the last two hours of each day, students and instructors from different schools safely and enjoyably fenced together. Everyone who attended the Historical Fencing Convention agreed that it was a huge success. A commitment was made to meet again, in July 2001 in Canberra.

The Australian Historical Fencing Convention 2001

by Stephen Hand

The Third Australian Historical Fencing Convention was hosted by the Finesse Academie of Fence in Canberra on July 14th and 15th 2001. Like the previous two conventions this one was a huge success.

We were welcomed to the convention by Julian Clark, the President of Finesse, the host club. Finesse teaches Classical Fencing, 18th century smallsword and 17th century rapier.

Short talks were given by Stephen Hand and Paul Wagner, both of Stoccata. As a regular guest at international symposia Stephen discussed the international scene. Paul, who had just returned from the UK talked about the thriving historical fencing community over there. Several other interesting talks were given over the course of the weekend. Nigel Poulton, Vice President of the Society of Australian Fight Directors and David Green, a local re-enactor discussed the differences between theatrical and real fencing and how the two communities can contribute to each other. Australian armourers Craig Sitch and Glenn Stokes discussed the problems of supplying the historical fencing community.

Outside the field of western swordsmanship we had fitness sessions from Finesse's inspirational fitness instructor JoJo Azurin and a demonstration by Elizabeth Halfnights, a local Tai Chi practitioner, who showed two different Tai Chi sword styles.

The meat of the weekend were the classes and demos of western swordsmanship which took up most of the two days of the convention. Scott McDonald, an army officer who runs the Australian College of Arms in Albury gave a class on half-swording, techniques with longsword. Julian Clark and Melissa Nesbitt of Finesse presented their interpretations of the rapier play of Salvator Fabris (1606) and the smallsword fencing of Domenico Angelo from his manual of 1763. Paul Wagner of Stoccata demonstrated grappling techniques using small shields, primarily from Manuscript I.33, the world's oldest fencing manual and also took a class in English quarterstaff. Stephen Hand presented a demonstration of sword and large shield techniques from Hans Talhoffer's 1467 fechtbuch and discussed why George Silver's English system of swordsmanship is so effective and easy to learn. Andrew Brew of Stoccata presented some interpretations of overhead cutting techniques and responses from Talhoffer's longsword. All the presentations showed a high degree of research skill, as well as martial ability.

Of course the main event for many people was the opportunity to test their skills against practitioners from other groups. There was a memorable series of bouts with Scott McDonald of ACA. Scott has embraced the author's interpretation of the English sword style of George Silver and in a very impressive and bruising display proved that imitation is indeed the sincerest form of battery.

At the end of the convention everyone parted firm friends and much the wiser for the experience.

Schola Saint George Swordsmanship Symposium 2001

by Brian R. Price

In the Summer of 2000, fresh from the outstanding SSI event in Houston, I mourned that with so many talented people not only on the West Coast but in the San Francisco Bay Area generally, that there were no sword events of any kind to be found.

By September I had decided to run an event of our own, sponsored by our local Company (and Schola) of Saint George. By December most of the instructors had been secured, and by February signups were in full swing and the date of the event was fixed at May 11th - 13th 2001.

With the assistant of our Schola Assistant Governor Robert Holland, we secured a local facility colloquially known as "The Barn," destined to be the site for Schola events for the next two years. Located in Livermore, California, just west of the San Francisco Bay Area, the site is a finished commercial hall that proved large enough—barely—to support two simultaneous classes, with more room available "on the green" just outside.

It proved fortunate that the space was available; beyond our wildest expectations, more than 134 people descended upon unsuspecting Livermore—home of a popular rodeo—to teach, to learn, to compete and to play.

We were truly blessed by the warm reception we received both from students and instructors, each of whom volunteered their valuable time and energy to help make the event a success. There is no way to thank each in print personally, but I think all were duly impressed by the depth of presentations and by the receptiveness of students from different backgrounds and approaches to consider the value in what others were / are pursuing.

The Schola event was set up with a wide cross-sectional sampling designed to cross-pollinate "sword" communities. As such, we focused classes not only on historical swordsmanship, but on equestrian arts, stage combat, and arms and armour.

Day 1

Opening Remarks
"Tournaments & the Medieval Martial Arts" (Paper)
    – Brian R. Price
"Mystery of Halfswording" – John Clements
"Introduction to Stage Combat" – Michael Cawelti
"Use of the Large Shield" – Stephen Hand
"Introduction to the Study of the Rapier" – William Wilson
"Introduction to Equitation" – Cliff Bassett
"Swordwork of Sigmund Ringeck" – Christian Henry Tobler
"Rapier of Salvatore Fabris" – William E. Wilson
"Introduction to the Joust" – Cliff Bassett
"Swordsmanship of Saviolo" – Stephen Hand
"Women in the Medieval Martial Arts" (roundtable)
"Sources in the Study of Medieval & Renaissance Martial Arts" – Greg Mele

Day 2

"Medieval Sword & Buckler: Royal Armouries MS. I.33"
    – Stephen Hand
"Stances & Guards in Medieval Longsword"
    – John Clements
"Rapier Tournament Formats" (roundtable)
"Jeu de la Hache" – Ian Johnson
"Rapier of Joseph Swetnam" – Steaphan Fick

Day 3 (All-Day Session)

"Swordsmanship of Fiore dei Liberi" – Bob Charron
"Swordsmanship for the Stage" – Randall Scott
"Fencing with the Case of Rapiers" – Gereg Jones Muller
"Achieving Realism in Choreography" – Michael Cawelti
"Voices of Experience" – Gereg Muller Jones

Most of the classes were hands-on *practicums* of the now-familiar sort, but there were also round-table discussions, lectures, demonstrations, and the thing we're perhaps known best for, tournaments. At this event there were two; a rapier tournament held on Friday night, sponsored jointly by William Wilson and the Adrian Empire staff.

The Company of Saint George has been involved in the sponsoring of medieval-style tournaments since the early 1990s, pioneering the format of the now-popular "pas d'armes" challenge format and digging out heaps of research to fuel our own tournaments. With the unearthing and presentation of the fighting treatises and *fechtbücher*, our focus has expanded to include the study of historical swordsmanship.

The other was our centerpiece tournament, a Grand Pas d'Armes celebrating Fiore dei Liberi. The twelve armoured combatants took part in a 15th century-style allegorical tournament, where Seeker of Prowess tried in vain to determine which of Fiore's four qualities (from the *Segno*) was dominant. Four ladies, arrayed in distinctive colors and bearing shields for each of the four animals, judged which of the combatants, during the course of the day, best displayed the respective qualities of *Prudentia, Fortituda, Celeritas, Audacia*.

The ladies of the Schola—led by Ann Price and Debora Saint-James, provided lunch and breakfast every day, as well as cooking a full medieval-style dinner for the pas-tournament revel Saturday night. In all, more than 700 meals were created by only six Schola companions.

Vendors were also present this year; our own Chivalry Bookshelf; Therion Arms; Mandrake Armouries; Christian Fletcher, Armourer; Albion Works; Gauckler Medieval Wares; Darkwood Armoury; and James Gillaspie, Master Armourer.

All in all, the weekend was marked by an unusually strong level of camaraderie; new inter-approach bridges were built.

Schola Saint George Swordsmanship Symposium 2002

by Brian R. Price

With the unexpected success of the Schola Saint George 2001 International Swordsmanship Symposium, we in the Schola looked for ways to improve the event for 2002, adding a third and even a fourth class track and expanding the focus of the event to include Eastern weapon arts as well.

Our May date became problematic, so we moved to June 7th – 9th, which worked out better for many of our previous year's participants and was easier for us, since we had to attend the Kalamazoo Medieval Conference (where Bob Charron and Gregory Mele presented) and the Bookseller's Expo.

The big news for the event was the support of the Royal Armouries at Leeds, who was kind enough to send Andrew Deane, one of the key members of their Fight Reconstruction team. Andy presented on Saturday, expositing the RA system without the usual "big institution" bias that I think many expected. Indeed, Andy proved more than approachable—he fit in perfectly and went home with a souvenir cowboy hat from the real American rodeo he managed to get himself lifted to.

Once again the numbers astounded us; 168 attendees and instructors from all over the globe. More than 875 meals were again created, and for the Friday-Sunday students crammed as much as they could with the over-generous instructors. Even more than the year before, open fencing "on the green" was extremely popular—many of the top combatants made themselves available for free-sparring work, including Maestros Paul MacDonald, Sean Hayes and Jeannette Acosta-Martinez. I participated as well—with impromptu poleaxe lessons—as did Bob Charron, Tom Leoni, Stephen Hand—and doubtless others I did not see.

The classes were again strong:

Day 1
"Year 2001 in the Western Martial Arts" – Brian R. Price
Keynote by Christian Henry Tobler
"Master Liechtenaeur's Art of the Longsword"
    – Christian Henry Tobler
"Sword & Buckler of Achille Marozzo" – William E. Wilson
"Creating Authentic Swordplay for the Screen"
    – Cawelti & Charron
"Backsword Techniques, 17th – 19th c." – Paul MacDonald
"Bad Rapier: The English Solution" – Stephen Hand
"Physical Conditioning, Folk Games…" – Pete Kautz
Cutting Workshop – Jim Alvarez & Gus Trim
"Master Liechtenauer's Art of Halfswording"
    – Christian Henry Tobler
"Introduction to Smallsword"
    – Jeannette Acosta-Martinez
"Fiore dei Liberi: Single-Handed Sword" – Bob Charron
"Combat with Two Swords" – Gereg Muller
"Drills for the Development of Indes & Fuhlen"
    – Brian R. Price
"Swordsmanship of Joseph Swetnam" – Steaphen Fick

Day 2
"Fighting Techniques at the Royal Armouries"
    – Andrew Deane
"Marozzo II" – William E. Wilson
"Teaching Swordsmanship to Women" – Steaphen Fick
"Extrapolated Techniques of the Scottish Dirk"
    – Dale Seago
"Armoured Longsword in Fiore dei Liberi" – Bob Charron
"19th c. Italian Duelling Sword" – Maestro Sean Hayes
"Mindset & Spirituality in the Western Martial Arts"
    – Paul MacDonald
"Techniques of the Japanese Naginata" – Miyako Tanaka

Day 3 (all-day sessions only)
"George Silver: The Last Medieval Swordsman"
    – Stephen Hand
"The Spanish Rapier" – Maestro Ramon Martinez
"Medieval Knife & Wrestling" – Pete Kautz
"Rapier of Salvatore Fabris" – Tomasso Leoni

The reception for the Eastern classes was so strong that we decided in 2003 to have a whole track dedicated to EMA. All of the classes were more in depth than had been the case with 2001, now that folks had a grounding in some of the arts and hungered for more depth. Each class was roughly an hour and a half to two hours, depending, except for the Sunday classes, which were planned to be all-day seminars. This too we will continue in 2003.

Once again there was much shopping to be done as the following were represented: Chivalry Bookshelf; Albion Works; Historic Arms & Armor; Snakepit Productions; Therion Arms; Purpleheart Armoury; James Arlen, Master Armourer; Gus Trim, Swordmaker; Mugen Daichi Company (supplier of the cool mats we did the cutting workshop with).

Once again there were tournaments; the Rapier tournament on Friday night was much more successful, a challenge-style list judged by the fencing Maestros; combatants called their own blows, but the best were selected by the panel for the honor of fencing in the final bouts. We had planned a blossfechten "unarmoured" tournament as well for the medievalists, but there was insufficient interest so only demonstration bouts were done. In the armoured tournament, the field was roughly the same size, but the quality of the displayed technique had improved dramatically.

Photographs and information on Schola 2003 (as well as information on our regular classes) can be found on the Schola Saint George website:

http://www.scholasaintgeorge.org

Fig. 1: *A sword from Oakeshott's collection. His personal swords are, according to his wishes, to be made available for the public to view.*

STUDYING ARMS WITHIN THE WIDER CIRCUMFERENCE OF HISTORY: A PERSONAL APPROACH

By Ewart Oakeshott

I was lucky enough when growing up to have a father who wrote historical novels as recreation from his work as a Civil Servant. He was a born teacher, and being a medievalist, led me deep into the lore of knights and deeds of valour from the time that I was five, passing on to me his great and abiding love for the study of history. But that is only half of the luck I had.

I also had an uncle, on the other side of my parentage – my mother's brother, who was the lion of romantic novelists throughout the second, third and fourth decades of the 20th Century. His name was Jeffery Farnol, and in his house at Brighton he had a magnificent collection of swords. In the Spring of 1937, when I was twenty years old, he moved from Brighton to Eastbourne; then a sort of heaven opened to me when (with my younger brother), I was invited to help him to clean, rearrange and hang those splendid weapons in his new home.

There, one day, as we were about to hang yet another fine sword, he took it and waved it out, saying

'I'll make my old fox fly about his ears'

as he did so. I knew what was meant by that – but I didn't know until he told me afterwards that he was quoting Ben Jonson. That was like him. He made it his business not to study history in an academic vacuum, but to read and learn all round its circumference in every way open to him, which, of course, included all the arts. And much, much more.

His favourite period was from c.1630 to c1820 A.D. He enlarged his already prolific knowledge of it, wherever possible, by making personal contact with living examples of the sort of characters he created in his novels, which in his young days were still part of contemporary society – gypsies, traveling tinkers, blacksmiths and tramps by the roadsides in Kent and Sussex, and shepherds and other farm workers out on the hills.

Then there were also the heroes of 'The Fancy', his devotion to the boxing-ring being almost obsessive, as his massive library showed; for there, among the many volumes recounting in detail the trials of highwaymen and smugglers, one would find others giving blow-by-blow descriptions of the many bare-knuckle 'mills' that were part and parcel of the mid-19th Century English scene. Thus he had all the references he needed literally at his fingertips, as well as in his prodigious memory, and above all in his heart. Could any youngster with a built-in yen for the tales and the trappings of the age of chivalry have been luckier than I was in those two – brothers-in-law who were as different in appearance as they were in character, whose thirst for history was an unslakable passion; who were rivals insofar as that they both wrote novels, yet who were the best of friends – and both of them wonderful companions for a boy with a similar passion of his own?

Now let us return to Uncle Jack, Ben Jonson, and 'the old fox'. I suspect that most of you reading this self-indulgent article will know quite well already to what it refers; but history and literature are twins, almost Siamese twins, though they are not always treated as inseparable, and in schools and colleges they can be separated from each other by the surgery of different 'disciplines'. What would 'the old fox' mean to many students in the 20th Century – students reading Eng.Lit., or as you would say, 'majoring in' that subject? Or for that matter, to some of their teachers?

Literal acceptance of the text as it stands is nonsense. Foxes do not fly – let alone at ear-level. To cope with such literary puzzles, successive editors of school editions of Shakespeare and his contemporaries have been wont to add explanatory footnotes – which often made confusion worse confounded, because even they were only 'making what they could' of what was on the page, and quite often got it wrong, sometimes offering solutions of their own making that are as much fantastic nonsense as the original appears to be.

The playwrights of the late 16th Century and the early 17th Century were writing for their own contemporaries who could be relied on to pick up topical references without the help of editors or footnotes, (as pantomime audiences do to this day); and to recognize allusion to military hardware as easily as we today recognize a reference to a BMW or a Harley-Davidson. But three hundred years on?

Which is why, many decades ago, my wife, herself both 'an educator' and a novelist, urged me to think about producing a 'military gloss' on Shakespeare. I liked the notion, but never got round to doing it. What I am doing now is to remind someone else that there may still be a need for such a work, and give a few examples of such allusions that may not be recognized as such at all, totally misunderstood, or made into laughable nonsense to those of us already 'in the know'.

The 'old fox' is one such example. Without wading through the very large and wordy mass of Jonson, I cannot put my finger on its source – or even swear that Uncle Jack quoted correctly – though I think he probably did, because we can pick up the same reference to the old fox in Bartholomew Fair (1614), Act 2, Scene 1.

> 'What would you have, sister, of a fellow who knows nothing but a basket hilt and an old fox in't?'

So what is the explanation? From a date as early as 1250 A.D., the sword-makers of Passau in Bavaria marked their blades with a schematic design of a canine animal – wolf, fox, or dog: we still don't know which. They went on using this mark until the 19th Century, with the result that 'old foxes' abound in modern collections.

It is hardly surprising that in 17th Century England the creature was seen as a fox; though wolves were still plentiful then on the continent, they had long since disappeared from England.

The second example I cite, from Troilus and Cressida, Act 3, Scene 3, is not so easy to decipher. It would be quite possible for the military allusion to be missed altogether, for two reasons. In the first place, this is one of the greatest of Shakespeare's many great speeches, a commentary on human nature and society in any age, as relevant to our own as it was, in Shakespeare's imagination, to Homer's.

The text is so dense, so closely woven, that any teacher of English literature would be exercised to point out all the examples of this consummate use of the English language, for instance the personification of two abstract concepts – by which Time is transformed into a beggar, and Oblivion into the collective noun for the fickle, ingrate public such as the pop-stars of today experience when their 'bubble reputation' bursts after a short period of fame and popularity.

(But I do not propose to conduct an English lesson – though my wife would love to!)

The second reason is that the meaning of so many of the words in this speech has changed almost beyond recognition. In England, we still use 'wallets' (usually made of fine leather) to keep our paper money, credit cards, airline tickets etc. safe, by carrying them in our breast-pockets. This is a far cry from the 'wallet' in this speech, which refers to the largish pouch which beggars once carried round the waist, into which they put such 'alms' (usually scraps of food) that were thrown to them. And so to the military allusion, and the word, 'monumental'.

The scene is set: Outside Achilles' tent.

The great Greek hero, famous for his feats of arms, Achilles, is having a long fit of the sulks, keeping to his 'tent' (?) and refusing to be involved in the Greeks' almost panic search for a champion to take on the Trojan champion, Hector, in single combat. The Greek leaders are of one mind that there is no other warrior as up to the task as Achilles. So wily old Ulysses, he of the golden tongue and the devious mind, sets out to either persuade or shame Achilles into doing his duty.

> 'Time has, my lord, a wallet at his back.
> Wherein he puts alms for Oblivion
> (A great-siz'ed monster of ingratitudes;)
> These scraps are good deeds past,
> Which are devour'd as soon as made,
> Forgot as soon as done.
> Perseverance, good my lord, keeps honour bright.
> To have done, is to hang, quite out of fashion
> Like a rusty mail, in monumental mockery.

So: we have metaphorical good deeds past hanging somewhere likened to a rusty mail. Good deeds past? Achievements.

Where might you find an out of fashion, rusty mail shirt hanging? Over a knight's monument, on show with the rest of his military 'achievements', above his tomb. As those of the Black Prince hung, until replaced by replicas earlier in this century, above his wonderful effigy in Canterbury Cathedral. His helmet, sword, shield, gauntlets and surcoat and the rest were all there once, till his great deeds were dishonoured by Time, his sword stolen, the little lion gadlings of this gauntlets fell off and disappeared, and his surcoat began to rot into shreds. His fame as a warrior forgotten, his 'achievments' hung in mockery, above his monument.[1]

But the word 'monumental' no longer means what Shakespeare meant it to mean. To a modern ear, it is likely only to mean large, massive, oversized, of great dimensions, obvious ('Don't be such a monumental idiot!')

Once you recognize the allusion, the passage falls into place – as history, as well as showing Shakespeare as the Great observer of mankind that he was, at his very best.

Next we'll turn to Hamlet, where such examples abound; some of which can be taken at face value; but some which are very obscure, and have to be worked on to ravel out the true meaning. Hamlet pretends to be mad. His wicked uncle the King of Denmark sets some of his erstwhile friends to watch him. Rosencrantz and Guildenstern. They pretend to humour him in his madness – till Hamlet (to let the audience know that he is 'on to' them and their purpose) says in an aside

'They fool me to the top of my bent'[2]

Well, it's easy enough to guess the drift of what he means by its context, but that does not explain his choice of words. That depends on whether you are acquainted with the word 'bent' as a noun. It can still be heard, usually in the plural, in common parlance in some isolated rural districts, especially in East Anglia, meaning reed-blades, or blades of grass. A bent is a synonym for 'blade' in general.

'To the top of my blade' then, i.e. 'right up to the hilt'. As far as a naked sword blade can possibly go to do its deadly work.

(Richard Burton, in his Book of the Sword, draws attention to the resemblance of a sword's shape to that of a reed-blade, suggesting, perhaps, that this part of a sword was so named because of its resemblance to the leaves of reeds, and not the other way round.)

Another splendid sources of allusions to sword-play is Romeo and Juliet. My Uncle Jack used to love to puzzle people viewing his collection by taking down a long rapier, making passes with it, declaring *'He is the very butcher of a silk button'*.

Then he would go on to quote Mercutio talking to Benvolio about the challenge sent by Tybalt to Romeo. (Act 2, Scene 4.)

Ben: *Why, what is Tybalt?*
Mer: *More than the prince of cats, I can tell you. O, he's the courageous captain of compliments. He fights as you might sing prick-song, keeps time, distance and proportion; rests me he minim rests, one, two, and the third in your bosom. The very butcher of a silk button, a duelist, a duelist. A gentleman of the very first house, of the first and second cause: Ah, the immortal passado! The punto reverso! The hai! –*

Ben: *The what?*
Mer: *The pox on such antic, lisping, affecting fantasticoes; these new tuners of accents! (etc. etc.)*

Again, taking this in context, one can easily see what Mercutio means. Let us look deeper. One of the great gambits of the 'professional' swordsman was to 'play with' his opponent, cutting off his clothes piece by piece, intimidating him before killing him. Viz. Cyrano de Bergerac: *'When I end the refrain I touch'*[3].

(It is interesting to note in passing, that Shakespeare must have read that immortal work, 'Paradoxes of Defence' by George Silver, Gentleman, published in 1599, in which the author makes great mock of the Italian masters of fence. Experts cannot agree about the exact date of Shakespeare's play as we now know it, but in my youth it was assigned to 1591; and I would like to put forward my support of that later date on the grounds I have suggested above).

The Merchant of Venice, Act 1. Scene 1.

'Why should a man, whose blood is warm within, sit like his grandsire cut in alabaster?'

A reference, of course, to the very many tomb effigies, mostly of men in complete amour, (some with their wives beside them) which fortunately for us, still abound in England. Most of these would be more than a century old by Shakespeare's time, so his audiences would know at once what he was implying. To people like us, they are a cache of information. It is from these, among other works of art, that we are able to relate surviving armours to the 14th and 15th Centuries, in order to given them *'a local habitation and a name'*, and therefore a (generally) reliable date; for these effigies are, in the main, carved (or cut), in exquisitely find detail, from alabaster.

Perhaps the most absurd misunderstanding I have ever met is to be found at the beginning of Hamlet, where Marcellus is telling the skeptical Horatio how he had seen the ghost of Hamlet's father, the late King of Denmark. Then the ghost appears. Horatio has no option but to believe what he has seen *'of his own eyes'*. Marcellus persists

Mar: *Is it not like the king?'*
Hor: *As thou art to thyself:*
Such was the very armour he had on,
When he the ambitious Norway combated.
So frowned he once, when, in an angry parle,
He smote the sledded Polacks on the ice.[4]

This is a difficult passage in any case. The late King of Denmark, at war with Norway, was engaged, before a battle, in a parley with the Norwegian commander. But who were 'the sledded Polacks'?

The editors of the 19ᵗʰ and 20ᵗʰ centuries seems unable to make head or tail of it. They decided that the 'Polacks' must be Denmarks' Polish allies. They were 'sledded' (according to several such 'glosses') because this all took place on frozen water; but where or why did Denmark 'smite' them on the ice?

Surely this has to be the silliest misunderstanding ever of an Elizabethan dramatist who knew perfectly well what he was saying. What he must have said, I believe, though quite incomprehensible to a lot of 20ᵗʰ century commentators was

He smote his leaded poll-axe on the ice.

Take the whole passage. We know that the king was angry; what more natural, then when he is 'engaged in angry parle' that a man should strike the butt of the weapon in his hand on the ground at his feet, in this case, ice? We can understand that this weapon was a poll-axe, but why was it 'leaded'? Well there are many references in 15ᵗʰ Century and early 16ᵗʰ Century 'fechtbucher' (fighting manuals) to poll-axes having sheet lead wrapped about the head to give the weapon greater weight and more striking-power. So, if Hamlet's father, fully armed and with his poll-axe in his hand, while speaking with his enemy, should bring it down on the ice to emphasize his anger or the point he was making, or both, what could be more natural – or dramatic, in the way a playwright would wish?

Puzzled editors, certainly those in my youth – made what they imagined the most sensible interpretation they could of it; but why the King should have thought fit to 'smite' his allies, in their sleds, on the ice, neither heaven, nor they apparently knew!

Now this is more than strange, because they were sometimes very thorough in their research into what Shakespeare himself wrote down for them.

Some decades ago I read a three-volume edition of Shakespeare produced in 1880, a most thorough, scholarly affair, abounding in footnotes. The editor queried the 'Sledded Polacks' and explained that they were 'Polanders', i.e., what we should refer to now as Poles: natives of Poland. He was more explicit in his footnote and translated 'the sledded Polacks' for the reader as the 'sledged Polanders' adding,

'though it may be doubtful whether the original 'Polax' was intended as singular or plural; many editors read 'Polack'.'[5]

Shakespeare had it right, first time – but they didn't believe him!

I have only given here a very few examples from the great mass of military allusions in the works of those early dramatists: in doing so I have enjoyed a self-indulgent trip into nostalgia with you, and present it in the hope that someone 'out there' among you will take up the idea, and carry it further?

- NOTES -

[1] In case any who have not yet visited this shrine to the Black Prince as it is now should regret that they never saw those 'achievements', let me hasten to tell you that what was left of the originals were taken down, restored as far as possible, and are now on show again in specially designed, preservative glass cases by the side of wonderful replicas hanging above. Time, luck and perhaps even conscience have restored other pieces, for example, many of the little lion gadlings. Perhaps, Time, too may yet restore the rest.

[2] William Shakespeare, Hamlet, Prince of Denmark, Act Three, Scene Two

[3] Edmond Rostand, Cyrano de Bergerac, Act One, Scene Four. The original text reads "a la fin de l'envoi, je touche" Translation by Stephen Hand

[4] William Shakespeare, Hamlet, Prince of Denmark, Act One, Scene One.

[5] It has been some decades since I read this footnote and though I remember it clearly, I did not have the foresight to note it down at the time. It is unfortunate that I have been unable to find the volume again. I expect that the original passage differs in detail from my recollection, though I am sure that I have captured its essence.

MUCH ADO ABOUT NOTHING,
OR THE CUTTING EDGE OF FLAT PARRIES

BY GREGORY MELE

The art of parrying, and more importantly the art of parrying and riposting is traditionally considered to be a key, if not *the* key, element of swordplay. A great deal of time and effort is spent learning the proper parries, counters and ripostes in the sport of modern fence, and in the formalized methods of theatrical combat.

It is generally accepted in modern fencing schools that the sword defends by moving into line to receive an attack, just as it is about to land, edge-to-edge:

> When threatened with a point thrust in saber, the same parrying technique is employed as that used in foil...

> When attacked with the cutting edge of the blade, the concept of parrying is quite different. I like to use the image of creating a triangular protective cage with my blade, and you can do this well with just three parries - three, four and five, or the head parry....

> In saber, the attack must be blocked with the forte of the blade, and one should avoid what I call fishing for the opponent's blade. Instead the parrying blade is brought to its position in my protective cage only when the attack is about to arrive on target...

> Parries are done with the cutting edge of the blade.[1]

This methodology seems to have been taught consistently by the military and civilian fencing masters of the 18th and 19th centuries:

> These defences, or parries, are so very similar to the parries of the foil, that I shall adhere in my lessons to the names given in foil fencing...

To Stop Cut 1

Quarte: *Turn the hand to quarte, carrying it a little to the left, raising the point slightly, and receive the cut on the forte as near to the shell as possible.*

To Stop Cut 2

Tierce: *Turn the hand to tierce, raising the point slightly, and carry the hilt a little to the right, edge to the right front, and thus receive the cut on the forte.*[2]

However, handling correctly fashioned replicas of medieval swords, and a study of period artwork, reveals two startling points. Firstly, that hard, edge-on-edge contact with a sharpened sword, rather than a dull cavalry saber or an edgeless, thrust-oriented smallsword, leads to the sword blade chipping, cracking, and often, breaking outright. Secondly, as will be shown, many of the fighting manuals of the 15th century clearly show the swords meeting either edge-to-flat or flat-to-flat. Sword scholar Ewart Oakeshott, is supported by many modern swordsmiths in his assertion that the flexibility of the sword across its flat is specifically designed to allow the flat, rather than the edge to absorb *and deflect* the impact of a parry.[3]

For the sake of clarity, let's define what we mean by a sword "edge." In simplest terms, the edge is simply the intersection point of the flats or "sides" of the sword that forms what would be, if sharpened, the cutting portion of the blade.

Now we have a clear definition of a sword's "edge." If we had such a clear definition of "edge parries," and "flat parries," I wouldn't need to write this article. Unfortunately, the lack of clarity in early texts, compared with modern methods and practical experimentation, has led to a host of theories about how the medieval and early Renaissance cutting sword was used to parry. These theories have led to a rather heated debate amongst modern practitioners, and have clogged Internet forums, private email, seminars, and book reviews with more verbiage than an unabridged dictionary.

A little knowledge is a dangerous thing...

There are a variety of reasons that modern students of the sword persist in the idea of hard blocks and edge-parries in medieval and early (pre-rapier) Renaissance swordplay. Firstly, the work of most stage combat shows precisely this. Secondly, the modern sport of saber fencing *does* use rigid edge parries, as did the 19th century military saber methods. The reasons for this are numerous, and beyond the scope of this article.[4]

This issue has often ironically been further clouded by reconstructionists of historical fencing. Since the late 19th century, some reconstructionists have relied upon modern fencing for apparent similarities between sabre fencing and medieval techniques, have created an essentially artificial system of pseudo-historical fencing, essentially based on the sabre.[5] This method is still used by some reconstructionists today, and carries the serious risk of distorting the historical work, based on what the student thinks they already *know*, as opposed to what the historical treatises actually *instruct*.[6]

Another problem in the reconstructionist community is that the majority of practitioners study, or have access to, the rapier-oriented manuals of the 16th and early 17th centuries, and have again, tried to force-fit their principles to earlier weapon systems. While this is perhaps a better fit than the modern sport sabre, a thrust-oriented, civilian sword is simply not the same as a cut-and-thrust weapon designed for use in duels, battles and tournaments, both in and out of armour.

The simple truth is that to study medieval swordsmanship, you have to study the medieval masters first and foremost. The works of 16th century masters who teach the older weapons "in the ancient fashion" form a useful second tier of study, but where they differ from their predecessors, and why, should be clearly noted.[7]

It's not technique, it's tactics

So what does this have to do with parrying? Not much, accept that anyone who claims that you *always* defend with your edge *or* your flat, or spends any great deal of time teaching parry-riposte concepts at all, is simply a poor scholar. You see, the medieval masters hardly speak of "parries" at all!

Rather, the guiding principle is avoidance and counter-attack, with the swords coming together in the meeting of two attacks, or in a momentary bind, but little-else.

This idea, and a good insight into the medieval mind-set of defensive actions is perhaps best expressed in a statement attributed to the 14th century German Grandmaster, Johannes Liechtenauer, from whom most of the surviving German school of swordplay is said to originate:

> *And beware of all displacements that poor fencers use. And remember: when he strikes, then strike also, and when he thrusts, then thrust also.*[8]

By this, Liechtenauer does not mean you do not defend yourself. Rather, he means that every action, in reality, should be directed towards the goal of slaying the opponent, and secondarily defend by time, distance, place, or counter-attacks with opposition. Thus even "defense," is really offense.

The "Hierarchy of Defense"

This guiding principle was still the foundation for defensive principles two centuries, later, when Joachim Meyer wrote his own, massive, fencing treatise[9].

In one simple set of instructions, Meyer neatly displays the variety of defensive options[10] taught with the longsword: deflecting parry with the flat, a flat parry and bind, or a deflective parry made by cutting into the on-coming attack:

> *However, if he strikes from above against your right, then take his blow on your flat and step out towards his right, or (when the swords have clashed together), remain with your blade on his, and wind the false edge in toward his head; turn the sword quickly out of the wind and come into the Longpoint, so that you send his following attack away from you with the true edge...*[11]

The German masters advised the student to defend himself in the following manner of decreasingly "perfect" technique.

1. Attack before your opponent.
2. Void the attack and strike simultaneously (in time)
3. Counterattack in time, parrying and striking in one action
4. Deflect the attack, either flat-to-edge, edge-to-flat, or by "attacking" the opponent's weapon, and immediately attack;
5. Static block and immediately attack;
6. Void the attack without counter attacking;
7. Static block of any variety.

As you can see, in this hierarchy, a parry of any sort is barely in the top half of the preferred responses, and simply parrying is really the least desirable method of defense. Meyer elaborates these principles in his only chapter on parrying with the longsword, entitled: *A useful warning concerning parries*

Meyer divides parries into two categories:

> *The first is when you displace [parry] without any particular advantage, out of fear, which is the common fashion, in which you do nothing else than*

displace the strokes that come from your opponent, using your own weapon against his.[12]

He then goes on to quote from Liechtenauer to show how, while this sort of defense is not altogether forbidden, it is frowned upon. Rather, says Meyer:

For more usefulness I will gladly here classify blows and parries executed in one stroke, and solely teach you how you should execute these blows for parrying, which may also take place in two ways.[13] *Firstly, you may set aside*[14] *your opponent's blow with a stroke; secondly when you press in upon him with a blow, having taken the forward part of his weapon.*[15]

The other way to parry is when you parry your opponent with a stroke that hits him at the same time, which the ancients especially praise as suitable.[16]

The remainder of the section goes on to describe how the basic vertical, diagonal, and horizontal blows can all be used to strike and parry in one blow. These simultaneous counter-attacks serve a secondary role of blocking with the edge, should the opponent's blow land. These instructions are identical to those of 14th and 15th century German masters:

Note: When your adversary strikes at you from his right side with an Oberhau (strike from above), then hit with a Zornhau (lit. 'Strike of Wrath') [diagonal blow down] from your right shoulder against it. Strike with your true edge and in your strong. When he is weak at the sword then, thrust into his face along his blade.[17]

Finally, Meyer also follows earlier German masters in relying upon false-edge blows and parry combinations:

These blows are especially invented so that you can parry and strike....when you are struck at with an Oberhau (from above), then step with the right foot towards your opponent's side, and strike across simultaneously with a Zwirch, (a horizontal blow with the false edge) so that you catch his blow on the forte of your blade near your cross guard, and hit his left ear with the outer part of your sword; thus you parry and hit in one.[18]

The other way to parry is when you parry your opponent with a stroke that hits him at the same time, which the ancients especially praise as suitable.[19]

Pasta and Pudding: Italian and English Traditions
The second "great tradition" of medieval swordsmanship is the Italian. Sadly, although we have the names of many 15th century Italian masters and their works, only the work of two masters, Fiore dei Liberi and Filippo Vadi, have thus come to light.[20] The *Flos Duellatorum* of dei Liberi was written in 1409, and refers to defensive blade actions as *coverta*. *Coverta* literally means "blanket", and is sometimes used to describe any sort of general "protection" (think of "to cover") from the enemy sword through blade contact. A "coverta" can be actively used against a cut, a thrust, or to passively protect the swordsman by simply closing a line of attack while entering.

Filippo Vadi was a Pisan master active in the third quarter of the 15th century. Vadi's manuscript is a plate-for-plate, and often, caption-for-caption, transmission of Fiore's earlier work. However, the manuscript's introductory material adds the Pisan master's own nomenclature, methodology, and concepts, so that the final work is more than simply a late 15th century redaction of the *Flos Duellatorum*.

Vadi, like Fiore, defines defensive actions that block or deflect an incoming attack as *coverta*:

Be well aware and understand my writing, if your partner strikes with the sword, be sure to cross the blades.

Be sure you never go out of the way, make a "coverta"[21] *and aim the point at your foe's face, and aim your blows at the head.*[22]

However, Vadi also adds a section to his manuscript where he discusses *parata*, or parries. Here, he is consistent with the German masters, in that the best way to intercept an incoming blow with your sword, is to cut into the attack:

When you parry, parry with fendente [blows from above] slightly push your sword away and press down the partner's sword.[23]

Why Vadi draws this distinction between *coverta* and *parata* is unclear. However, a clue may exist in how Vadi discusses executing parata. These actions are a made by striking into the oncoming attack (usually with a fendente), whereas coverta seem to be a more general defensive action.

The entire known corpus of 15th century English fencing material, are three anonymous manuscripts on the use of the longsword.[24] Sadly, they are not comparable in detail or clarity to the handful of surviving Italian manuscripts. Besides the obtuse character of the Middle English they are composed in, these manuscripts do not really discuss parrying at all; they are essentially solo drills or one side of a paired drill.

In the Harleian MS, there is a "a reuence to ye cros of thy hilte" that may be a guard or a parry. One intriguing line does suggest something in sympathy with what we see in German and Italian sources of the period, namely counter a blow with a blow:

Greue not gretly thov yu be tochyd a 1yte
ffor a aftr stroke ys betr yf thou dar hÿ smyte[25]

and, likewise:

Wt a renyg qrtr sette hÿ oute of hys way.[26]

The first readily understandable native text of English fencing, are George Silver's *Paradoxes of Defence* (1599) and his unpublished *Bref Instructions Upo My pradoxes of Defence*. Although published in the late 16th century, Silver's work is based on the traditional English method being taught before the introduction of the rapier, and there is little reason to suspect that this method had changed notably in the prior century.[27]

Silver has little interest in detailing *how* to parry, merely telling the student to *ward*,[28] and sometimes mentioning which guard position they will move into, in the process. Silver's guiding principle, however is to strike *from cover*, and finish *in cover*, and he seems to care little with which part of the sword is used to affect this:

yf ii Men fight both upo open fyght, he yt first breaketh his distance, yf he attempts to stryke at the other's hed, shalbe surely stryken on the hed himself, yf the patient Agent strike ther at his Comynge in, & slyp a lyttle back wt all, for yt slydinge back maketh an indirection, wherby yor blow Crosseth[29] his hed, & maketh a true ward for yor owne, this will yt be, because of his length of tyme in his comynge in.[30]

This is much the same technique as the German *Zornhau*, in which an oblique cut forms a simultaneous edge parry, should the opponent's blow land. Silver's work, in particular, makes heavy use of "stops" - blocks made by intercepting the attacker's blow with your forte, at the start of his cut, before the blow gains momentum. Yet, his work also relies heavily upon the True Guardant ward, identical to the single-handed hanging guard shown in Talhoffer, and which can just as easily be used to deflect or counter-cut blows without taking a hard block on the edge.[31]

So Prove It!
Which is all well and fine, and shows just how your edge might be used to actively parry and counter-cut with opposition in both single and double-time defense,[32] but does nothing to prove the contention that the flat was in anyway used to deflect or parry. The question may be asked, "how do we know this as a fact? Do any of the historical Fechtbücher (fencing books) describe how to parry in detail?"

Actually, prior to the 16th century, the historical Fechtbücher don't really describe *how* to parry in detail, as will be seen below. Examples of sword-on-sword blocks in Medieval artwork are notably rare, reinforcing the notion that avoiding a cut is preferable to trying to parry it. The most efficient and effective response to an attack is to counter-attack, rather than parry and riposte. This is *precisely* what is described, time and again, in the surviving fencing treatises of the 14th and 15th centuries. Where parries are used, they are almost universally single time with longer weapons, and double-time with shorter weapons, like the messer.[33]

In fact, we hear little about blade-to-blade contact at all before the latter half of the 16th century. When a shield is present, this seems to be the primary defense,[34] and for two-handed swordplay, the goal seems to be to step and counter-attack. One interesting anecdote does appear in the Norse saga <u>Kormac's Saga</u>. In a Holmganga (formal duel), Kormac parries Bersi's sword Hviting using the edge of the sword Skofnung, which he has borrowed from his friend Skeggi. In the duel, Kormac is caught off-guard and makes a desperate parry with his sword's edge. He breaks the point off of Bersi's sword, but in the process badly nicks and chips Skofnung. The skald's tell us that Skeggi was "greatly annoyed" that Kormac did not take better care of his weapon.[35]

But one paragraph in one Norse saga does not a system of defense make. So we must support our premise with iconographic evidence, textual analysis, and practical research. Let's hit the books:

Tower Manuscript I.33 c.1275 - 1300 AD
The oldest known fighting manuscript ('Fechtbüch'), the anonymous 13th century German sword and buckler manuscript seems to show rather clearly the use of the flat in a variety of deflecting parries and flat-to-flat binds. The actual text never describes a parry, more than to say "here the scholar puts aside the blow and then...," [paraphrase mine] all without referencing the part of the sword. More importantly, most of the time the blades are shown in contact with one another, the text calls it a *bind* rather than a block or parry of any sort.

While the art of this period is only semi-representational, a clear picture of the methods of I.33 can be discerned, in which the sword wards and binds, the buckler then continues this bind or press, freeing the sword to make an immediate counter-attack. When we compare the seeming "flat parries" of I.33 with later depiction in the works of Hans Talhoffer (1443, 1459,1467) and the manuscript illustrated by Albrecht Dürer (1512) we will find that the art may be more reliable than we thought.

Fig. 1: Royal Armouries MS I.33.

Fiore dei Liberi, *Flos Duellatorum, 1409*

Fiore dei Liberi was born sometime around 1350 in Cividale del Friuli, a small town on the river Natisone in Italy. Very little is known about Fiore, except for what is written in the prologue of his treatise. As a young man he to learn and train in swordsmanship under a variety of German and Italian masters. He participated in numerous battles in and around Italy for the last 20 years of the 14th century. Around 1400, he entered the court of Niccolo III d'Este, Marquise of Ferrara, as the master at arms. He then began to write the *Flower of Battle* for the Marquise's knights, at Signore di Ferrara's bequest.

Unarmoured Combat
Figures 2 - 7

Although the artwork is very simplistic, the artist is still able to show wrist positions, weight distribution, and movement, so the art cannot be discounted out of hand.

The figures in this section all refer to a series of instructions in which Fiore details what to do anytime the swordsmen has crossed blades with his opponent. Since Fiore does not advise straight vertical blows, this will most often arise from two diagonal blows bringing the sword edges together in at an oblique angle. However, at the same time, the "opponent" in Fiore's instructions is sometimes said to make *colpi villani* (villainous blows), which are strong, vertical cuts, so both sorts of blow must be taken into account.

Since Fiore's straight thrust is made with the edges vertical, Fig 2 shows flat-to-flat or flat-to-edge contact in a thrust with opposition:

> "This is a cruel fight with the sword's end [point], but there is not a more dangerous thrust. You used your thrust, and with the point I hit you. It can be made safer by moving out of the way."[36]

Fig 3 is more difficult to analyze. Flat-to-flat, or flat-to-edge? The text suggests a thrust at the grip's conclusion, which works best in reconstruction if the swords meet flat-to-flat, and this technique is viewed as a follow-on to the previous action:

> "As I hold your sword's handle,
> I hit you in the face with the point."[37]

Fig 4 Carefully study the arm/wrist positions of the combatants. The right-hand man's backhand cut (squalembratto roverso) is parried with the flat. *However,* the same picture could represent a vertical cut being deflected by a counter-cut to the blade, edge-to-flat. Either way, the text does indicate a parry:

> "This is a parry[38] of a blow that comes from the left-hand side. It is used to deceive the opponent."[39]

Fig 5 shows the contact from Fig 4 contact maintained against the right-hand attacker's edge with the left-hand man's flat, as he closes to grapple.

> "Through my left parry, I have blocked you,
> From close combat and wounds you cannot flee."[40]

Armoured Combat (*Duellatorum in Arnis*):
Fig 6 Shows a fendente parried at the half-sword, using a flat parry.

Fig 7 In this plate, the blow parried in Fig 6 is pushed aside with the flat, and the counter-attack made.

> "From the Maestro's parry comes this thrust,
> As other techniques could as well come from it."[41]

Talhoffer's *Fechtbuch*, 1467

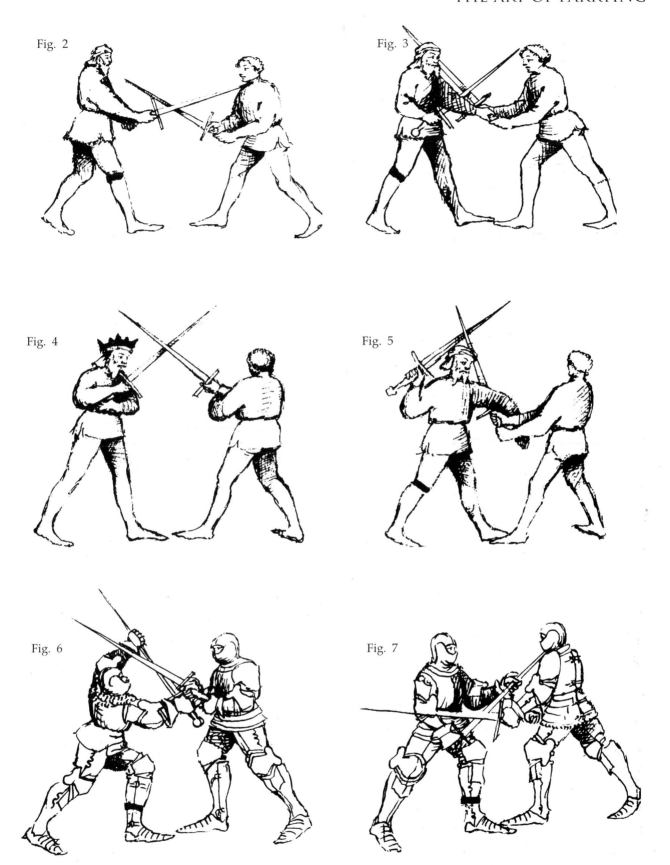

Fig. 2

Fig. 3

Fig. 4

Fig. 5

Fig. 6

Fig. 7

Fig. 8

Fig. 9

Fig. 10

Fig. 11

Talhoffer is the best known of the Liechtenauer school, primarily because of the numerous editions of his manual he created while in service to various Swabian lords. Hans Talhoffer may have been born c. 1410-1420 and wrote about swordsmanship, poleax play, wrestling and dagger fighting. There were at least six editions of his work, of which the best known, the 1467 Gotha Codex, is analyzed here.

Single Sword and Messer (a long, single-edge knife): Plate 226 (Fig 8)
A flat parry is made with the messer against an *Oberhau* (overhand cut) made high inside to the left side of the face. The defender's hand is completely turned over, striking into the blow with the flat of the knuckle side of the hand, as described in the caption:

> *"The swordsman on the right deflects the cut aside with a turned-around hand and will step forward and wrench his blade around to the other side."*[42]

Compare with Plate 240 and Plate 5 of Albrecht Dürer's Fechtbüch, below, as well as Tower MS I.33, above.[43]

Sword and buckler:
Plate 234 (Fig 9)
Note the similarity between this plate, and Plate 227, above. The left-hand figure is binding the blade with his flat as he closes with his opponent for the grip. This technique only works if you ward by simply gliding your blade past his. The caption reads:

> *"Here he has displaced his opponents cut from above, shoves him away, and is going to wrench his blade around for a counter attack."*[44]

Plate 236 (Fig 10)
Again. This time the right-hand figure blocks with both weapons, but his sword is clearly turned to receive the blow on its flat. The caption reads:

> *"The swordsman on the right sets aside the cut with both sword and buckler, and rushes into his opponent."*[45]

Plate 240 (Fig 11)
Similar to Plate 226, only this time, in the sword and buckler section. The caption reads:

> *"Then displace **with the upside-down hand** [emphasis mine] and turn and cut the one standing behind me."*[46]

Here, even the caption makes it clear what we are seeing, the hand is turned,[47] so that the blades will meet, and the defender's flat will glide across the attacker's edge, as he continues around to cut at the second opponent behind him. [48]

<u>Longsword</u>

Plate 12 (Fig 12)

Here, a "free" thrust from the guard *Ochs* (Ox) so that the defender can then kick his opponent's belly, as the opponent's sword is received on the flat of the sword's forte.[49] The thrust is a safety precaution to cover the head and to draw the attention (and the blade) away from the kicking leg.

Plate 18 (Fig 13)

This is a counter-thrust made against the cut from above. The swordsmen on the left strikes around his head from right to left, deflecting the cut with his flat, and thrusting in the same time.

Plate 26 (Fig 14)

I have included this as an example of half-swording techniques. The sword is indisputably being parried flat-to-flat to facilitate the bind.

Plate 36 (Fig 15)

Another half-swording technique. Here the flat is being used to parry a vertical cut, and counter-thrust with opposition.

Plate 39 (Fig 16)

This is the *brentschirn*, or the bind in the half-sword position, and the blades are clearly meeting flat-to-flat in order to bind.

Codex Wallerstein

A rather unusual "amalgam" Fechtbüch, the *Codex Wallerstein* is comprised of at least two fechtbücher that appear to have been illustrated by two, and possibly three, different artists. Portions of this work may date to c1380 – 1410, while the rest is dated to the later half of the 15th century, while the written text appears to be consistent throughout the manuscript. The present fechtbuch or **Codex Wallerstein** is written in German and contains extraordinary images, many depicting fully armoured individuals engaged using longsword, spear and pollaxe weapons.[50]

Like other German treatises, the Codex Wallerstein often deflects incoming attacks by using the short edge to strike into blow. This is clearly illustrated in the two following examples:

No 17, Plate 9 (Fig 17)

> *"Before/Next, you bind someone on the sword, and he strikes strongly at your head, so deflect with your short edge and run on him so that he has to strike;*

Fig. 12

Fig. 13

Fig. 14

Fig. 15

Fig. 16

if he strikes you from the other side, put your sword on his left shoulder, so that you hit his ear, and this is called 'the placed' and this is called 'before.'"[51]

No 18, Plate 10 (Fig 18)
"After/Next, one strikes you strongly from above, so wait and parry his blow with your short edge; but if he is quick and strikes while you could lay his sword on him, so let him strike freely, and hit with the short edge in his sword as it is depicted here: this way, you bind him on the sword and hit him in his ear and the back of his head."[52]

Use of the flat to deflect an attack is called out clearly in the section on fencing with the messser/falchion. In reconstruction, lead to similar positions as those seen in MS I.33, and are clearly active actions made against the incoming attack. This is clearly seen in the illustrations from Albrecht Dürer's reinterpretation of the Codex Wallerstein.

The following sequences also note the importance of not merely relying on iconography when interpreting medieval fencing treatises. In each of these cases, the plate shows the riposte from the parry, rather than the parry itself. Only the text instructs how the defense is made.

No 65, Plate 57

"Then, you fight someone with the falchion. If he strikes at you, deflect with your falchion to the side with your flat and on your crosspiece, and go quickly forward with your left foot, and hit him with the pommel in his arm as it is depicted here, so that you strike him in his head."[53]

No 69, Plate 61

"Next one strikes downwards at your head, so deflect with your flat and on your crosspiece, and push his falchion to the side, so that he has to strike, and when he wants to strike, find the openings and chop his arm off, as it is depicted here."[54]

Oplodidaskalia sive Armorum Tractandorum Meditation, aka "Albrecht Dürer's *Fechtbuch*, 1512
Yes, *that* Albrecht Dürer. Dürer's work is considered to be a re-working of the earlier Wallerstein Codex. [55] As a master artist known for his attention to detail, his work is particularly important. Perhaps even more importantly, Dürer shows the same flat parries and turned hand positions we find in the "non-representational" artwork of Manuscript I.33.

<u>Longsword/Greatsword</u>
Plates 9, 10 and 12 (Fig 19 - 21)
In plate 9, the right-hand swordsman has cut with a *Krumphau* causing the swords to cross in the hanging guards, while the left-hand figure turns this into a thrust into his opponent's abdomen as his blade is struck on the flat. In practical reconstruction, the blades essentially meet at oblique angles.

In Plate 10, the left man's vertical cut is displaced with a simultaneous scalp cut with the false edge. The displacement occurs edge-to-flat. This is a recurring technique in the German school.

In plate 12 we see the reverse of this technique, as the scalp cut with the false edge is put aside by the right-hand swordsman, who simultaneously turns his point into his opponent's belly.

Figure 17: Codex Wallerstein No. 18, plate 9

Figure 18: Codex Wallerstein No. 18, plate 10

Fig. 19

Fig. 20

Fig. 21

Fig. 22

Fig. 23

Fig. 24

Fig. 25

Fig. 26

Fig. 27

Fig. 28

Fig. 29

Messer/Falchion

Plate 5 (Fig 22)
In this plate, the right-hand swordsman clearly parries and binds with the flat to turn a vertical cut.[56] The bent wrist is clearly detailed, and the plate *suggests* that the parry sets up a thrust with opposition. Compare this with Tower Ms. I.33, and Plate 240 in Talhoffer's 1467 manuscript, above.

Plate 8, 10, 12 and 13 (Fig 23 - 26)
These are half-swording techniques used with the messer/falchion. Again, note that the defender's flat is clearly used to defend against the edge or flat.

Plates 20, 22 and 26 (Fig 27 - 29)
In plate 20 we do know who is the attacker, or who is the defender. However, note a back-edge strike/parry from the right-hand swordsman vs. a thrust/flat parry with opposition from the left.

In plate 22 the thrust is met with a vertical blow, cutting edge to flat.

In plate 26 the left-hand figure clearly parries with his flat against a vertical cut.

Joachim Meyer, *Gründtliche beschreibung der freyen ritterlichen und adelichen kunst des fechtens*, 1570
As we have seen above, Meyer is primarily a text manual, and as we have already seen, he clearly describes cutting into the opponent's attack or redirecting (*absetzen*) the incoming blade with your true or false edge.

Meyer also details a series of "displacements" (*versetzen*), done with the flat of the blade.

from *Handwork*:

"Running Off"
> "From whichever side you bind the opponent on his sword, when the blades meet then reverse your hands and let it run-off your flat with the false edge down; while you pull your hilt up high for a blow; and do this for both sides."[57]

"Pressing the Hands"
> "For example, if an opponent strikes down with a hard blow, then go under his blow with the Crown, or else a higher parry, or displace him with the Hanging-point [a hanging guard], and catch his sword on the flat of your blade, thus coming to him from below his sword."[58]

"Pressing the Hands"
> "For example, if an opponent strikes down with a Buffalo strike (a hard, sweeping blow), then go under his blow with the Crown, or else a higher parry, or displace him with the hanging- [see below], and catch his sword on the flat of your blade, thus coming to him from below his sword."[59]

Hanging
> "Hanging is easy to understand from the previous technique. It is done thus: When you stand in the Plow [a guard with the tip pointed at the opponent's face, hands mid-level] and your opponent strikes at you, then lift your hilt so that the blade hangs toward the ground and his blow is caught on the flat of your blade; then work with winding to the nearest opening."[60]

And least we start to give the appearance that the more familiar edge parry on the flat is not shown, from the notes on the guard of the Key:

> "...and at the same time as you thrust, turn the true edge against his incoming stroke; now when you have caught his blow on the forte of your true edge, remain hard on his blade, and wind inward and outward to his head."[61]

Much Ado About Nothing
So where does this leave us?

As I said at the beginning of this paper, the historical fencing community has largely been divided into two camps: those that only parry and block with the edge, and those that only use the flat. Yet, in reality, a study of the actual master's work reveals a far more complex picture:

1. Parrying was simply not a favored response in the methodology of 14th - 16th century masters. Of the manuscripts surveyed in this article, *any* form of parry only occurs between 25 and 33% of the time.

2. The preferred defensive methods for combat with edged weapons were avoidance, a variety of single-time counter-attacks, and time-cuts or thrusts.

3. Of those parries used, the flat was clearly preferred for deflection-riposte actions, the edge for single-time counter-attacks, and recieving the blow on the forte to stop and bind the opposing steel in order to close to grips.

4. Except when seeking to close to grips, these parries, in their various forms, were neither *stops*, *blocks*, nor static *crosses*, as has been taught in modern sabre fencing, but rather, are dynamic actions, moving almost simultaneously into an attack.

5. The reason for all of this has far less to do with

preserving the sword's edge, than it does an understanding of timing and biomechanics - two of the key factors underlying all martial arts.

Which means that the entire parrying debate has been "much ado about nothing." The staunch defenders of either camp are simply *both* wrong,[62] their arguments based largely on what they think they know, rather than a detailed study of what the master's actually wrote.

As a final irony, it seems many of those same *fin de siecle* fencing instructors, who have been accused of spreading so much misinformation about historical fencing, were well aware of all of this:

> *"The sixteenth-century swordsman had, in general, four ways of meeting or attempting to meet, an attack. First, he could interpose his left hand, armed or unarmed...In the next place, he could avoid it by a displacement of the body, with or without a corresponding movement of the feet. As a third measure, he could cross and close the line of it before it reached him, by a similar attack of his own. This was the parry and riposte in single-time. Or, in the fourth case, he could stop it by a time-cut or thrust at the person of his attacker."[63]*

If you would study, practice and teach late medieval swordsmanship, then you must use your edge and your flat. The *when, why* and *how* that flat and edge are used must be based on an understanding of the underlying defensive principles and biomechanics taught explicitly and implicitly by the medieval masters themselves. Finally, as *Kormac's Saga* illustrates, when your life is on the line, you do what you must. As with all aspects of martial arts, there are no absolutes.

Acknowledgments
The author is particularly indebted to Jörg Bellinghausen and Stephen Hand for helping him to make this paper much more than it might otherwise have been. Special thanks to Grzegorz Zabinski and Bartlomiej Walczak for providing information on the Codex Wallerstein at the eleventh hour.

Translational assistance courtesy of Jörg Bellinghausen, Stefan Dieke, Luca Porzio, and Grzegorz Zabinski. Thanks also to Steve Hick for his assistance with the Harleian Ms.

Peer Reviewers
This article was peer reviewed by Jörg Bellinghausen, Stephen Hand, Steve Hick and Russell Mitchell.

Bibliography

Primary Sources

Anonymous, <u>Manuscript I.33</u>, unpublished Ms. c.1275 - 1300. Royal Armouries, UK. (Note a translation and analysis of I.33 by Dr. Jeffrey Forgeng (previously Singman) will be released by the Armouries sometime in 2003.)

Anonymous, <u>Harleian Manuscript 3542</u>, unpublished 15th century Ms. British Museum, UK.

Anonymous, <u>The Life and Death of Cormac the Skald ("Kormak's Saga"), Translation by W.G. Collingwood & J. Stefansson (Ulverston, 1901).</u>

Anonymous, <u>Solothurner Fechtbuch</u>, reprinted by the city of Solothurn, Charles Studer, editor. The exact date and origin of this fechtbuch is currently debated. Although it has been claimed to be as early as 1423, the clothing and armour depicted are from no earlier than the late 1460s. The paper used for this manuscript is of Italian origin and dated to 1504-1516, and it is very likely a copy of one of Paulus Kal's works, not of Talhoffers. See, Amberger, J. Christoph: *The Death of History: Historic European fighting arts in the Mis-information Age*, first published in Fencers Quarterly Magazine, Spring 2001, also available online at: http://www.swordhistory.com/excerpts/masters.html

Dei Liberi, Fiore, <u>Flos Duellatorum in arnis, sine arnis, equester, pedester</u>; Italy, 1409 (MS Ludwig XV.13, Getty Museum, Los Angeles)

Dei Liberi, Fiore, <u>Flos Duellatorum</u>; Italy, 1409 (this is the lost Pissani-Dossi manuscript reprinted by Francesco Novati; Padova, 1902)

Dürer, Albrecht, <u>Fechtbuch</u>, 1512, in Dornhoffer, Friedrich; <u>Albrecht Dürers Fechtbuch</u>; *Jahrbuch der Kunsthistorisches sammulungen des allerhochsten Kaiserhausen*; Wein, Liepzig F. Temsky, G. Freytag (vol. 27, 1907/09)

Meyer, Joachim, <u>Gründtliche Bechreibung der Freyen Ritterlichen und Adelichen kunst des Fechtens</u>, Strasbourg, 1570 (English translations courtesy of Jörg Bellinghausen and Stefan Dieke)

Ringeck, Sigmund, <u>Commentaries on Master Liechtenauer's Fechtbuch</u>; c.1440. translated by Christian Tobler in <u>Secrets of Medieval German Swordsmanship</u>, Chivalry Bookshelf Press, 2002 (Including portions translated by Jörg Bellinghausen)

Silver, George, Paradoxes of Defence; London, 1599

_____, Bref Instructions upo my Pradoxes of Defence; Unpublished MS, c.1605
(unpublished until Cyril Matthey's edition of 1896)

Talhoffer, Hans, Fechtbuch (1443) reprinted by Gustav Hergsell, Prague, 1901.

Talhoffer, Hans, Fechtbuch (1459) reprinted by Gustav Hergsell, Prague, 1890.

Talhoffer, Hans Fechtbuch; 1467, translated in Medieval Combat by Mark Rector, Greenhill Publications, London 2000. (A 1998 German reprint of Talhoffer is also available from VS-Books, Carl Schulze & Torsten Verhullsdonk GbR, 44635 Herne, Germany.)

Vadi, Filippo, Arts Dimicandi Gladiatoria, 1482-1487 (translations courtesy of Luca Porzio, Chivalry Bookshelf edition, 2002).

Von Baumann, Codex Wallerstein, c.1470 Universitätsbibliothek Augsburg: Cod.I.6.40.2

Secondary Sources
Anglo, Sydney, The Martial Arts of Renaissance Europe, Yale University Press, New Haven and London, 2000

Cass, Eleanor Baldwin, The Book of Fencing; Lothrop, Lee & Shepard Co., Boston, 1930.

Cole, Michael D et. al, Swords and Hilt Weapons; Weidenfeld and Nicholson; London, 1989

Edge, David and Miles, John, Arms and Armour of the Medieval Knight; Crescent Books, 1988

Galas, S. Matthew, "Kindred Spirits: The Art of the Sword in Germany and Japan Journal of Asian Martial Arts, VI (1997), pp. 20 - 46

Hutton, Alfred, Cold Steel; London, 1889
_____, Old Swordplay; London, 1892

Oakeshott, R. Ewart, Records of the Medieval Sword; Boydell Press, 1991
_____, The Sword in the Age of Chivalry; Boydell Press, 1994 (reprint)

Shaff, Jo, Fencing; McClelland and Stewart Ltd., 1982.

Singman, Jeffrey, "The medieval swordsman: a thirteenth century German fencing manuscript", Royal Armouries Yearbook, II (1997), pp. 129-36

Smith, Raymond, Art of the Sword in the Late Middle Ages; PhD dissertation presented to Catholic University of America, 1992. (Reprint available through UMI Dissertation Services, Ann Arbor, MI. Document #9221887)

Notes

[1] Jo Shaff, Fencing, 1982 pp. 84 - 5.

[2] Capt. Alfred Hutton, Cold Steel, 1889, pp. 34 - 36. Hutton's work is particularly interesting, since it relied heavily on English backsword treatises of the 18th century, in which this method of parrying cuts by blocking with the forte, was already established. Nor was the method unknown to earlier masters, as will be seen, it was usually only favored when seeking to grip or grapple the opponent.

[3] Personal correspondence, January 2000

[4] Better educated fencers sometimes refer to the Italian dueling saber, another 19th century innovation, which does not really use edge or flat parries, but rather, when used properly, uses fast moulinellos to deflect attacks with its edge, not block them. Although this is not entirely inconsistent with medieval practice, as will be shown, it was not the primary method of defense.

[5] See Hutton's system of sword and buckler and two-handed sword fencing in Old Swordplay. While ostensibly based on Marozzo's Opera Nova (1536), Hutton replaces Marozzo's guards and parrying instructions with modern sabre guards and parries, and advises against thrusting, to give the fencing a more "antique" flavor. This last instruction is particularly ironic, since many of Marozzo's techniques with both the single-handed and two-handed sword makes use of the thrust.

[6] For examples of modern-historical fusions today, see the on-line article On Marozzo (http://www.thehaca.com/essays/Marozzo1.htm) and the recent Italian edition of Flos Duellatorum by Giovanni Rapisardi.

[7] Joachim Meyer, Gründtliche beschreibung der freyen ritterlichen und adelichen kunst des fechtens, 1570. Although Meyer begins his 1570 Fechtbuch with the longsword, he clearly shows that it has become a weapon of the training hall, and not the battlefield: ...according to the use of the old German fighters, who allowed both cut and thrust, nonetheless, with us Germans nowadays, attacks are made chiefly at the head, especially in the handwork and winding...[3v] Transcribed and translated by Jörg Bellinghausen.
Meyer's actual techniques often rely on a succession cuts and slaps with the flat of the blade, when a lethal thrust would have been taught a century earlier. Fortunately, when comparing Meyer's techniques to the earlier ones, it becomes apparent when he has departed from the older method. See especially Meyer's description on the guard "Eisenport" (lit.

'Iron Door'), where he states that "...thrusting among us Germans nowadays has been totally abolished..."(folio VIII r.) Translated by Jörg Bellinghausen.

[8] The Verses of Master Liechtenauer, as set down in Sigmund Ringeck's Fechtbuch, c.1440 (Dresden, State Library of Saxony, Ms. Dresd. C 487). Translation by Christian Tobler. *Vnd hyt dich vor allen versetzen, die die schlechten vechter tryben. Vnd merck: wen er hawt, so haw och, vnd wen er sticht, so stych och.*

[9] Joachim Meyer, *Gründtliche bechreibung der freyen ritterlichen und adelichen kunst des fechtens,* 1570

[10] There are two distinctive defensive actions in the German school. *Versetzen* literally translate as "displacements" and are deflective parries of any sort. *Absetzen* (lit: "to set aside") is a timed counter-attack that deflects the incoming blow with the edge as the cut is made. In this article's German translations, *versetzen* has been translated as "displace" or "parry," based on clarity, while *absetzen* is always translated as "set-aside."

[11] Ibid., 39v. *Hauwet er aber gegen deiner Rechten von Oben/ so fange sein Streich auff dein flache klinge/ unnd trit aus gegen seiner Rechten/ oder bleib mit deiner klingen (in dem die Schwerdter zusamen geruehrt haben) an der seinen und winde ihm die kurze schneide einwerts zu seinem Kopff/ verwende behend mit dem Schwerdt aus dem winden in das Lang ort/ also das du ihm sein nach arbeit mit Langer schneide von dir abweisest...* Transcription and translation by Jörg Bellinghausen.

[12]Meyer, 15r - 17v. *...das erste ist da du ohn allen sondern vortheil/ gemeniglich nur aus forcht versetzest/ in welchem du nichts anders thuost/dann mit deinem Wehr/ so du deinem gegenfechter entgegen helst die streich die von im beschehen auffahest...* Transcription and translation by Jörg Bellinghausen.

[13] Ibid., 15v *Aber umb mehrer nutz willens/ will ichs hauwen und versetzen so mit einem streich geschicht alhie abtheilen/ und dich lehren allein wie du solche Haeuw zuo versatzung brauchen solt/ welches dann auch auff zweierley weiß mag beschehen/Erstlichen da du deinens gegenparts streich zuovor abtregst/ oder mit einem Hauw abweisest/darnach wenn du ihm die vorwehr genommen/ mit einem Hauw seinem leib zuoeilest.* Transcription and translation by Jörg Bellinghausen.

[14] The German word used here is *Absetzen*, literally "to put aside."

[15] Either by taking his weapon off-line, or by binding against it.

[16] Meyer, 15v. *"Die ander Art zueversetzen ist/ da du dein widerpart in einem streich zuogleich versetzest und verletzest/ welches die alten fürnemlich wie de billich loben..".* Translated by Jörg Bellinghausen

[17] Sigmund Ringeck, *Commntaries,* c. 1440. Transcribed and translated by Jörg Bellinghausen

[18] Meyer, 16r. *"Dann solche verkehrte Haeuw sind fürnemlich dazuo erfunden/ das damit zuogleich versetzt und getroffen wirdt...wirt denn auff dich von oben her gehauwen/ so tritt mit dem Rechten fuoß gegen deines widerparts seiten/ und hauw mit einer Zwirch das ist/kurtzerschneid oberzwerch zuo gleich mit hinein/ also das du sein Hauw auff die sterck deiner klingen/ nahe bey deiner Kreutzstangen aufffangest/ und mit dem eussern theil deines Schwerdts sein Linck Ohr treffest so hastu denn zuogleich versetzet und getroffen mit einander."* Transcribed and translated by Jörg Bellinghausen
This is the *Zwerchau* (Cross Cut), one of the five *Meisterhau*. See note 14, above.

[19] Meyer, 15v. *"Die ander Art zueversetzen ist/ da du dein widerpart in einem streich zuogleich versetzest und verletzest/ welches die alten fürnemlich wie de billich loben.."* Translated by Jörg Bellinghausen

[20] A third master, Pietro Monte, also wrote a massive martial arts compendium in the 1490s, published as part of his *Collecteana*, in 1509. However, Monte was a Spaniard living in Italy, and his exact relationship to the Italian school is not yet known.

[21] Interestingly, Vadi uses both *coverta* and *parata* in his manuscript, a distinction not made in Fiore. This may be similar to the German distinction between *absetsen* and *versetsen*. Because of this distinction, I have translated *parata* as "parry" in all Vadi quotations, and have left *coverta* untranslated.

[22] Filippo Vadi, *Ars Gladiatoria Dimicandi,* 1482

[23] Vadi, Chapter 11. Translation by Luca Porzio.

[24] Harleian MS. 3542, Add. 39564

[25] Ibid.

[26] Ibid. Alfred Hutton translated *renyg* as "furious," but I interpret this word as the same as *rengyng,* or "ringing." Either seem to convey the same general meaning: *With a ringing/furious quarter set him out of his way.*

[27] Admittedly speculative. However, the English fencing masters were notoriously conservative, and Silver's sword and sword and buckler instructions are far more consistent with 15th century German masters, than they are many English masters that followed.

[28] In Silver's nomenclature, *ward* is both an action and a position. *To ward,* is to parry, while *a ward,* is a guard.

[29]Silver seems to use 'cross' for both engagement and parry.

[30] George Silver, *Bref Instructions upo My Pradoxes of Defence* p.10R

[31] Interestingly, while I tend to favor deflections with the flat, yet interpret this as an edge parry, Stephen Hand of the Stoccata School of Defence, who slightly favors edge parries, interprets this technique as a vertical countercut, which results in a parry with the flat. This serves as a reminder that any written text or illustration is subject to interpretation.

[32] A *single-time* defense (Italian: *stesso tempo*) is an action that is a parry and a counter-attack made in one action. A *double time* (Italian: *dui tempi*) defense is a defense and return attack made as two distinct actions, i.e.: the classic parry and riposte.

[33] For a more detailed analysis of this theory, see *Counterattacks with opposition: The influence of weapon form* by Stephen Hand, in this issue.

[34] The glaring exception to this rule is the buckler, which is shown being used both as a primary defense, and in concert with the sword. This "double parrying" method is clearly shown in Ms. I.33, and is expressly detailed by Silver: "*Sword & Buckler fight, & sword & dagger fyght are al one, saving yt yo may safly defend both blowe & thrust, syngle wt yor buckler only, & in likesort yo may safly ward both blowes & thrusts dubble, yt is wt sword & buckler together wch is a great advantage against ye sword & daggr, &c., & is the surest fight of al short weapons*". - Bref Instructions upo My pradoxes of Defence, Cap. 9 p. 25R

[35] *The Life and Death of Cormac the Skald ("Kormak's Saga")*, Translation by W.G. Collingwood & J. Stefansson (Ulverston, 1901).

[36] Fiore dei Liberi, *Flos Duellatorum*, (Pissani-Dossi Ms.), 1409. Carta 20 B. Fig 3 "*Aquesto è de punta un credelle schanibar:/ In l'arte più falsa punta de questa non se pò far./ Tu me trasisti de punta e questa io t'ò dada;/ E piu seguro se po far schiuando la strada.*" Translation by Greg Mele and Luca Porzio.

[37] Ibid., Carta 20 B, Fig 4. "*Per tuo mantinger che io in mia tegno/Cum la punta in lo uolto io te faço segno.*" Translation by Luca Porzio.

[38] The word translated as "parry" throughout the *Flos Duellatorum* is *coverta*. See note 17 above.

[39] Ibid., Carta 23 B, Fig. 1. "*Questa e coverta de la riverssa mano/ Per far zoghi de fortissimo ingano.*" Translation by Greg Mele and Luca Porzio.

[40] Ibid., Carta 23 B, Fig. 2. "*Per la coverta de la riverssa mano aqui t'ò aserato:/De zogho streto e de feride non sera' guardato.*" Translation by Luca Porzio.

[41] Ibid., Carta 23 B, Fig. 2. "*De la coverta de lo magistro ese questa punta/ E li altri zoghi dredo che asay ben monta..*" Translation by Luca Porzio.

[42] Hans Talhoffer, *Fectbuch aus dem Jahre 1467*, as translated by Mark Rector in Medieval Combat, Greenhill Books, 2000. "*Der howt Fry von Dach. - Der hatt versetzt mit gwenter hand und wyl für tretten und Ryssen.*"

[43] This plate is rife with possible interpretations. Jörg Bellinghausen adds the following comments: "This is either an active strike into the attack done with the flat, or, more possible, a simultaneous thrust into the opponent's face, the edge turned into the direction of the incoming attack. The opponent must react to this thrust, or be hit in the face. His reaction would very likely be to redirect his attack with a clockwise turn of his edge to the left, beating the thrust out of line. The energy of this beat is used by the defender to hook the pommel of his weapon over the attacker's wrist in a clockwise motion. [For comparison see the instructions for #65 (Fig 21) from the Codex Wallerstein, below.] In the mounted combat section (plate 25 lff.), Talhoffer depicts a similar situation in more detail. The caption on the plate that depicts the beginning of the technique reads: "*Der will mit dem stosz versetzen* (This one will parry with the thrust. Translation by Mark Rector)." In the second plate, you see the attacker being hit in the face with the thrust, the hand of the defender being in the same position as in plate 226."

[44] Ibid. "*Da hatt der Im versetzt und Stoszt In von Im und Ryszt mit dem Messer*"

[45] Ibid. "*Der Statt für den Stich. -Der Wyl In stechen.*"

[46] Ibid. "*Das Ist der Notstand wen zwen über ain Sind. Hie wyl ich uff In howen. -Da versetzt der mit Eppicher hand und wirt sich wenden und howen zu dem hindn. -Hie wyl der och howen.*"

[47] Likely, creating a "slapping" motion of the flat into the attack, as discussed in Plate 234, and note 43, above.

[48] On a cross-cultural, hopological note, a nearly identical "gliding" parry is seen in Filipino sword and stick arts.

[49] Talhoffer's text calls for the counter attack to be a thrust, creating the single-time attack and parry on the flat. This action is illustrated in much the same way as a *Zwerchau* (Cross Cut), one of the German Meisterhau. The Zwerchau would be made so as to cut into the attack -and the attacker- with the short-edge, creating a simultaneous counter attack and edge parry.

[50] This Fechtbüch also formed the basis for a later work by the famed artist, Albrecht Dürer (1471-1528). Friedrich Dörnhöffer discussed this relationship, and re-structured transposed the original Bavarian dialect of the Codex Wallerstein in his study of the manuscript: Friedrich Dornhöffer, <u>Albrecht Dürer's Fechtbüch</u>; Jahrbuch der Kunsthistorisches sammulungen des Allerhöchsten Kaiserhauses; Wien, Leipzig. F. Temsky, G. Freytag (vol. 27, 1907/09)

[51] *Vor - Also, wenn du jemandem an das Schwert bindest, und er schlägt dich stark zu dem Kopf, so versetze mit deiner kurzen Schneide und dringe in ihn, daß er schlagen muß; wenn er dann in die andere Seite schlägt, lege ihm dein Schwert auf seine linke Achsel, wie es hier gemalt ist, daß du ihn in seinem Ohr schlägst: das heißt „ein gelegt" und heißt „vor."* Transcription and translation by Grzegorz Zabinski

[52] *Nach/ Also, wenn jemand dich stark von oben haut, warte und versetze den Schlag mit der kurzen Schneide; wenn er denn schnell ist und haut wann du dein Schwert auf ihn legen könntest, so lasse ihm frei hauen und schlage mit der kurzen Schneide in sein Schwert, wie es hier gemalt ist, daß du ihn bindest und schlägst ihn in das Ohr und Hinterkopf.* Transcription and translation by Grzegorz Zabinski

[53] *Also, du kämpfst mit jemandem mit dem Messer. Wenn jemand*

dich von oben einhaut, versetzte mit deinem Messer nach außen mit der Flache auf dem Nagel, und gehe schnell vorwärts mit dem linken Fuß und schlag ihm mit dem Messerknauf über seinen Arm, wie es hier gemalt ist, daß du ihn in den Kopf schlägst. Transcription and translation by Grzegorz Zabinski

[54] *Also, wenn jemand dich von oben zu deinem Kopf haut, versetze mit der Flache und auf dem Nagel, und schiebe ihm sein Messer weg, daß er schlagen muß, und wenn er schlagen will, suche die Blößen, und schneide ihm den Arm ab, wie es hier gemalt ist.* - Transcription and translation courtesy of Grzegorz Zabinski

[55] Friedrich Dornhöffer, Albrecht Dürer's Fechtbuch; *Jahrbuch der Kunsthistorisches sammulungen des Allerhöchsten Kaiserhauses*; Wien, Leipzig. F. Temsky, G. Freytag (vol. 27, 1907/09)

[56] In practical reconstruction, the author has found that this action can work with the blade parrying with the flat, or with the edges meeting at a very narrow angle, as the defender's hand moves to this position. The important aspect is that the defender finish with his hand turned with the edges vertical, as shown in the plate.

[57] Meyer, 18v. *"Ablauffen: Ist/ von welcher Handt du dem mann an sein Schwerdt bindest/ so verkehr in dem es riert dein Hand/ und laß mit halber schneid undersich ablauffen/ und zuck under des dein Heft obersich in die höh zum streich/ und solches treib zu beiden seiten."*

Transcription and translation by Jörg Bellinghausen.
[58] Ibid., 21v. *"Hendtrucken: Als oberlaufft dich einer mit Bueffelschlegen/ so underfahr ihm seine streich mit der Kron/ oder sonst hoher versatzung/ oder undergehe ihm mit verhengen/ und fang ihm sein Schwerdt auf deiner klingen fleche/ und so du ihm under sein Schwert kommen/..."*
Translation by Stefan Diecke.

[59] Ibid., 21v. *"Hendtrucken: Als oberlaufft dich einer mit Bueffelschlegen/ so underfahr ihm seine streich mit der Kron/ oder sonst hoher versatzung/ oder undergehe ihm mit verhengen/ und fang ihm sein Schwerdt auf deiner klingen fleche/ und so du ihm under sein Schwert kommen/..."*
Transcription by Stefan Dieke.

[60] Ibid., 22r. *"Hengen: Hengen ist auß dem vorigen klar zuoverstehen/ das mach also/ Wann du im Pflug stehest/ und dein widerpart auf dich hauwet/ so fahr mit deinem gefeß obersich das die kling etwas gegen der erden hang und und empfach damit seinen streich auff deiner klingen fleche/ als denn arbeite mit Winden der nechste Bloesse zuo."*
Translation by Stefan Dieke.

[61] Ibid., 38v. *"...und wende zuogleich in solchem fuertschieben die Lang Schneid gegen seinen herfliegenden hauw/ wann du nun seinen Hauw auf dein Lange schneide in die sterck empfangen hast/ so blein hart an seiner an seiner klingen/ und winde behendiglich hinein/ und außwerts zuo seinem Kopff"*
Translation by Stefan Dieke.

[62] "Both wrong" as opposed to "both right," in that the

historical material necessitates the use of both methods, each for a specific purpose.

[63] Eleanor Baldwin Cass, The Book of Fencing, 1930, p.56. Cass, although American, was an associate of Archibald H. Corble, Alfred Hutton, and Egerton Castle, and shared their views on "antique swordsmanship." Like them, she viewed these earlier methods as being "imperfect," compared to the modern method, but whether or not these fencers' biases impaired their understanding of *why* the old masters had utilized these methods, they clearly understood that these were the methods being taught.

COUNTERATTACKS WITH OPPOSITION: THE INFLUENCE OF WEAPON FORM

BY STEPHEN HAND

Introduction

In studying the use of different European weapons we can observe many similarities in technique. For instance the techniques of *Giocco Stretto* (literally close play) shown by Fiore de Liberi[1] and Filippo Vadi[2] in 15th century Italy bear a striking resemblance to the *Grypes* of George Silver, described in the early 17th century[3]. Are these similarities the result of either fashion or tradition, or are there more fundamental reasons why similar techniques are described by different authors for use with what are often dramatically different weapons? An argument can certainly be made that in some instances fashion and tradition are important motivational forces. A handful of years after George Silver wrote his *Bref Instructions Upo my Pradoxes of Defence*, Joseph Swetnam[4] described a quite different style of combat with the backsword. Swetnam's style was more suited to civilian combat between men in normal street clothes than Silver's more military style. Silver's techniques, as noted above, bear more in common with the longsword play of two hundred years earlier than to the fashionable practices of Jacobean England. For a period of years, two quite different styles of using the same weapon co-existed in England, the fashionable modern style and the unfashionable traditional style. Which style was better and whether fashion or tradition led to a more effective fighting system is not the subject of this paper, but clearly factors other than pure martial effectiveness were at work.

It is also possible in some instances, to state with confidence that similarities in technique are the result of the nature of the weapon dictating that it be used in a particular way. In his article *Kindred Spirits*, S. Matthew Galas argues persuasively that German and Japanese longsword play in the 14th to 16th centuries was broadly similar in style, with the major differences resulting from the physical differences between German and Japanese longswords[5].

This article will discuss a group of actions known variously as time thrusts and cuts or counterattacks with opposition. By examining these actions and looking at why certain weapons do or don't use them, it will be possible to establish whether the reason for their presence or absence is weapon form, or whether we have to look for another reason.

What Are They?

The mid-19th century author Gomard wrote, "The time-thrust is the action of counter attacking (thrusting) on the adversary's attack. The time-thrust, that is not ordinarily composed of more than one movement, must be taken with opposition which when found guarantees the enemy's steel."[6] In other words, a time-thrust or counterthrust with opposition is a thrust intended to strike your opponent while simultaneously providing protection through opposition. Opposition is defined by the same author thus; "Opposition is the obstacle brought by the steel of the fencer to the steel of the enemy for him to close the line straight to the body."[7] So according to Gomard the time thrust is made on the adversary's attack and is made in such a way as it closes the line of the original attack.

Gomard does not specify when, during the attack, the counterattack must be made. Later definitions of the time-thrust, such as that used in the *Manuel D'Escrime* of 1877 restrict the time-thrust to those counterattacks made with opposition against the last action of a compound attack. "The time thrust is a surprise attack on the adversary in the preparation of his attack; it is therefore an attack executed on the absence of the foil, a feint too large or a direct attack in the low line, or a poorly executed attack in which the departure of the feet precedes the deployment of the arm.

On a feint to the outside of the body, or a direct attack in the low line deploy the arm in the high line without searching for the blade and touch with a straight thrust.

The time thrust is therefore a unique movement that comes into being at the time of the parry and the riposte; it is parry and riposte indivisible. It consists in short to prevent the adversary in the final execution of his complex attack and closes the line to which he wants to strike. It is preferable to take it in the line above than in the line below because then he is less exposed to the double hit."[8]

This is not the same action as the arrest or stop-hit which may be made at any point in the attacker's action. The *Manuel D'Escrime* defines the action thus; "The stop thrust is the live attack executed on another's moving attack, preceded by a lot of feints. It is the time thrust done in the adversary's march."[9] So the time-thrust "always *intercepts the final action of the attack*, even if the attack is in one motion."[10] This is not the case for the arrest or stop hit.

It can be seen that even in the space of 30 years the definitions of time-thrust and opposition changed. The definition used in the *Manuel D'Escrime* is very precise, but rather limited compared to the broad definition used by Gomard. Later definitions become more precise and limited still. For example, the following definition of opposition, quoted from Dr William Gaugler's *A Dictionary of Universally Used Fencing Terminology*, is from 1973. "2. French. a sort of pressure executed with the strong of the blade on the weak of the adverse steel, in a progressive and uninterrupted fashion, right up to the completion of the attack."[11] While this definition is useful for modern fencing it does not take into account weapons other than those used in the modern sport.

When dealing with weapons as diverse as the longsword, the rapier and the spear we have a range of possibilities, not all of which are open to us with a foil or an epee. We can oppose a thrust with a counterthrust or with a countercut. Similarly we can oppose a cut with a counterthrust or with a countercut. The mechanics of each action are different, but certain similarities exist. In each of these actions a counterattack is made in stesso tempo, or single time[12]. The line of attack is always covered by the counterattack. Counterthrusts with opposition are made in the same line as the attack which they oppose. This is not always the case with countercuts. For example a fendente or oberhau (a downward blow) to the head can be opposed with a tondo or zwerchhau (a horizontal cut) to the side of the head (see below). The weapon is always used to defend against the attack. This may be done by deflective opposition of a thrust, as in the definition of opposition above, by a hard block against a cut (for example the counterthrust with opposition against a rapier cut described by Saviolo below), or by crossing the line of the incoming attack and beating it aside in the same fencing time as the counterattack lands (as in the case of the zwerchhau mentioned above and described below).

Gomard's definition of opposition given above ("Opposition is the obstacle brought by the steel of the fencer to the steel of the enemy for him to close the line straight to the body.") is valid for all these actions (it is worth noting that for some of the weapons under discussion opposition is a critical element of attacks as well as counterattacks)[13]. Similarly his definition of a time-thrust (though written with only the counter thrust vs another thrust in mind) is a valid description of all the actions which constitute a counterattack with opposition. If we substitute the word attack for thrust Gomard's definition reads very well. "The time-attack is the action of counter attacking on the adversary's attack. The time-attack, that is not ordinarily composed of more than one movement, must be taken with opposition which when found guarantees the enemy's steel." Of particular note is Gomard's perceptive comment "that is not **ordinarily** composed of more than one movement" (author's emphasis). In the past, as today, the completion of a counterattack with opposition in one movement was an ideal, not always achieved.

To understand more about counterattacks with opposition, it is necessary to examine specific examples described in fencing treatises. The reasons why these defensive actions were used with some weapons, but not with others must also be examined. Through this it is hoped that it will be possible to determine what the most important factors are in determining whether or not counterattacks with opposition form part of the defensive repertoire of a particular fencing system.

An Examination of Counterattacks with Opposition with various Weapons

The longsword
The longsword is a weapon approximately 40-50 inches (102-127cm) in total length, with a seven to nine inch (18-23cm) grip and weighing between three and five pounds (1.35-2.25lb).[14] It was designed for use in one hand on horseback or accompanied with a shield and two hands when used aone on foot.

Counterattacks with opposition were common with the longsword, more so in the German texts, though they are shown in both German and Italian treatises. In Flos Duellatorum, Fiore De Liberi's treatise of 1409, at least one counterthrust with opposition is shown. In illustration 170 at the bottom left of Carta 20B the right hand fencer has made a rising thrust or stoccata. The left hand fencer has thrust immediately after his opponent, deflecting the latter's point to the outside and striking him in the throat.[15]

Figure 1 Fiore De Liberi 1409
The fencer on the right thrusts. In response, the fencer on the left thrusts in the same line, deflecting his opponent's longsword and striking him with the point in the throat.

Sigmund Ringeck, writing in the 1440s[16] is typical of longsword masters from the Liechtenauer tradition.[17] He includes several examples of counterattacks with opposition, one of which is described below.

"The Zwerchhau
The Zwerchhau counters (literally "breaks") all downward strikes made from above. Do it like this: If he strikes an Oberhau at your head, "jump" (make a large, explosive step) to his left side with your right foot, while you jump, turn your sword, so that your hilt is high in front of your head and your thumb is down (on the flat of the blade) and strike at his left side with your short edge. So you catch his strike with your hilt and hit him simultaneously on the head."[18]

This defence is one of the meisterhau (master cuts), "the most prized techniques in Liechtenauer's repetoire."[19]

A quarter of a century later Talhoffer[20] described a thrust in the high outside line in opposition to an oberhau. This technique is possibly the most commonly used counterthrust with any weapon.

Figure 2: [22] *Talhoffer 1467--A counterthrust with opposition against an oberhau.*

Figure 3: Talhoffer 1467: *A similar counterthrust, done at the half sword.*[24]

Figure 4: Durer 1512--*A counterthrust in opposition to a Krumphau or Crooked Cut.*

Figure 5: Durer 1512--*Compare the counterthrust by the fencer on the right with the one shown in Figure 2.*

"Plate 18
The Swordsman on the left makes a crosswise thrust. His opponent cuts from above."[21]

In a variant of the same technique Talhoffer's defender deflects the descending cut at the half-sword, in other words, by grasping his blade in his left hand. As the cut is deflected, the point strikes the attacker's throat, though for the parry and thrustcomponents of the counterthrust to be truly simultaneous in this technique requires superb judgement. The left hand must be kept out of the path of the attacker's blade. If it is incorrectly placed, the counter may be done in dui tempi (double time)[23] deflecting the attack and then thrusting the point into the attacker's face or throat.

Durer (1512) also contains examples of counterattacks with opposition. Two of these are described by Greg Mele in this volume.

"In plate 9, the right-hand swordsman has cut with a *Krumphau*" (crooked cut) "causing the swords to cross in the hanging guards, while the left-hand figure turns this into a thrust into his opponent's abdomen as his blade is struck on the flat. In practical reconstruction, the blades essentially meet at oblique angles."[25]

and

"In plate 12 we see the reverse of this technique, as the scalp cut with the false edge is put aside by the right-hand swordsman, who simultaneously turns his point into his opponent's belly."[26]

As late as 1570 Meyer describes the Zwerchau in almost identical terms as Ringeck, 130 years earlier. This is surely an indication of the effectiveness and resiliency of the German tradition based on the writings of Johannes Liechtenauer.

"Because those turned around cuts have been invented primarily for displacing and hitting at the same time.
...
Place yourself in the Zornhut (guard of wrath)[27] / if you are cut at from above / then step with your right foot to your opponent's side / and cut with a Zwirch that is / shortedge horizontal at the same time in such a way that you catch his cut on the strength of your blade / close to the cross-bar / and hit him with the further part of your sword at the left ear / in this way you did displace and hit together at the same time."[28]

Meyer also gives the following general discussion of counterattacks with opposition.
"Again for the sake of being more usefull / I want to separate cutting and displacing if it happens in one strike / and teach you solely how you shall use those cuts for displacement / which then may happen in two ways. First that you displace your opponent's cuts first / or turn away with a cut / hereafter when you moved away his protection / rush towards his body with a cut.

The other way to displace is / when you displace and injure your opponent at the same time with one cut / which the old ones praise as suitable. From this derives the proverb: a real fencer does not displace but if someone cuts he cuts as well / if someone steps he steps as well / if someone thrusts he thrusts as well."[29]

According to Meyer there are two types of parry done with an attack. The first is the attack into the opponent's blade as he attacks. Examples of this style of defence will be given in the section on the Messer, below. After the opponent's weapon is parried, and a riposte is made in opposition.secondly, Meyer mentions the stesso tempo counterattack with opposition, speaking more highly of it than the other method.

Looking at a range of longsword treatises we can see that counterattacks with opposition were the preferred defence in most German works, and figured in every treatise examined, both German and Italian.

The rapier
The rapier is a dominantly thrusting civilian weapon. Based on the weapons illustrated in rapier fencing manuals it is approximately 44 and 54 inches (112-137cm) long with a hilt six to seven inches (15-18cm) long and consequently a blade between 37 and 48 inches (94-122cm) in length. The rapier weighs between 2lb 2oz and 3lb 8oz[30]. Outwardly the rapier is a quite different weapon to the longsword, but an examination of rapier texts reveals that counterattacks with opposition were just as popular with the rapier as they were with the longsword. The importance of opposition is indicated by Capo Ferro in 1610 when he writes...

"However, with my guard, the only precaution necessary is to hold the sword straight in front and cover the 'weak' of the adversary's blade, so as to have power over it without touching it, before the movement of delivering the thrust, either on the inside or the outside, according to the occasion."[31]

Vincentio Saviolo[32] is typical of Italian rapier masters, with the very first technique he describes being a counterthrust with opposition.

"then shall the maister begin to teach him, moving his right foot somewhat on the right side in circle wise, putting the point of his Rapier under his schollers Rapier, and so giving him a thrust in the belly.

L. And what then must the scholler doo?

V. At the selfesame time the scholler must remove with like measure or counter-time with his right foote a little aside, and let the left foote follow the right, turning a little his bodye on the right side, thrusting with the point of his Rapier at the belly of his teacher, turning readily his hand that the fingers be inward toward the body, and the joint of the wrist shall be outward. In this sorte the saide scholler shall learne to strike and not be stricken,"[33]

As the maister attacks with a step forward and right (Di Grassi's slope half pace[34]) the scholler takes a circular step

(Di Grassi's circular half pace[35]) to the right with each foot, simultaneously turning his hand into quarta[36] and counterthrusting in opposition to the belly.

As well as using counterthrusts with opposition against other thrusts, Saviolo recommends that they be used against cuts. The resultant techniques closely resemble the counterthrusts made against the same cuts with the longsword.

"and if he offer you a Stramazone[37] to the head, you must beare it with your swoord, passing forward with your lefte legge, and turning wel your hand, that your point maye go in manner of an imbroccata[38], accompanied with your left hand, so that your poynt respect the bellye of your adversary, and break this alwaies with the point of your sword, for of all stoccataes[39], riversaes[40], and Stramazones, I finde it the most dangerous."[41]

Saviolo recommends that in response to a riverso stramazone[42] the correct response is to pass forward with the left leg, turning the hand into Prima and thrusting into the attacker's belly. The phrase "accompanied with your left hand" has been interpreted by the author to mean that the blade is braced against the cut with the left hand, a thrust at the half sword very similar to that shown in figure three.

An attack to the other side of the head is also dealt with using a counterthrust with opposition, albeit a slightly different variety.

"and then the maister shall goe backe with his right foote toward the left side of his scholler, in breaking with his lefte hand the saide imbroccata outward from the lefte side, and shall strike a downe right blowe to his head, because that by beating aside his foyne[43] with his hand, he shall finde him naked and without garde.

L. And what then, cannot the Scholler defend him selfe?

V. Yes very easilye with a readie dexteritie or nimblenes, for at the same time that the maister shall give the saide mandritta[44], the scholler shall doo nothing else but turne the pointe of his foote toward the bodye of his maister, and let the middest of his left foote directly respect the heele of the right and let him turn his body upon the right side, but let it rest and staye upon the lefte, and in the same time let him turne the Rapier hand outward in the stoccata or thrust, as I have given you to understand before, that the point be toward the bellye of his maister, and let him lifte up his hand and take good heede that hee come not forward in delivering the saide stoccata, which is halfe an incartata[45], for how little forever hee should come forward, he would put himselfe in danger of his life:"[46]

As he parries the thrust with his left hand, the maister steps to the right with his right foot, cutting at the left side of his scholler's head with a "downe right blowe" (a mandritta squalambrato[47]). The scholler steps to the right with his left (rear) foot (a half incartata), turns his body counter-clockwise and thrusts at the maister's belly with his hand in quarta. The scholler raises his hand high as he thrusts, so that the forte of his rapier guards the left side of his head.

Salvator Fabris[48] describes counterthrusts with opposition against cuts in almost identical terms to Saviolo. In chapter 8 "On Good and False Parrying"[49] he states,

"If you are forced to parry by a cut you must give the opposition with your forte where the adversary's sword is about to fall, and at the same time drive the point in with great swiftness, in order that it may arrive before your adversary's falls, so that he may neither avoid it nor be able to hit."[50]

An example of this sort of defence is given on Plate 38. The text reads,

"Now follows another hit in quarta, this time against a quarta, arising in this manner. You have tried to engage your adversary, who was in terza on the outside. He has planned out a mandiritto in sgalembro[51] at the face, keeping his arm in line and working from the wrist only. You have suddenly brought the left foot forward with the point of the foot turned outwards; at the same time you have brought your hand into quarta; extending the arm and bending the body as far as possible, you have met your adversary's sword in its descent, before it was in line, excluded it and hit him in the throat. This is the true method of parrying a cut of mandiritto at the head, when you are forced to parry, for by bringing forward the left foot in this manner, not only does the sword reach further, but it is stronger and can better resist the shock of the cut; with the right foot it is weaker."[52]

As you attempt to engage your opponent in terza in the outside line he disengages, probably by a cutover and cuts at the left side of your head. Passing forward with the left foot, you turn your hand into quarta and counterthrust with opposition to your opponent's throat.
Like Saviolo, Fabris also uses counterthrusts against thrusting attacks. One example is shown on Plate 23 of his treatise.

"This is a hit in quarta against a terza. It has suceeded because both were in terza within wide distance[53] and you have moved your sword and tried to engage the adversary's on the inside. He, seeing your plan and that you were uncovered below the sword hand, has lowered his point in order to hit in terza in that line. But you, who have moved the point only, seeing

him coming in below have abandoned the attempt to engage and directed your point at his body, turning your hand into quarta. By carrying the hilt to his debile[54] you have parried and hit at the same moment."[55]

As you attempt to engage on the inside your opponent drops his point to avoid the engagement and strike you in the low line. You have dropped your point and counterthrust in quarta to his thigh, gaining opposition and deflecting his point off to your right.

A third of a century after Fabris, the anonymous author of *Pallas Armata The Gentlemans Armorie*[56] describes remarkably similar uses of counterthrusts with opposition. This technique differs from the one above only in the fact that the thrust and counterthrust in Fabris' example are made in the low line, while in the example from Pallas Armata the thrusts are in the high line.

"An example how to use the Tertz *without*
9. If thine adversary lye open within, then *stringere* him within, as soone as hee makes a thrust at thee without, then thrust him over the *Secunde* or weakest part of his Rapier with a *Tertz*, and with thy Hilt goe low."[57]

Stringering[58] is a form of engagement. As you attempt to engage on the inside your opponent disengages by a "Cavere"[59], thrusting in your exposed outside line. As he does this you should counterthrust in the same line, with your hilt low, to provide opposition. A similar technique is described below.

"An example how to use the Quarte *within*
10. If thine adversary lie open without, then *Stringere* him without, as soone as he doth make a thrust at thee within, then thrust with the *Quarte* close to the *Secunde* or the weakest part of his Rapier betweene his right arme and his right breast, and when thou hast performed thy thrust, then presently *stringere* within."[60]

As you attempt to engage on the outside your opponent disengages by a "Cavere" and thrusts at your exposed inside line. As he does this you should counterthrust with opposition

Figure 6: Salvator Fabris 1606
A counterthrust in quarta against a mandritto squalambrato.

Figure 7: Salvator Fabris 1606
A counterthrust in quarta against a thrust in terza in the low line.

in the same line. Upon completion of the thrust you should engage him on the inside, i.e. in the same line you thrust in. The latter seems to be reminding the fencer that even a successful thrust may not kill their opponent. Therefore it is important to immediately assume a defensive posture on completion of the thrust.

So, a range of rapier fencing manuals describe counterthrusts with opposition against both cuts and thrusts. As with the longsword, the single time defence of counterattacking with opposition was the preferred style. As Salvator Fabris described it,

> "In treating of the rule of the dui tempi, although it may succeed against some, it is not to be compared with the rule of parrying and hitting at the same time, because the true and safe method is to meet the body as it advances, before it has had time to withdraw and recover."[61]

The spear
The spear is once again, a very different weapon from those already discussed. Not a great deal is written in historical fencing treatises about how to fence with a spear, but what we do have points to counterthrusts with opposition being an important part of spear defence. Plate 127 of Fiore de Liberi's Flos Duellatorum shows two spearmen in guard positions with eight to nine foot long spears. The text to the plate reads,

> "I'm waiting on this guard with a short spear because I'm used to parrying and thrusting with my lance and I'll thrust the lance into your chest. Your spear is long and mine is short"[62]

Plates 128 and 129 show attacks from the guard positions shown in plate 127. In plate 129 the spearman on the right has thrust at his opponent's face. The spearman on the left has passed (it's impossible to establish whether the attack was delivered on a forward pass and the counterattack on a backward pass or vice versa) and has changed his line, simultaneously thrusting into the attacker's face and providing opposition which covers him in the line of the

Figure 8: Fiore de Liberi 1409
Two spearmen on guard

Figure 9: Fiore de Liberi 1409
The spearman on the right has thrust. The spearman on the left counterthrusts with opposition.

attack. The text reads,

> "What I wrote is the way in which the three masters hit their opponents and so their spear should go into the face or into the chest of the opponent."[63]

In each of the three weapons studied thus far, the preferred method of defence has been by counterattacking with opposition. However, there were weapons where this was not the case. By examining them, and asking how they differ from the three weapons described above, we may be able to establish what it is that dictates whether or not counterattacks with opposition are used with a particular weapon.

The shortsword and backsword

When we come to the shortsword (a straight bladed, double edged, single handed sword that was not at all short[64]) and the backsword (a straight bladed, single edged sword , otherwise similar to the shortsword) counterattacks with opposition become less frequent. George Silver describes the three actions available to a defender who is at the correct distance.

> "Certaine general rules wch must be obsyrved in yt prfyt use of al kynde of weapons. Cap. 2....
> 2. Let al yor lyinge be such as shal best like yorself, euer consyderinge out what fight yor Enemye chargeth yo, but be sure to kepe yor distance, so yt nether hed, Armes, hands, body, nor legges be wtin hys reach, but yt he must fyrst of necessytie put in his foote or feet, at wch tyme yo haue the Choyse of iii Actions by the wch yo may endangr him & go free yorself.
> 1. The fyrst is to strike or thrust at him, at yt instant when he haue gayned yo the place by his cominge in.
> 2. The second is to ward, & Aftr to strike him or thrust from yt, remembringe yor gournors
> 3. The thyrd is to slippe alyttle backe & to strike or thrust after hym."[65]

So, Silver's three options are to counterattack in single time, to ward and strike, or in other words parry and riposte and lastly to move out of distance and attack after the initial attack has fallen short. The first of these options includes all possible single time actions, so it is necessary to examine specific examples to see whether or not counterattacks with opposition are amongst those actions.

The following passage is typical of Silver's single time defences for shortsword.

> "yf he lye a loft & strike as aforesaid at yor head, yo may endanger him yf yo thrust at his hand, hilt or Arme, turninge yor knuckles dounwarde, but fly back wtall in the instant yt yo thrust."[66]

As a cut is launched at your head from above Silver recommends that you move back out of distance and simultaneously thrust at the underside of the attacker's hand or arm. This defence is not a counterattack with opposition. It relies on moving the target (in this case the head) out of distance while attacking the arm which will be extended and therefore in distance.

There is one example of a countercut with opposition in *Bref Instructions*...

> "yf ii Men fight both upo open fyght he yt first breaketh his distance, yf he attempt to stryke at the others hed, shalbe surely stryken on the hed himself, yf the patient Agent strike ther at in his Comynge in, & slyp a lyttle back wtall, for yt slydinge back maketh an indirection wherby yor blow Crosseth his hed, & maketh a true ward for yor Owen, this will yt be, because of his length of tyme in his Comynge in,"[67]

Compare this with the description of Ringeck's Zwerchau above. Silver's cut is with the true edge[68], but is otherwise similar. One difference is brought about by the different lengths of the weapons. Silver's sword is barely long enough to simultaneously strike the opponent and provide opposition against his descending blade. The cut which ideally would be made with the third quarter of the blade must be made with the fourth quarter. This is the only counterattack with opposition described by Silver for sword. When making it, it is apparent that the sword is only barely long enough to perform both offensive and defensive tasks simultaneously. Attempting this action using a sword without a basket hilt or knuckle bow risks a blow to the hand, even if the counterattack is sucessful.

The emphasis in Silver is on the second type of defence, ward and strike. The same is true of Joseph Swetnam, writing in 1617. In his section "The guard for the Backe-sword." Swetnam writes,

> "Carrie your Sword-hilt out at the armes end, and your point leaning or sloping towards your left shoulder, but not joyning with your enemies weapon, as this Picture seemeth, but so long as you lie in your guard, let there be three foote distance betwixt your weapons, but if your enemie do charge you, either with blow or thrust, carrie your Sword over your bodie against your enemies assault, and so cross with him according to the Picture, beare also your point steadie over your bodie, something sloping towards your left shoulder; I meane the point must goe so farre as the hilt, but not turning your point the contrarie waie, but carrie both together. I will make it plainer by and by, because I would have thee to understand it wisely, for having with a true defence defended by your enemies blow or thrust by crossing with him, or by bearing your weapon against his assault (as beforesaid) the danger being past, then presently at the same instant, and with one motion turne downe the point of your Sword, turning your knuckles inward, and so thrusting it home to your enemies thigh, but with all, steppe forth with your foote and hand together."[69]

Swetnam recommends that a cut to the unguarded line should be opposed with a parry, immediately followed by a riposte of a thrust to the thigh. Looking at the counterthrusts mentioned above, the question must be asked, why doesn't Swetnam simultaneously parry and riposte with a thrust to the thigh. As with Silver, blade length is the answer. If a cut is launched at the body and is opposed by a thrust to the belly or thigh in the same line as the cut, then the defender's blade must be long enough to reach from the attacker's belly or thigh to his weapon. If it isn't then either the counterattack must fall short or if the counterattack lands, then the attacker's weapon will pass unimpeded behind the defender's hilt and the latter will be struck.

Pallas Armata: The Gentlemans Armorie is even more illustrative of the difference between longer weapons such as the rapier and shorter weapons such as the short or backsword. As was shown in the rapier section, above, the author of *Pallas Armata* describes quite a number of counterthrusts with opposition in the chapters on the rapier. However, none are described in the chapters on the sword. Instead, the defences that are described are parry ripostes, or ward and strike to use Silver's terminology. The following is typical,

"1. If thine adversary doth make a blow at the inside of thy Sword, towards thy head, *parere* his blow towards thy left side downewards with a *Secunde*, onely turning thy wrest and thy point towards thy left side, when thou hast *parered* his blow, then strike with a back blow, and a *Secunde* towards thy right side at the outside of his right arme, and instantly *stringere* him within, when thou hast performed thy blow."[70]

Compare this with the the following counterattacks with opposition described above for use with the lonsword and rapier respectively against similar blows.

Here is Ringeck's countercut with the false edge against a descending cut with longsword.

"The Zwerchhau
The Zwerchhau counters (literally "breaks") all downward strikes made from above. Do it like this: If he strikes an Oberhau at your head, "jump" (make a large, explosive step) to his left side with your right foot, while you jump, turn your sword, so that your hilt is high in front of your head and your thumb is down (on the flat of the blade) and strike at his left side with your short edge. So you catch his strike with your hilt and hit him simultaneously on the head."[71]

and here is Saviolo's counterthrust against a mandritta squalambrato with a rapier.

"at the same time that the maister shall give the saide mandritta, the scholler shall doo nothing else but turne the pointe of his foote toward the bodye of his maister, and let the middest of his left foote directly respect the heele of the right and let him turn his body upon the right side, but let it rest and staye upon the lefte, and in the same time let him turne the Rapier hand outward in the stoccata or thrust, as I have given you to understand before, that the point be toward the bellye of his maister, and let him lifte up his hand and take good heede that hee come not forward in delivering the saide stoccata, which is halfe an incartata, for how little forever hee should come forward, he would put himselfe in danger of his life:"[72]

So, is weapon length a critical requirement for using counterattacks with opposition?

The messer
The hypothesis that a critical weapon length is required for counterattacks with opposition to be practical is supported by examining the messer, the long German knife (a straight or slightly curved single edged sword approximately the length of the arm). Only one example will be analysed. Plate 26 of the messer section of Albrecht Durer's Fechtbuch shows a typical ward and strike technique. What is significant about this plate is the position of the weapon of the combatant on the left. The attack from the combatant on the right is being parried, in anticipation of the combatant on the left pivoting his messer clockwise, passing forward and striking to the right side of his opponent's head. However, the position of the left hand combatant's blade as he parries is such that his point is directed at the right hand combatant's face. With a messer the point is a foot from the right hand combatant's face (fig. 10). With a longsword or rapier in the same position the point would have struck the right hand combatant in the face (fig. 11). Figure 12 shows a further modification. The arm of the left hand figure has been extended so that he is striking the right hand figure in the face with his standard length messer. The messer is too short to simultaneously counterattack and

Figure 10: Albrecht Durer
If the blade of the weapon on the left were a foot longer it would be striking the right hand figure in the face.

Figure 11
A modification of figure 10. The left hand figure has a longer weapon and his point is striking the right hand figure in the face.

parry and the left hand combatant is now unguarded. The messer is simply too short to simultaneously parry an incoming cut and make a counterattack.

The examples discussed above suggest that a weapon needs to be of a critical length for a counterattack with opposition to be physically possible. If this is so, what is this length? Attacks with both cutting and thrusting weapons are made

Sword and Buckler –*The exception that proves the rule.*
The swords used by the sword and buckler fencers in Manuscript I.33[74] are simple medieval cross hilted swords, shorter than Silver's "shortsword" but longer than the messer. Therefore, it is somewhat surprising to see a considerable number of counterattacks with opposition used in I.33. However, examination of these techniques reveals that they are very much the exception that proves the rule.

The counterattacks with opposition shown in MSS I.33 are thrusts and are referred to as stichslac, or stabknocks[75]. What allows a counterthrust with opposition to work with such a short weapon is the fact that I.33 places such a great emphasis on keeping the sword and buckler hands together to provide protection with the buckler for the right forearm. Therefore the sword and buckler are often moved together, as if they were a single weapon, lengthening the distance from 'forte' to point.

The first mention of the stab-knock is in the first sequence that commences on plate three. The protagonists in I.33 are the Priest, clearly the instructor, and the Scholar. In the first sequence the Priest adopts the first ward, underarm, and the Scholar responds with the counter-ward of half-shield. The text reads,

> "When half-shield is adopted, fall under the sword and shield; If he is ordinary he will go for the head; you should use stab-knock"[76]

The stab-knock is not described in this passage. It is used again on plate 19 and is illustrated there (fig 14). The accompanying text reads,

> "Here, however, when the Priest is in the action of binding above he teaches the Scholar what is to be done against this, namely stab-knock, which he is generally accustomed to use. Here it is shown by example."[77]

As the Priest attempts to bind the Scholar's sword in the low line the Scholar passes forward rotating his sword and buckler together in a clockwise direction. He thrusts at the Priest's face and simultaneously closes the outside line by pressing his

with a straight arm. Therefore, for a weapon to be able to defend against such an attack and simultaneously reach the attacker's head or body the blade must be longer than the attacker's arm. In fact, the weapon needs to be substantially longer than this. A cut will overlay the target and a thrust will enter it. In addition, an attack will never be parried on the forte, exactly at the guard. Parries will be made over at least the first six inches (15cm) of the blade. Allowing six inches margin for error and another six inches for the weapon overlaying or penetrating the target adds approximately 50% to the blade length required. The practical minimum length to simultaneously parry an attack made with a straight arm and strike the opponent is therefore approximately three feet (92cm). This is greater than the blade length of most medieval

Figure 13: MSS I.33 Plate three Upper Illustration
The Priest is in underarm. The Scholar responds with half-shield

swords and is about the length recommended by Silver for his "short sword."[73] It is less than than the blade length of most longswords and rapiers.

Is this the full story? No it isn't. There are two instances where counterattacks with opposition are made with weapons with blades shorter than three feet. An examination of these two cases will help in the understanding of how counterattacks with opposition work and how they are influenced by weapon form.

Figure 14: MSS I.33 Plate 19 Upper Illustration

hands across to the right, creating opposition. The sword and buckler are used as a single unit, so the buckler acts as a blade extension. In effect the buckler lengthens the blade and allows the use of techniques better suited to longer weapons.

Moving back to the situation shown on plate three, the Priest will "fall under the sword and shield". In other words he attacks with a horizontal backhand cut to the opponent's right side[78], aiming his attack just under the hands of the Scholar (a very awkward cut to counter). If the Scholar "is ordinary he will go for the head", that is he will cut down onto the Priest's head, turning his buckler under his arm to parry the incoming attack. Turning his own buckler over his arm, the Priest turns his cut into a thrust with opposition, just as shown in figure 14 (though the Scholar will obviously not be in the same position as the Priest in figure 14; he will be part way through a vertical cut launched from the position shown in figure 13). Again, the buckler is used in unison with the sword, covering the hand. This effectively extends the blade by about a foot, giving extra length that can be used for defence, while the blade is used for attack.

To those used to using sword and buckler independently, it may seem strange to consider these actions to be counterthrusts with opposition. However, with the hands held together, the angulation of the blade is as critical in I.33 as it is with a longsword or a rapier. In fact I.33's stab-knock is quite similar to Fiore de Liberi's counterthrust with opposition with longsword, illustrated at figure 1.

So, in MSS I.33 the buckler is used on occasion to create an ad hoc longsword. Without the extra parrying area provided by the buckler alongside the forearm, the stab-knock would not be possible.

Smallsword – *The Exception that Disproves the Rule?*
Another apparent exception to the "rule" that a critical weapon length is needed for counterattacks with opposition to be used successfully, is the smallsword. The smallsword is a very light, often quite short weapon, designed almost exclusively for thrusting. Smallswords in the Wallace Collection typically weigh around one pound (450g) and have blades between 27 and 33 inches long (69-84cm)[79]. Although smallsword defence is based primarily on the dui tempi (double time) defence of the parry-riposte, counterthrusts with opposition are known. One such thrust is described by Scorza & Grisetti in 1803,

> "Section 228 The inquartata against the same[80].
> In turn the adversary thinking on drawing his force, on his edge, it will be rendered easy to wound him with the inquartata[81]. Properly therefore on his time, goes the cavazione[82] then thrust at great velocity executing an inquartata, sustaining the fist on the line of offense and placing your sword with the arm in an obtuse angle, on whose vertex the enemy sword will be obstructed from using the line of offense and securing your body, which you have deviated from this line."[83]

However, Scorza and Grisetti were Italians, known for their longer weapons. What length weapon are they discussing

when they talk of the counterthrust with opposition? We are lucky that they discuss weapon length in the folowing passage.

> "The length of the blade is indeterminate and not precisely settled. It depends on the fact that all things are seen under varied aspect, and in contemplating them our bias is nearly always our guide. Some are intimately persuaded that the short blade is added advantage, seeming to act with consummate celerity of the point, while others, for good reasons, recognize the long blade as the superior one. There is no need to demonstrate and convince, since everyone knows that the long blade can hit from greater distance and prevents the enemy from coming close. The Neopolitans and the Sicilians, recognizing these properties in all their extent, embrace the sword of four palms' length of blade, which then they call the measure, because the make use of these in the duel. It is common in the rest of Italy to carry swords of three palms and a half, or four less a third part of the blade; and it is certainly well to understand that if it were shorter it would be disadvantageous for him it would have to serve."[84]

A palm is 25cm, so four palms is one meter or 39.37 inches. Four palms less a third is 91.75cm or 36.15 inches and three and a half palms is 87.5cm or 34.45 inches. Scorza and Grisetti followed the Neapolitan system and therefore presumably recommended the longer weapon of one meter in length. This is significantly longer than the 92cm mentioned above. In fact a thrusting weapon with a blade one meter in length is arguably a rapier. However, there is no discussion of the effect of length on particular actions, no recommendation not to perform counterthrusts with a shorter northern Italian weapon.

Writing in 1818 La Boëssière the Younger also wrote of the time thrust. He states that "the time thrust is a thrust in opposition".[85] We do not know the length of La Boëssière's sword, but French smallswords of the early 19th century all have blades shorter than 92cm.

Alberto Marchionni in 1847 wrote that "The time thrust (colpo d'arresto d'incontrazione) is a counterthrust along the adversary's steel, in other words a glide that is effected the instant the opponent thrusts."[86]

Arguably, by 1847 the smallsword had been replaced by the duelling sword, the precursor of the modern epee, but the fact remains that counterthrusts with opposition formed a minor, but significant part of the defensive armoury of early 19th century fencers. The weapons used by these fencers were sometimes a little longer than the 92cm or three foot "critical length" discussed above, sometimes a little shorter. The evidence presented here could probably be ignored, as it does not seriously dent the "critical length" hypothesis. However, let us instead take this opportunity to explore counterattacks with opposition in more detail. The counterattacks described by the three 19th century authors above are all counterthrusts made against attacking thrusts. Are thrusts vs thrusts a special case that work with a slightly shorter weapon? Let us examine the mechanics of the four different combinations of counterattack with opposition in an effort to see whether this is so.

The Mechanics of the Counterattack with opposition
Cuts vs cuts

A classic example of a countercut vs a cut is Ringeck's Zwerchau described earlier.

> "The Zwerchhau
> The Zwerchhau counters (literally "breaks") all downward strikes made from above. Do it like this: If he strikes an Oberhau at your head, "jump" (make a large, explosive step) to his left side with your right foot, while you jump, turn your sword, so that your hilt is high in front of your head and your thumb is down (on the flat of the blade) and strike at his left side with your short edge. So you catch his strike with your hilt and hit him simultaneously on the head."[87]

This is a remarkably simple action. From a ward of Alber[88] or right side Pflug[89] you form a ward of left side Ochs[90], striking your opponent in the left side of his head as you do. The countercut does not block the attack. Rather it closes the line of attack, catching the descending cut in the angle between blade and crossguard. For this to occur your blade must be able to reach from the attacker's blade to his head. Part of the blade must overlay the target. Allowing six inches (15cm) for uncertainty gives us the critical length mentioned above; three feet (92cm). Other cuts require the same blade length for the same reason.

Therefore countercuts with opposition against cuts are only possible with longer weapons.

Cuts vs thrusts

I have been unable to find an example of a countercut with opposition against a thrust. Possibly a cut is slower or requires better timing than a thrust against the same attack. The reasons for excluding these techniques constitute a study in themselves, one which it is not my intention to pursue here.

Thrusts vs cuts

The simplest and most widely described counterthrust against an attacking cut is that described above from Saviolo.

> "and then the maister shall goe backe with his right foote toward the left side of his scholler, in breaking with his lefte hand the saide imbroccata outward from the lefte side, and shall strike a downe right blowe to his head, because that by beating aside his foyne with his hand, he shall finde him naked and without garde.
>
> "L. And what then, cannot the Scholler defend him selfe?
>
> "V. Yes very easilye with a readie dexteritie or nimblenes, for at the same time that the maister shall give the saide mandritta, the scholler shall

doo nothing else but turne the pointe of his foote toward the bodye of his maister, and let the middest of his left foote directly respect the heele of the right and let him turne his body upon the right side, but let it rest and staye upon the lefte, and in the same time let him turne the Rapier hand outward in the stoccata or thrust, as I have given you to understand before, that the point be toward the bellye of his maister, and let him lifte up his hand and take good heede that hee come not forward in delivering the saide stoccata, which is halfe an incartata, for how little forever hee should come forward, he would put himselfe in danger of his life:"[91]

In the above counterthrust, and indeed in any other, for the cut to be parried at the forte with any certainty the thrust must be completed a fraction of a fencing time before the parry is made. There are several reasons for this. Firstly, if the parry precedes the completion of the thrust, the impact upon the blade will reduce point accuracy dramatically. Secondly, the action is an attack which closes the line, not a defence which also attacks. Thirdly, related to the first point, if the line is closed before completion of the thrust then the hand will be moving towards the opponent at the time the cut lands. This is an inherently weak position in which to resist a forceful cut. If the thrust is completed before the line of attack is closed then the forte of your blade is moving to meet the defender's forte at the moment the cut lands. This is inherently a very strong position in which to resist a forceful cut. Finally, and perhaps most importantly, completing the thrust first is a lot quicker than closing the line first.

The necessity to complete the thrust before the line of attack is completely closed is illustrated by a variant of the same counterthrust, also made by Saviolo.

> "At the selfesame time that the scholler goes back, the maister shall play a little... and withall shall give a mandritta at the head of his scholler, at which time the scholler must remove with his right foote, following with his lefte, and let him turne his Rapier hand as I have saide, and that the scholler observe the same time in going backe as the teacher shall, to the end that his point maye be toward the bellye of his maister, and let him lifte up his other hand with his ward on high, that he be not stricken on the face with the mandritta, or in the belly with the thrust or stoccata."[92]

The 'maister' strikes at the head with a mandritta squalambrato. The 'scholler' who has finished the previous move left leg forward must make the same counterthrust described against the same attack in the previous example. Because his sword is refused the 'scholler' must exchange his feet to be in an appropriate position to make the counterthrust. He does this with two passes, or removes as Saviolo calls them. The first pass is forward and right. The right foot is brought next to the left foot, both facing forward. The second pass is back and right with the left foot, behind the right foot, the last part of the action being the same as the half incartata described above and taking the 'scholler' into exactly the same position. As the first of these two passes is made, the sword arm naturally comes forward with the body. If the line was to be closed before the counterthrust was completed this natural forward motion would have to be stopped and converted into a motion of the sword hand to the left. Then, as the second pass was made the sword hand would naturally move to the right with the body. The hand would be moving away from the cut, hardly a suitable way to meet a powerful stroke.

Conversely, if the thrust is made with the first pass then the second pass naturally closes the line, by moving the body to the right, under the protection of the rapier, without the line of the blade having to be changed at all. This manner of making the counterthrust is so completely natural and the other so slow, awkward, weak and unnatural that no one who did both could be in any doubt which is correct.

If counterthrusts are made such that the thrust lands fractionally before the parry is made, then the counterthruster's arm must be fully extended at the moment the parry is made. Therefore the blade must be long enough to simultaneously thrust into the opponent and cover the target, in this case the head. In a counterthrust against a cut the counterthsutser's blade must be greater than the critical length of three feet.

Therefore counterthrusts against cuts are only possible with longer weapons.

Thrusts vs thrusts
The final category of counterattack with opposition and the one most familiar to students of modern or classical fencing is the counterthrust vs a thrust. Unlike the other categories of counterattack, the counterthrust is made in the same line as the thrust it opposes. For example, in the following example from Pallas Armata (1639) a rapier thrust is made to the outside line (it can be made high or low, it doesn't matter) and is opposed by a thrust in the same line.

> "An example how to use the Tertz without 9. If thine adversary lye open within, then stringere him within, as soone as hee makes a thrust at thee without, then thrust him over the Secunde or weakest part of his Rapier with a Tertz, and with thy Hilt goe low."[93]

The two thrusts are moving in almost opposite directions towards each other. The initial thrust is made with the intention of striking the target. The counterthrust is made with the intention of striking the target AND closing the line of attack. This allows the counterthrust to be angled so that a stronger part of the blade meets a weaker part of the opponent's blade. This deflects the attacking blade, progressively more as the thrust nears completion. The attacking blade is deflected out of the line of attack and misses its target.

This deflection, or more accurately opposition, is the key to understanding how counterthrusts can be made with weapons that are not long enough to simultaneously strike the opponent and cover the target. In a counterthrust versus a thrust the weapon does not have to simultaneously strike the opponent and provide opposition against a fully extended attack. The opposition begins only a fraction of a

second before the counterthrust lands, but, particularly with shorter weapons such as the smallsword, this is enough to compensate for the lack of blade length.

So, counterthrusts against thrusts are a special case. Because the counterattack moves along the same line as the attack it 'picks up' the incoming thrust before it lands. Therefore it doesn't have to simultaneously reach from the attacker's forte into his body.

Therefore counterthrusts against thrusts are possible with weapons shorter than the critical length of three feet.

Conclusions
Although modern fencing texts only refer to the time thrust, or counterthrust with opposition, the counterthrust against a thrust is only one of four possible combinations of cuts and thrusts that together comprise counterattacks with opposition. Counterattacks with opposition made against cuts require a blade that is long enough to reach from the cutting weapon at full extension into the attacker's body. This length is approximately three feet. Under this length counterattacks with opposition against cuts are simply not possible. Judging from the fact that no examples were found by the author, countercuts with opposition were either not done against thrusts or were extremely rare. Therefore, against thrusting attacks only counterthrusts were used. These do not require a blade long enough to reach from the attacking weapon at full extension into the attacker's body. However, I am not aware of any counterthrusts with opposition done with weapons shorter than the smallsword. The counterattack with opposition requires one blade to find the other while both are moving at speed. The shorter the weapons the harder this will be. In addition, a time thrust with a shorter weapon requires the attacking arm to be forced back or away to reduce the distance between the point of opposition and the point being attacked. This also becomes harder, the shorter the weapon.

There is also the matter of weapon weight. The smallsword and duelling sword are lighter weapons than the others discussed. Although they can be used to counterthrust with opposition they have less inertia and move more quickly than weapons like the rapier. This means that the time available to deliver a counterthrust is less for a fast moving smallsword than it is for the relatively slower rapier. Hence the fencer's timing must be better to use these techniques with a smallsword than with a rapier. Coupled with the fact that smallsword fencers are able to make two hand movements faster than one foot movement[94], it is no surprise that smallsword defence was largely in dui tempi (double time, for example the parry-riposte) rather than stesso tempo (single time, for example the counterthrust with opposition). Counterattacking with opposition is mostly confined to heavier weapons where the duration of each fencing time is longer.

If weapon length is the single most important determinant factor in whether or not counterattacks with opposition can be used, it does not necessarily have much bearing on whether or not they will be used. For example, Joseph Swetnam recommends a rapier "foure foote at the least"[95] This translates to a blade length of 41 or 42 inches (104-107cm), easily enough to allow all categories of counterattack with opposition to be made. However, Swetnam does not include a single example of these techniques. In contrast Pallas Armata, another English rapier fencing manual describes counterthrusts with opposition with rapier, but not with sword. Pallas Armata may be typical, but Swetnam reminds us that factors unrelated to weapon form still played a large part in dictating what was actually done with weapons.

Acknowledgements

In examining a subject of such breadth it is inevitable that I would require the assistance of other historical fencing practitioners whose areas of expertise differ from my own. Without exception they have proved more than generous with their time and expertise. All those named here have proved themselves members of a true community of scholars.

I would like to thank Dr Jeffrey Forgeng (formerly Dr Jeffrey Singman) for providing the translation of MSS. I.33 and Philip Abbott of the Royal Armouries for his help with the plates. The plates from I.33 are used by permission of the Royal Armouries. Plates from Hans Talhoffer's Fechtbuch of 1467, reprinted in Medieval Combat are used with kind permission from Lionel Leventhal of Greenhill Books.

Paul Wagner was of major assistance, touching up and modifying some illustrations. Paul also helped with examples of counterattacks with opposition using pole weapons. Christian Tobler, Greg Mele, Maestro Paul McDonald and Steve Hick provided invaluable assistance in finding specific examples of counterattacks with opposition with the longsword. Maestro Jeanette Acosta-Martinez is to be thanked for her help finding examples of counterattacks with opposition with the smallsword.

My thanks are due to Christoph Kaindel and Jörg Bellinghausen for making their translation of Sigmund Ringeck's fechtbuch publicly available, to Stefan Dieke for providing translations of passages from Meyer, to Bob Charron for sending me text from his translation of the three versions of Fiore dei Liberi, to Maestro Jeannette Acosta-Martinez for her translation of passages from Italian and French smallsword works and to Maestro Sean Hayes for his translation of text from Scorza and Grisetti. Thanks are also due to Grzegorz Zabinsky for kindly providing a translation of text from the von Bauman fechtbuch (aka. the Codex Wallerstein) which unfortunately revealed that what looked at first glance like a counterthrust with opposition was in fact one of the "Winden".

Steve Hick, Maestro Jeannette Acosta-Martinez, Maestro Sean Hayes, Stefan Dieke and Milo Thurston reviewed the paper and each offered useful suggestions which have resulted in improvements to the final paper. Maestro Acosta-Martinez is to be particularly singled out for her recognition of an oversight by the author and for her generous help assisting the author in fixing this.

Bibliography

Anonymous. MS I.33 c. 1300 Royal Armouries, Leeds

Anonymous. *Pallas Armata The Gentlemans Armorie.* London 1639

Capo Ferro, Ridolfo. *Gran simulacro dell'arte e dell'uso della scherma.* Siena, 1610

Castle, Egerton. *Schools and Masters of Fence from the Middle Ages to the Eighteenth Century.* London 1885

Clery, Raoul . *L'escrime.* Paris, 1973

Dörnhoffer, Friedrich, *Albrecht Dürer's Fechtbuch* in *Jahrbuch der Kunsthistorischen Sammlungen des Aller höchsten Kaiserhauses,* (XXVII, 1907-1909)

Fabris, Salvator . *De Lo Schermo Overo Scienza D'arme.* Copenhagen 1606

Forgeng, Jeffrey . *The Walpurgis Manuscript.* Royal Armouries Monograph (in prep.)

Galas, S. Matthew. *Kindred Spirits: The Art of the Sword in Germany and Japan.* in *The Journal of Asian Martial Arts* (Vol.6 No.3, 1997)

Gaugler, William. *A Dictionary of Universally Used Fencing Terminology* Bangor, Maine 1997

Gaugler, William. *The History of Fencing* Bangor, Maine 1998

Gomard, A.-J.-J. Posselier *La theorie de l'escrime.* Paris, 1845

Grassi, Giacomo di. *His true Arte of Defence.* Translated by I.G. Gentleman, London 1594

Le Ministere De La Guerre. *Manuel D'Escrime.* Paris, 1877

Liberi, Fiore dei. *Flos Duellatorum in Armis, sine armis, equester, pedester.* ed. Francesco Novati. Bergamo, 1902.

Mann, Sir James . *Wallace Collection Catalogues. European Arms and Armour. Volume II Arms.* London 1962

Meyer, Joachim. *Gründliche Beschreibung der freyen Ritterlichen unnd Adelichen kunst des Fechtens.* Strasbourg, 1570

Ringeck, Sigmund . *Fechtbuch.* c. 1440

Saviolo, Vincentio. *His Practise. In two Bookes.* London 1595

Scorza, Rossarol and Grisetti, Pietro. *La scienza della scherma,* Milano 1803

Scorza, Rossarol and Grisetti, Pietro. *La scienza della scherma,* (second edition) Nocera Inferiore 1871

Silver, George. *Paradoxes of Defence.* London 1599

Silver, George. *Bref Instructions Upo my Pradoxes of Defence,* Unpublished MSS Sloane 376. British Library c. 1605

Swetnam, Joseph. *The Schoole of the Noble and Worthy Science of Defence.* London 1617

Talhoffer, Hans. *Medieval Combat: A Fifteenth-Century Illustrated Manual of Swordfighting and Close-Quarter Combat.* Translated and Edited by Mark Rector. London. 2000

Vadi, Filippo. Liber *de arte gladiatoria dimicandi.* c. 1482-7, Fondo Vittorio Emmanuele, MS 1342, Biblioteca Nazionale, Rome

Notes

[1] Fiore De Liberi . *Flos Duellatorum* 1409 in Novati, Francesco. *Flos Duellatorum in Armis, sine armis, equester, pedester.* Bergamo, 1902.

[2] Filippo Vadi. *De Arte Gladiatoria.* c. 1482-7

[3] George Silver. *Bref Instructions Upo my Pradoxes of Defence* Unpublished MS. c. 1605 (Sloane MS 376, British Library)

[4] Joseph Swetnam. *The Schoole of the Noble and Worthy Science of Defence.* London 1617

5 S. Matthew Galas. *Kindred Spirits: The Art of the Sword in Germany and Japan.* in Journal of Asian Martial Arts Vol.6 no.3 1997. The primary physical differences are that the western blade has a straight blade which facilitates thrusting and allows use of the false edge, and has a substantial crossguard which allows hooking actions.

6 A.-J.-J. Posselier Gomard. *La theorie de l'escrime.* Paris, 1845. p. 247 Translated by Maestro Jeannette Acosta-Martinez. The original text reads "Le coup de temps est l'action de tirer sur l'attack de l'adversaire. Le coup de temps, qui n'est ordinairement compose que d'un mouvement, doit etre pris avec une opposition telle qu'on se trouve garanti du fer ennemi."

7 A.-J.-J. Posselier Gomard. *La theorie de l'escrime.* Paris, 1845. p. 133 Translated by Maestro Jeannette Acosta-Martinez. The original text reads "L'opposition est l'obstacle apporte par le fer du tireur au fer ennemi pour lui fermer la ligne droite vers le corps."

8 *Manuel D'Escrime,* Approuve par M. Le Ministere De La Guerre, Paris, 1877. p. 36 Translated by Maestro Jeannette Acosta-Martinez. The original text reads

"Coup de temps.

"Le coup de temps est une attaque surprenant l'adversaire dans la preparation de la sienne; c'est donc une attaque executee sur une absence d'epee, une feinte trop large ou une attaque directe dans la ligne basse, ou une attaque decomposee par le depart du pied, avant le deploiement du bras.

"Il se produit sur une feinte en dehors du corps, ou une attaque directe dans la ligne basse, en deployant le bras dans la ligne haute, sans chercher l'epee et en touchant par le coup droit.

"Le coup de temps est donc un mouvement unique qui forme a la fois parade et riposte; c'est une parade et une riposte indivisees. Il consiste, en resume, a prevenir l'adversaire dans l'execution finale de son attaque composee, en lui fermant la ligne ou il veut frapper. Il est preferable a prendre dans la ligne de dessus que dans la ligne de dedans, parce qu'alors il expose moins au coup double. A pres avoirbien familiarise l'eleve avec les engagements, les attaques, les parades et les ripostes, il est bon de l'initier aux differents coups de temps."

9 *Manuel D'Escrime,* Approuve par M. Le Ministere De La Guerre, Paris, 1877. p. 37 Translated by Maestro Jeannette Acosta-Martinez. The original text reads "Le coup d'arret est l'attaque vive, executee sur une autre attaque en marchant, precedee de beaucoup de feintes. C'est le coup de temps pris dans la marche de l'adversaire."

10 Maestro Sean Hayes Pers. Comm. July 3rd 2001

11 Raoul Clery. *L'escrime.* Paris, 1973. quoted in William Gaugler, *A Dictionary of Universally Used Fencing Terminology* Bangor, Maine 1997 p.45

12 In other words in one fencing time or more simply in one action. The term stesso tempo is used by several masters, for instance by Salvator Fabris. *De Lo Schermo Overo Scienza D'arme.* Copenhagen 1606 who uses the term on p. 9 and elsewhere. See note 32.

13 As for example in the anonymous *Pallas Armata: The Gentlemans Armorie.* London 1639. On page four and five the author states "When thou dost thrust at thine adversary without, over his right arme, thou must doe it with a *Secunde.* When thou makest a thrust at thine adversary within, thou art to doe it with a *Quarte.*"

14 Based on measurements of approximately twenty longswords held in the Wallace Collection. Sir James Mann. *Wallace Collection Catalogues. European Arms and Armour. Volume II Arms.* London 1962

15 Fiore De Liberi. *Flos Duellatorum,* 1409. Plate 170, Carta 20B. in Novati, Francesco. *Flos Duellatorum in Armis, sine armis, equester, pedester.* Bergamo, 1902. The Novati version has abridged text. It reads,

"A questo e de punta un audelle schambiar
In l'arte piu falsa punta de questa non semper fare
Tu mi brasisa de punta e questa io to dada
E piu seguro se po far schivando la strada"
Which has been translated by Bob Charron to read,
"This is concerning the thrust one dares to exchange
In the art a more false thrust than this is not ever made
Through your thrust to my arm and this one I return to you
And more will follow if I can make the voiding step."

The caption to the identical plate in the Getty version of the manuscript (MS Ludwig XV.13, Getty Museum, Los Angeles) reads,

"This play is called "trading of thrust" and that same is made in this way. When one makes a thrust into you, then advance your foot that is in front making a step and with the other foot pass a la traversa again making a step. Cross your sword with your arms low. And with the point of your sword high in the face or in the chest as drawn." Translation by Bob Charron

The original text reads,

"Questo zogho si chiama scambiar de punta e se fa pro tal modo zoe. Quando uno te tra una punta, subito acresse lo tuo pe che denanzi fora de strada e cum laltro pe passa a la traversa anchora fora di strada, traversando la sua spada cum cum (sic) gli toi brazzi bassi. E cum la punta de la tua spada erta in lo volto o in lo petto come depento."

16 Sigmund Ringeck. *Fechtbuch* (this manuscript is undated and unpublished, but is thought by S. Matthew Galas in his paper *Kindred Spirits: The Art of the Sword in Germany and Japan.* in Journal of Asian Martial Arts Vol.6 no.3 1997 to have been written in the 1440s)

17 "Nearly all of the surviving German manuals bear the mark of Johannes Liechtenauer, an influential sword master of the 14th century." S. Matthew Galas. *Kindred Spirits: The Art of the Sword in Germany and Japan.* in Journal of Asian Martial Arts Vol.6 no.3 1997 p. 21

18 Sigmund Ringeck. *Fechtbuch,* Translation into New High German by Christoph Kaindel and from there into English by Joerg Bellinghausen. The original text reads,

"Merck, der zwerhaw bricht alle hew, die von oben nyder gehawen werden. Vnd den haw tryb also: Wen er dir oben jn hauwet zuo dem kopf, so spring mit dem rechten fuoß gen jm vß dem hawe vff sin lincken sytten. Vnd jm springen verwent din swert - mit dem gehultz houch vor deinem haupt, das din doum vnnnden kome - vnd schlach jn mit der kurtzen schniden zuo siner lincken sytten. So vahestu sinen haw jn din gehultz vnd triffest jn zuo dem kopff."

19 S. Matthew Galas. *Kindred Spirits: The Art of the Sword in Germany and Japan.* in Journal of Asian Martial Arts Vol.6 no.3 1997 p.33

20 Hans Talhoffer. *Fechtbuch.* 1467 (unpublished). The translation is by Mark Rector from the book, Hans Talhoffer. *Medieval Combat: A Fifteeenth-Century Illustrated Manual of Swordfighting and Close-Quarter Combat.* Translated and Edited by Mark Rector, London, 2000

21 Translation by Mark Rector. The original text reads "Der das geschrenckt ortt macht. Der hout von tach." Stefan Dieke (pers.

comm. July 2nd 2001) states that " 'Geschrenckt' refers to the crossed position of the hands which occurs when you turn the true edge of the Longsword to the right side. The more you turn the true edge to the right or to the top the more the hands become crossed (geschrenckt)."

[22] Talhoffer plates used with the kind permission of Lional Leventhal, owner of Greenhill Books, publishers of *Medieval Combat: A Fifteeenth-Century Illustrated Manual of Swordfighting and Close-Quarter Combat.*

[23] The term dui tempi is used by several masters, for instance by Salvator Fabris. *De Lo Schermo Overo Scienza D'arme.* Copenhagen 1606 who uses the term on p. 6 and elsewhere.

[24] Hans Talhoffer. *Medieval Combat: A Fifteeenth-Century Illustrated Manual of Swordfighting and Close-Quarter Combat.* Translated and Edited by Mark Rector, London, 2000. Plate 36

[25] Greg Mele. *Much Ado About Nothing, or the Cutting Edge of Flat Parries*, this volume

[26] Ibid.

[27] A guard where the blade slopes vertically down the back.

[28] Joachim Meyer. *Grüntliche Beschreibung der freyen Ritterlichen unnd Adelichen kunst des Fechtens.* Strasbourg, 1570 p. 16R Translation by Stefan Dieke. The original text reads,

"Dann solche verkehrte Hauew sind fürnemlich darzu erfunden / das damit zugleich versetzt und getroffen wirdt.

...

"Schick dich in die Zornhut / wirt denn auff dich von oben her gehauwen / so tritt mit dem Rechten fuß gegen deines widerparts seiten / und Hauw mit einer Zwirch das ist / kurtzerschneid oberzwerch zu gleich mit hinein also das du sein Hauw auff die sterck deiner klingen / nahe bey deiner Kreutzstangen aufffangest / und mit dem eussern theil deines Schwerdts sein Linck Ohr treffest / so hastu denn zugleich versetzet und getroffen mit einander."

[29] Ibid. pp. 15v-16R. Translation by Stefan Dieke. The original text reads,

"Aber umb mehrer nutz willens / will ichs Hauwen und versetzen so mit einem streich geschicht alhie abtheilen / und dich lehren allein wie du solche Haeuw zu versatzung brauchen solt / welches dann auff zweierley weiß mag beschehen / Erstlich da du deines gegenparts streich zuvor abtregst / oder mit einem Hauw abweisest / darnach wenn du ihm die vorwehr genommen / mit einem Hauw seinem leib zueilest.

"Die ander Art zuversetzen ist / da du dein widerpart in einem streich zugleich versetzest und verletzest / welches die alten fürnemlich wie denn billich loben / daher das sprichwort erwachsen / ein rechter Fechter versetzed nicht / sonder Hauwet man so Hauwet er auch / trit man so tritt er auch / sticht man so sticht er auch. Translator's note: "I translate 'ander' literaly as 'other'. In enumerations in those books it's used as '2nd' like: erster Teil, ander Teil, dritter Teil ... - first part, other part, third part ..."

[30] Bryan Maloney Pers. Comm. May 20th 1997. These results are based on measurements of 100 surviving rapiers in various arms and armour collections.

[31] Ridolfo Capo Ferro. *Gran simulacro dell'arte e dell'uso della scherma.* Siena, 1610 p. 22 Translation by Egerton Castle (see Egerton Castle. *Schools and Masters of Fence from the Middle Ages to the Eighteenth Century.* London 1885, p. 110)

[32] Vincentio Saviolo. *his Practise. In two Bookes.* London 1595

[33] Ibid. pp.14V-15R (also labelled 8V-9R)

[34] Giacomo Di Grassi. *his true Arte of Defence.* London 1594 pp. 15V-16R (illustrated on page 16V)

[35] Ibid.

[36] The hand positions referred to here are the standard ones of Italian rapier fencing, prima, with the palm to the right, seconda with the palm down, terza with the palm to the left and quarta with the palm facing up. This terminology is best explained by Salvator Fabris. *De Lo Schermo Overo Scienza D'arme.* Copenhagen 1606 Chapter 2, pp. 1-2

[37] A slicing cut with the fourth quarter of the blade.

[38] A thrust launched from over the opponent's hand.

[39] Thrusts launched from below the opponent's hand.

[40] Attacks from the left (i.e. to the opponent's right)

[41] Vincentio Saviolo. *his Practise. In two Bookes.* London 1595 p.24V (also labelled 18V)

[42] A slicing cut to the right side of the face with the fourth quarter of the rapier blade.

[43] A thrust: Saviolo restricts the term to imbroccatas.

[44] An attack from the right (i.e. to the opponent's left)

[45] In 1595 the words incartata (inquartata) and volte were synonomous.

[46] Vincentio Saviolo. *his Practise. In two Bookes.* London 1595 p.15V (also labelled 9V)

[47] A diagonal downward cut to the left side of the opponent.

[48] Salvator Fabris. *De Lo Schermo Overo Scienza D'arme.* Copenhagen 1606

[49] Ibid p.9 Translation by the author

[50] Ibid p.9 Translation by A.F. Johnson. The original text reads "& pero essendo astretto a parare da qualche taglio fa dimestieri andare alla diffesa col forte da quella parte, oue la nimica spada uiene a cadere, & che nelo stesso tempo la punta uada a ferire con tanta prestezza, che gionga prima, che la detta nimica, habbia colpito nell' altra, accioche nel darli sopra non si suiasse,"

[51] A mandritta squalambrato or in other words a diagonal forehand cut downwards from right to left.

[52] Ibid p.65 (illustration on page 66) Translation by A.F. Johnson (modified by the author). The original text reads, "Vedesi segvire vn' altra ferita di qvarta, ma contra una medesima quarta, laquale puo essersi caggionata dall'essere quello, che ha ferito andato a trouare la nimica, che era in terza di fuori, & dall'hauere il detto nimico uoltato di un mandiritto in sgalembro per la faccia tenendo il braccio in giustezza, con operare solamente il nodo della mano, onde, quello che ha ferito, subbito e passato del sinistro piede inanzi, & con la punta di esso piede uoltata infuori, & con uoltare similmente la mano in quarta slongando il braccio, & piegando il corpo, quanto che piu ha potuto, ha incontrata la nimica che discendeua prima, che sia caduta in presenza & l'ha esclusa di fuori ferendo il medesimo nimico di

detta quarta nella gola, & questo e stato, & e il uero modo, col quale si dee parare il mandiritto per testa, quando l'huomo e astretto di parrare, perche passando col sinistro piede in questa forma, oltre che la spada ua piu inanzi a ferire, e ancophi forte, & puo meglio resistere alla percossa del taglio, doue che col destro piede e molto piu debile."

[53] The distance where a hit cannot be made without advancing with the foot. See Salvator Fabris. *De Lo Schermo Overo Scienza D'arme.* Copenhagen 1606 Chapter 5

[54] Italian for the foible or the weak part of the blade nearest the tip.

[55] Salvator Fabris. *De Lo Schermo Overo Scienza D'arme.* Copenhagen 1606, text p.50, illustration p.51. Translation by A.F. Johnson. The original text reads, "La quarta, che qvi si vedra havere ferito una terza, e successa perche ambidui erano in terza nella misura larga, & collui, che ha ferito si e mosso con la spada, & andato per aquistare la nimica dalla parte intenore, & l'altro cognoscendo il disegno dell'auerslario, & uedendolo scoperto disotto dalla mano della spada ha abbassato la punta perferirlo di detta terza in quella parte, ma quest'altro, che non haue a mossa se non le punta uedendolo uenire disotto per ferire restando di andare alla spada, ha dirizata essa punta al corpo uoltando la mano in quarta, & portando il finimento al debile nimico ha parato, & ferito in medesimo tempo,"

[56] Anonymous. *Pallas Armata The Gentlemans Armorie.* London 1639.

[57] Ibid. p. 13

[58] Ibid. "*Stringering* is the touching of thine adversaries point with thy point, which thou art to doe upon any occasion, that thou mayst secure thy selfe on eyther side from a thrust, which is commonly termed binding." p. 5

[59] Ibid. "To *Cavere* is to turne thy point under thine adversaries Rapier on the other side when thou art bound, or he doth thrust at thee." p. 5

[60] Ibid. pp.13-14

[61] Salvator Fabris. *De Lo Schermo Overo Scienza D'arme.* Copenhagen 1606 p.6 Translation by A.F. Johnson. The original text reads, "Hora per trattare della raggioni de' dui tempi diciamo, che se bene contra di alcuni potrebbero riuscire, nondimeno non hanno da equipararsi alle raggioni di parare, & ferire in tempo medesimo, perche il uero, & sicuro modo e di incontrare il corpo nel punto medesimo; che quello si spingie inanzi, altrmenti egli subbito s'allontana."

[62] Fiore de Liberi. *Flos Duellatorum.* 1409 Caption to plate 127, Carta 15B. in Novati, Francesco. *Flos Duellatorum in Armis, sine armis, equester, pedester.* Bergamo, 1902. Translation by the Royal Armouries

[63] Fiore de Liberi. *Flos Duellatorum.* 1409 Caption to plate 129, Carta 15B. in Novati, Francesco. *Flos Duellatorum in Armis, sine armis, equester, pedester.* Bergamo, 1902. Translation by the Royal Armouries

[64] In his *Paradoxes of Defence* (London, 1599) George Silver explains that the perfect length for a sword is "The blade to be a yard and an inch for meane statures, and for men of tall statures, a yard and three or foure inches, and no more." (Paradox 14, page 25)

[65] George Silver. *Bref Instructions Upo my Pradoxes of Defence* Unpublished MSS. c. 1605 (Sloane MS 376, British Library) pp. 6R-6V

[66] Ibid. p9V

[67] Ibid. p10R

[68] He doesn't state this, but the action doesn't work when done with the false edge.

[69] Joseph Swetnam. *The Schoole of the Noble and Worthy Science of Defence.* London 1617 pp. 124-5

[70] Anonymous. *Pallas Armata The Gentlemans Armorie.* London 1639. p. 52

[71] See note 18

[72] Vincentio Saviolo. *his Practise. In two Bookes.* London 1595 p.15V (also labelled 9V)

[73] George Silver. *Paradoxes of Defence.* London 1599. Paradox 15 p. 25 Silver states "The best lengths for perfect teaching of the true fight to be vsed and continued in Fence schooles, to accord with the true statures of all men, are these. The blade to be a yard and and inch for meane statures, and for men of tall statures, a yard and three or foure inches, and no more."

[74] MSS I.33 is currently the oldest known treatise on swordplay. It is held by the Royal Armouries at Leeds and is also referred to as the Tower Fechtbuch.

[75] Jeffrey Singman. *The Walpurgis Manuscript.* Royal Armouries Monograph (in prep.) The initial mention of the stichslac accompanies plate three of the original MSS.

[76] Ibid. The original text accompanying plate three reads, "Dum ducitur halpschilt cade sub gladium quoque scutum; Si generalis erit recipit caput, sit tibi stichslac"

[77] Ibid. The original text accompanying plate 19 reads, "Hic vero, cum esset sacerdos in actu superius ligandi, informat scolarem quid sit faciendum aduersus hec, videlicet stichslac, quod generaliter ducere consueuit. Patet hic per exemplum."

[78] In Italian terminology a roverso tondo

[79] Sir James Mann. *Wallace Collection Catalogues. European Arms and Armour. Volume II Arms.* London 1962

[80] "The same" being the fianconate (modern, flanconade) an attack to the flank, commonly made with a bind.

[81] A pass forward and right with the left (rear) foot such that the left heel is aimed at the opponent.

[82] disengagement

[83] Rosaroll Scorza & Pietro Grisetti. *La Scienza Della Scherma* (second edition) Nocera Inferiore 1871 (the first Edition was published in Milan in 1803) p. 103 Translation by Maestro Jeannette Acosta-Martinez. The original text reads,

"Section 228
"L'inquartata contro la stessa.
"Volti tutt'i pensieri dell'aversario sugli sforzi, e su i filli, vi si rendera agevole il colpirlo colla inquartata. Dovete percio in quell tempo, chi'egli fa la cavazione, tirare velocissimamente inquartando, sostenendo il pugno sulla linea di offesa, e facendo la vostra spada col braccio un angulo ottuso, il di cui vertice impedisca all spada nemica di uscire dalla linea de offesa, e seguire il vostro corpo, che avete dalla stessa linea deviato."

[84] Rosaroll Scorza & Pietro Grisetti. *La Scienza Della Scherma* Milano 1803. pp. 3-4 Translation by Maestro Sean Hayes. The original text reads,

"La lunghezza poi dell lama e é indeterminata, e non si puo esattamente stabilire. Questo dipende da che tutte le cose si presentano agli occhi degli nomini, sotto vario aspetto, e che nella loro contemplazione, i nostri pregiudizj ci sono quasi sempre di guida. Taluni sono intimamente persuasi, she la lama corta sia di sommo vantaggio, sembrando loro di agire consomma celerita di pugno, mentre altri, indotti da ragioni plausibili, riconoscono nella lama lunga una grande superiorita. Non fa d'uopo di dimonstrazione per convincersene, poiché ognuno si avvede, che colla lama lunga, si colpisce a maggior distanza, e s'impedisce al nemico di avvicinarsi. I Napoletani, ed i Sciliani, riconoscendo queste proprieta in tutta la loro estensione, cingono Spada di quattro palmi di lama, che poi denominano di misura, perché di queste propriamente fanno uso ne'loro duelli. Si suole comunemente nel resto d'Italia portare delle Spade di tre palmi, e mezzo, o quattro meno un terzo di lama; e conviene tenere per certo, che se fosse più corta, sarebbe svantaggiosa per chi se ne dovrebbe servire."

[85] William Gaugler. *The History of Fencing* Bangor, Maine 1998. p. 100

[86] Ibid p.140

[87] see note 18

[88] The Fool's Guard. The blade is held in front of the body sloping forward and down so that the point almost touches the ground. S. Matthew Galas, *Kindred Spirits: The Art of the Sword in Germany and Japan.* in *The Journal of Asian Martial Arts* (Vol.6 No.3, 1997) p. 32

[89] The guard of the Plough. The hilt is held by the hip (in this case the right hip) with the point angled up at the opponent's throat. S. Matthew Galas, *Kindred Spirits: The Art of the Sword in Germany and Japan.* in *The Journal of Asian Martial Arts* (Vol.6 No.3, 1997) p. 31

[90] The Guard of the Ox. The hands are above the head (in this case to the left of the head) with the blade extended forward at the opponent's face. S. Matthew Galas, *Kindred Spirits: The Art of the Sword in Germany and Japan.* in *The Journal of Asian Martial Arts* (Vol.6 No.3, 1997) p. 31

[91] Vincentio Saviolo. *his Practise. In two Bookes.* London 1595 p.15V (also labelled 9V)

[92] Ibid. pp. 15R-V (also labelled 9R-V)

[93] Anonymous. *Pallas Armata The Gentlemans Armorie.* London 1639 p. 13

[94] Stephen Hand. *A Matter of Time.* in *Hammerterz Forum* (Vol.5 No.1, November 30th 1998) pp. 11-14

[95] Joseph Swetnam. *The Schoole of the Noble and Worthy Science of Defence.* London 1617 p. 184

DOM DUARTE AND HIS ADVICE ON SWORDSMANSHIP

STEVE HICK

Today the renown of the House of Alvis in Portugal rests with the efforts of one its princes, Henry the Navigator, who created the school for navigators at Sagres and guided the efforts of Portuguese exploration during the early and middle 15th century.

However, his brother, Dom Duarte, the Philosopher King, was equally well respected within and without Portugal for his learning and his military prowess. He successfully joined the exercise of weapons (with) the knowledge of letters and sciences.[1] Prior to and during his reign, Dom Duarte produced many articles and writs where he attempted to convey his knowledge and insight to his people in the many areas his interest lead him, including the martial arts and training. It is this insight into noble practices that forms the core of this paper.

Detail of this sort about a knightly skill is unusual. Gaston, Count de Foix in his 1387 work on mounted hunting, Livre de la Chasse makes no mention of the skill of riding, with which any noble reader would be familiar. Dom Duarte's works therefore provide an almost unique insight into the martial arts of Europe in the early 15th century from the point of view of one of its noble proponents.

This has been recognized recently by a number of historians. Dom Duarte's early, detailed and unique treatment of jousting forms the core several analyses of the martial history of Europe including of Barber and Barker's book Tournaments, and several articles by Sydney Anglo that is reprised in a section of his new book.

The Author and His Works

Dom Duarte, "The Eloquent", lived 1391 –1438 and reigned 1433-1438, was the second king of the House of Alvis and the 11th King of Portugal. He was the son of Dom João I, king of Portugal and his queen Philippa of Lancaster, and grandson of John of Gaunt, Duke of Lancaster. He was the great-grandson of Edward III, King of England, after whom he was named, and cousin to Henry IV of England. His was also the brother in law to Duke Philippe of Burgundy, uncle to Duke Charles of Burgundy, and married to Leonor of Aragon, daughter of Ferdinand I of Aragon, and therefore the uncle of Ferdinand I, king of Spain.[2]

During his life, Dom Duarte was famed for his intelligence, culture and his large and valuable library. His present renown rests upon two of his literary works, his Leal Conselhiero (Loyal Counselors) and Livro da ensinança de bem cavalgar toda sela {Book on the Knowledge of Good Horsemanship). The former is written to the newly noble that supported the House of Alvis in the previous generation's dynastic disputes with Castile and describes how best to be good citizen and servant of the king. The latter is a remarkable work that details the art of horsemanship, including sections on the use of weapons from horseback.

Unfortunately, as Professor Anglo notes[3], his reign was a disaster for Portugal. Dom Duarte and his brothers were knighted after the successful attack that took Cueta in Morocco from the Moors during their father's reign; he acquiesced to his brothers Dom Enrique and Dom Fernando and allowed them to lead an attack on Tangiers. The attack was an utter disaster, and Dom Fernando was captured. His ransom was the loss of Cueta to the Moors, even though he died prior to his return to Portugal. Dom Duarte died the next year of the plague, or as it is poetically affirmed, of remorse[4].

Locating the Regimento

Carl Thimm[5] and Baron Leguina[6] both mention the "Regimento para aprender a jogar as Armas" in their bibliographies. Neither supplies a date or location for the manuscript, nor citing any authority. In Baron Leguina's bibliography, it is listed among other 15th century sources, half provided without date[7]. Dom Duarte's work is the earliest cited, all of the other works, except Dom Duarte's and two others that remain lost, do not concern themselves with swordsmanship at all.

Jose Almirante's historical bibliography of Iberian military works, cited by both as the source for other early Iberian material, notes the "Regimento para aprender a jogar as armas" of Dom Duarte[8], as the earliest work on fencing produced in the Iberian peninsula in his index, along with citations of the Leal Conselhiero and Bem Cavalgar. Due to the vagaries of time, the former two works were found not in Portugal but in the National

REGIMENTO PERA APRENDER ALGUAS COUSAS D'ARMAS
(REGIMEN TO LEARN SOME THINGS ABOUT ARMS)

Portuguese version, after Dias' [11]transcription:

Regimento pera aprender alguas cousas d armas:
[01] a ora de Terça se va algus dias ensayer/ e o
[02] ensayer seJa este, ele se ha d armar de todas
[03] armas e hir a pe por hua costa açima hu grande
[04] pedaço e mais riJo que poder, e depois se torne [05]
pera casa, e aly tenha armas de fynos ferros
[06] pera outros homens, e tenha lanças e fachas e
[07] espadas de pao/ e quando se quiser prouar
[08] com alguem arme se com armas mais pesadas
[09] hua vez e mea mais que aquelas que ouuer de
[10] trazer no dia da peleJa e este prouar que fizer
[11] com estes, faça por aprender alguas maneyras
[12] e gardas e offensas que outros sabem fazer, e
[13] se em oito ou dez dias non vier nynguem a se
[14] ensayer. // Pode se emsayer con quem quyser,
[15] e esta maneira faz ter bom foleguo, e aprender
[16] de hus e dos outros em feito d armas

English:

Regimen to Learn Some Things of Arms:
[1] On the third hour (Tierce) on some days he goes to practice.
[2] And to practice he should arm himself with all
[3] weapons and goes on foot a great distance up a [hill] for a long
[4] length (piece or section) to strengthen himself. Later he returns
[5] to his house, and there he has arms of fine steel
[6] but for other men, he has there lances and axes
[7] and wooden swords. And when wishing to test (himself)
[8] with a particular weapon (arm) he does so with a heavier weapon
[9] which is something more than of those seeking
[10] to carry on the day of combat. And in proving (himself)
[11] in using these, he ends in learning various ways
[12] and guards and offences (attacks) that others know how to do.
[13] and if in eight to ten days there is no one with whom to
[14] practice. //He may rehearse (practice) with anyone with whom he wants.
[15] And in this manner one will have good courage, and learn
[16] of the uses of others in feats of arms.

Library of Paris in 1820, and were first published in Lisbon in 1843. He notes that the location of the third work seems was unknown; it apparently had never been published. He provided no basis for his citation. Recourse was made to general bibliographies of Portuguese works.

Barbosa Machado's bibliography of Portuguese authors and their works[9] provides the location of the Regimento manuscript at some time prior to his publication. It was part of the Da Misericordia M.S., kept in the Carthusian Convent of Scala Caeli in Evora. This collection contained several works, including Da Arte de domar os Cavallos (alt. title to Bem Cavalgar) and Memorias varias (various records). Barbosa Machado lists the Regimento para aprender a jogar as armas as the last entry under this heading "Memorias varias" along with other, miscellaneous items. Nicolás Antonio's

Bibliotheca Hispana vetus, a collection of all works published in Iberia from Roman times through 1500 lists the Regimento para aprender a jogar as armas as being in Evora as well.[10] It is no longer in Evora within the convent whose collection has been disbursed. In the interim, the collection has been renamed and relocated to an extent that Portuguese bibliographers could not find the work.

Fortunately an effort has been underway to index all significant Iberian materials. The collection had been renamed; the Memorias varias had been copied and collected into a separate collection, la Livro da Cartuxa (Book of the Carthusians), alternately entitled Livro dos Conselhos de el-Rei d. Duarte (Book of the Advice of the King, Dom Duarte). And the title of the entry in all previous works was based on that of a 17th century copy, and not that used within the index.

At this time there are at least 4 different copies extant. One is in the Torre do Tombo Collection in Lisbon, two are in the National Library in Lisbon, and the fourth is in the municipal library in Santarem. The Torre do Tombo version is the authoritative version that formerly belonged to the Carthusian Convent in Evora. The Livro dos Conselhos contains many different items, part of it are parts of "Leal Conselheiro " (Loyal Counselors), although this latter work is only a fraction of the manuscript. Among other advice Dom Duarte provides his people are items on personal hygiene and medicines against common ailments including toothache, diarrhea and the pestilence. It appears to be a fairly random selection of notes made during Dom Duarte's reign. It is aptly named "Memorias varias" (various records).

It appears that all the bibliographers were working from an index of a specific collection, the one currently in the Biblioteca Nacional in Lisbon. The scribe for this version apparently added a new title to the section, it was not originally entitled "Regimento para aprender a jogar as armas" (Regimen to learn to play at arms) but instead "Regimento pera aprender alguas cousas d'armas" (Regimen to learn some things of arms).

As such, it represents the earliest work cited related to fencing from Iberia currently known, and is presented herein in translation derived from the Torre do Tombo version as transcribed (see previous page).

In synopsis, this seems trivial at first glance, but continued reading provides good sound basic advice, almost 600 years old.

1- Start training early in the morning.
2- Do roadwork in armor, including climbing hills.
3- Have spare weapons and armor at your house for anyone who comes over.
4- Have wooden weapons for training.
5- When you train use heavier weapons than you would for battle.
6- Training with capable partners helps you to learn new techniques
7- If no one comes over, train anyway.

Item 2 is reminiscent of training of the Mareschal de Boucicaut as described by Professor Anglo in his monograph.[12]

"One has only to recall Boucicuat's punishing, body-building routine towards the end of the fourteenth century. He would run for miles in full armor to develop 'longue haleine'…"

Item 4 is interesting, as it supports the contention that wooden weapons were used in the training of the knightly classes. This is consistent with the 15th century poetic Poem of the Pell[13] that also recommends wooden weapons (of extra weight) "Of double wight a mace of tre to welde."

Item 6 – The first group of people are those somehow selected as those from whom it was especially worthwhile to learn something of ways and guards and offenses. The second group are those with whom, in the absence of this first group you may practice to some avail.

Dom Duarte's advice echoes that of a work (ghost) written for a Norweigian king, probably Haakon IV (ca. 1240). The author of this work also advises other activities to promote health and martial vigor.

"But if you are in a borough or some such place where horses cannot be used for recreation, you should take up this form of amusement: go to your chambers and put on heavy armor; next look up some fellow henchman (he may be a native or alien) who likes to drill with you and whom you to be well trained in fight behind a shield or buckler. Always bring heavy armor to this exercise, either chain-mail or a thick gambison, and carry a heavy sword and weighty shield or buckler in your hand. In this game you should strive to learn suitable thrusts and such counterstrokes as are good necessary and convenient. Learn precisely how to cover yourself with the shield, so you may be able to guard well when you have to deal with a foeman. If you feel that it is important to be well trained in these activities, go through the exercise twice a day, if it is convenient; but let no day pass, except holidays, without practicing this drill at least once; for it is counted [213] proper for all kingsmen to master this art and moreover, it must be mastered if it is to be of service."[14]

Advice How to Wound With the Sword

This is not all the advice that Dom Duarte provided to the swordsman. Within Bem Cavalgar, there is a slightly longer section on how to wound with a sword (Da maneira do ferir de spada) (122v - 123 v in the Paris MS].[15] Together with the Regimento, this contains Dom Duarte's method of using the sword.

In his chapter on how to wound with the sword (Da maneira do ferir de spada), Dom Duarte presents a quick survey of the most important aspects of mounted combat: horsemanship, swordsmanship, linking the force of horse and rider, and fighting tactics. He concludes with a short section on training and gaining familiarity with using weapons on horseback.[16]

Duarte writes that he offers what he has learned and what he has verified by his own experience. While the customs of other lands might be different, what he presents is good practice.

E por que a husança das terras e dos tempos mudam as manhas e os custumes, poderá seer que a algûû parecerá o contrairo desto que screvo; e porem saibham que o screvy segundo mynha speriencia, a qual concorda com a mais geeral boa pratica que ao presente se husa em estes Reynos delrrey, meu senhor e padre, cuja alma deos aja.

And while there may be little tricks that others teach that may seem to give advantages to their students, what he has written represents the best way to do things.

E aquesto nom digo por meu gabo, ainda que destas pequenas manhas horhem possa dizer sem empacho o que com verdade sentir, mes eu o faço por dar autoridade de mynha leitura, conhecendo os que esto leerem que nom screvo do que ouvy, mes daquello que per grande custume tenho aprendido.

Horsemanship

In the Book of the Courtier,[17] it is noted that horsemanship forms the basis of fighting on horseback, as wrestling forms the basis for fighting on foot. Dom Duarte also advises that he who wishes to fight with the sword on horseback to be as ready to ride as to walk.

E tam bem se devem de vezar saltar sobre a ssella assey vestidos como andarem, se muyto pejados nom forem

Also that he must habituate himself to riding without favoring either horse or saddle,

que se vezem alguas vezes a cavalgar do chããu sem nem hua avantagem sobre suas sellas, nom lhe teendo outrem o cavallo per as redeas nem per cadahua das strebeiras.

and accustom himself to using either his right or left hand equally well

Em aquesto se custumen assy da mããu derita como da ezquerda.

Duarte also advises that he who wishes to fight should keep in practice as did the Roman equites (*cavalleiros romããos*) citing the "*Regymento dos Principes*", who kept wooden horses in their homes to practice upon in armor.

Ca scripto he no livro do Regymento dos Principes que os cavalleiros romããos, quando cessavam da suas guerras, tiinham cavallos de madeira postos em suas casas os quaaes ellavam e se vezavam armados a cavalgar du hua parte e da outra, conhecendo quanto esta manha he proveitosa.

Swordsmanship

Dom Duarte in Bem Cavalgar recognizes four principle ways to wound with the sword

Sobre os avysamentos para ben ferir de spada, a mym parece que razoadamente a cavallo se pode ferir per quatro maneiras.

These are across, reverse, straight down, and the thrust.

Primeira, de talho travesso. Segunda, de revés. Terceira, fendente de cima pera fundo. Quarta, de ponta

Of these, he advises that the first two are the best. Despite this, later in the section he advises another blow, an oblique blow, neither across nor up and down

faça seu golpe nom todo travesso nem de cima pera baixo, mes envyees pera fundo

as the "finest blow" (*fremosos golpes*). The Italian master, Fiore Furlan dei Liberi in 1410 catalogued the same cuts, and likewise shows a preference for the diagonal fendenti[18].

"…Fendenti…cleaving teeth and down to the knee along the same direction … sottani blows… begin from the knee, and we go in the middle of the forehead, following the path of the fendenti. And from the way we rose, we come back; …..mezzani blows … in the middle between the blows soprani (fendenti) and sottani. And we go with the true edge from the right side, and from the reverse side we go with the false edge. … the cruel and deadly punte, and our way is on the center of the body…"

Linking the Force of Horse and Rider

In order to be effective, and he keeps harping on this, the mass and force of the rider must be linked, but the arm free to strike, all precisely together.

E pera dar grande golpe de talho, deve ferir da viinda do cavallo e do corpe e da soltura do braço todo juntamente

He indicates that if you try and strike while you and the horse just stand there, you are not likely to strike an effective blow, but if you do as stated above, it will be to your advantage.

ca se eu feria stando quedo do braço solamente, dava assaz pequeno golpe, e sse em viindo o cavallo da soltura do corpo [e] do braço juntamente, o golpe era mayor em grande avantagem.

He further elaborates how you link sword, man and horse together—you have to stand firmly on your legs, ensure that you can freely move your body and your arm and firmly press the sword into your hand.

que poucas vezes feira senom da viinda, firmandosse sobre as pernas, solte bem o corpo e o braço com a espada bem apertada na maao

If you do not use your momentum to attack, your arm will grow tired and your blows weak and small.

E por que os golpos dá de spaço, o braço nom cansa.... os braço cansam logo, e a pequeno spaço os golpos parecem aos que os vée assaz bem fracos.

For traverse blows and descending blows, he advises this approach, for reverses, ensure the arm is freed and lengthened in attack.

E pera ferir de revés, da ssoltura do braço sollamente se deve fazer, e em pelleja quando comprir

Fighting Tactics

The swordsman should not continually turn this way and that in the middle of the field, but instead drive through, preferably from the side or behind.

E pera esto compre nom fazer voltas curtas em grande torneo, nem teer teençom em hûû, salvo se o filhar de tal avantagem de tras ou dilharga

Note that this differs from the training advice in The King's Mirror.

... Train your good steed to veer about when at full gallop...[19]

And passing the first after attacking him, then attack the next one without recovering and turning until you pass through the entire field

e como der a hûû, logo vaa a outro sem curar de fazer volta ataa que nom passe todo o campo.

Dom Duarte notes that this approach will get you better noticed by the high and mighty

requerindo os lugares das principaaes vistas... que he mais visto

However, he notes that practically, it allows you to identify and to wound whom you will. Note here that Professor Anglo cites "ssa voontade" as meaning "will power". But given the practicality Dom Duarte has shown, I read this not as "will power"; it's "by his will," or, in the usual English "at will." It's "disposed to wound at will, without any obstruction", with no mystical connotations.

dá seus golpes mayores, por que fere em quem lhe praz; [e] muytos achará bem despostos pera os ferir aa ssa voont[a]de sem algúu embargo

And it allows you a chance to get outside the fray occasionally to rest man and horse, galloping only when it works to good effect

Terceira, que anda el e seu cavallo folgadeamente; por que o nom deve aficar em correr nem voltar, mas a gallope trazer geeralmente quando quyzer fazer algúa certa chegada

If you find yourself surrounded, attack the one in front and push through to another and wound him in turn, and not make short rollbacks as it will tire you (and your horse).

E onde vyr que algúus dos seus stam em pressa cercados doutros, ferindo ryjo antr'elles, spalhandoos da viinda do cavallo, logo passe e vaa ferir em outro.

Training

But Dom Duarte says once learned it must be practiced, and not lost, so that you will strike with authority.

E por que, segundo disse, husança [h]e principal fundamento de aprender todallas manhas [e], desque som aprendidas, nom viirem em squeecimento, porem os que desejarem aver esta, husem todavya cortar de spada de cavallo e de pee, trazendoa boa, por que receberá della tal avantagem que lhe acrecentará desejo de o fazerem mais vezes, [e] o custome lhe dará vantagem na manha.

This latter theme, that practice is the best teacher, resonates with both the Regimento, and the advice of other Iberian authors of the joust.

Conclusions

While there is little technical detail in Dom Duarte's works on the sword when compared to other contemporary works on the sword, e.g., Sigmund Ringeck's Fechtbuch of 1440 or those of the Italian Fiore dei Liberi's of 1410. What he writes about is the practical and sensible approach to becoming successful in combat. In the Regimento he recommends rising early, exercising and focused training. In Bem Cavalgar the key to fighting on horseback is horsemanship – the best blow to use from horseback is to use the horse's momentum to develop power, along with proper body positioning and freedom of movement. And to not obviate the power advantage of the horse and your martial focus by dithering hither and yon in the fray, but cut in and out.

But Dom Duarte in both the Regimento and Bem Cavalgar is interested most in training, how to learn to be a good fighter-learn through experience. He doesn't cover a plethora of techniques as familiarity with these is assumed; that's why you are to invite those well-trained individuals to practice at ways, guards and offenses.

Bibliography

Almirante, José, Bibliografía militar de España, por José Almirante,Madrid, M. Tello, 1876

Anglo, Sydney, "How to Win at Tournaments – The Techniques of Chivalric Combat", Antiquaries Journal, LXVIII, Part ii (1988), p.p. 248-64.

Anglo, Sydney, 'Jousting – the Earliest Treatises', Livrustkammaren. Journal of the Royal Armoury (1991-1992), pp 3-23.

Anglo, Sydney, The Martial Arts of Renaissance Europe (New Haven and London 2000)

Anonymous, The King's Mirror (Speculum Regale – Konungs Skuggsjá) trans. by Laurence Marcellus Larson, Twayne Publishers, NY 1917

Anonymous, Poem of the Pell, Cotton Library: Titus A XXIII fol. 6-7

Antonio, Nicolás, Bibliotheca Hispana vetus, Madrid : Visor, 1996

Barbosa Machado, Diôgo, Biblioteca lusitana histórica, crítica e cronológica.(t.I. A.-E. 1741), 2. ed., Lisboa, 1930-35.

Barber, Richard W . & Barker, Juliet, Tournaments : jousts, chivalry, and pageants in the Middle Ages, (New York 1989)

BIBID1334 João José Alves Dias, Ed. Livro dos Conselhos de el-Rei d. Duarte (Livro da Cartuxa){M}. Edição diplomática. Imprensa Universitária, 27. Lisboa: Editorial Estampa, 1982., http://sunsite.berkeley.edu/Philobiblon/BITAGAP/BIB/BIB1334.html

BITAGAP Manid 1479 : Lisboa: Torre do Tombo, Ms. da Liv. 1928. (f. 272r-v. . Author- Duarte, Title-Regimento para aprender algumas cousas das armas., 1433 - 1438. , Text type-prose, Title-Regime~to p~a apre~der algu~as cousas darmas.). http://sunsite.berkeley.edu/Philobiblon/BITAGAP/1479.html,

BITAGAP Manid 1480: Lisboa: Biblioteca Nacional, COD. 3390 (f. 204v. Author- Duarte, Title-Regimento para aprender algumas cousas das armas., 1433 - 1438. , Text type-prose, Title-Regim.to p.a aprender algu~as cousas darmas.) http://sunsite.berkeley.edu/Philobiblon/BITAGAP/1480.html

BITAGAP Manid 1704: Lisboa: Biblioteca Nacional, PBA. 147. (f. 210 f. 210r. Author –Duarte, Title – Regimento para aprender algumas cousas das armas., 1433 - 1438. , Text type-prose, Title – Regimento pera aprender a iugar as armas.), http://sunsite.berkeley.edu/Philobiblon/BITAGAP/1704.html

BITAGAP Manid 3154: Santarém: Biblioteca Municipal, 31 - 7 - 10(f. 132r-v, Author –Duarte, Title – Regimento para aprender algumas cousas das armas., 1433 - 1438. , Text type-prose), http://sunsite.berkeley.edu/Philobiblon/BITAGAP/3154.html

Castiglione, Baldassarre, The book of the courtier [by] Baldesar Castiglione, translated and with an introduction by George Bull, Harmondsworth, Penguin, 1967

Duarte, King of Portugal, Leal conselheiro : o qual fez Dom Eduarte, Rey de Portugal e do Algarve e Senhor de Cepta. Ed. crítica e anotada / organizada por Joseph M. Piel , e preparada pela Faculdade de Letras de Coimbra, sob o patrocínio do Instituto para a Alta Cultura, Lisboa : Livraria Bertrand, 1942.

Duarte, King of Portugal, 1391-1438., Livro dos conselhos de el-Rei D. Duarte : (livro da cartuxa) / transcrição de João José Alves Dias , introdução de A.H. de Oliveira Marques e João José Alves Dias , revisão de A.H. de Oliveira Marques e Teresa F. Rodrigues., Ed. diplomática., Lisboa : Editorial Estampa, 1982

Duarte, King of Portugal, Livro da ensinança de bem cavalgar toda sela que fez el-Rey Dom Eduarte de Portugal e do Algarve e Senhor de Cueta. Ed. crítica / por Joseph M. Piel., [Lisbon] : Impr. Nacional-Casa da Moeda, 1986.

Edward, of Norwich, 2d Duke of York, The master of game; the oldest English book on hunting. Edited by Wm. A. and F. Baillie-Grohman, (New York 1974)

Gaston III Phoebus, Count of Foix, The hunting book of Gaston Phébus : manuscrit français 616, Paris, Bibliothèque nationale / introduction by Marcel Thomas and François Avril , commentary by Wilhelm Schlag, (London 1998).

Fiore Furlan dei Liberi da Premariacco, Fior di Battaglia, Getty Museum 83.MR.183 Call Number: MS LUDWIG XV 13

Fiore Furlan dei Liberi da Premariacco, Fior di Battaglia, Pierpoint Morgan Library, M. 383

Fiore Furlan dei Liberi da Premariacco, F. Novati, Flos duellatorum: Il Fior di battaglia di maestro Fiore dei Liberi da Premariacco/ed. F. Novati, Bergamo, 1902

Leguina y Vidal, Enrique de, Bibliografia e Historica de la Esgrima Espanola, Madrid, Est. Tip. De Fortanent, 1904 & Martino Pub., Mansfield Center, CT, 2000

Rui de Pina, Crónica D'El-Rei D. Duarte, ed. of Alfredo Coelho de Magalhães, Port, Portuguese Renaissance, 1914

Saincte-Marthe, Scevole & Louis de, Histoire généalogique de la Maison de France, (Paris 1617)

Santos, Graziela Skonieczny, DOM DUARTE E O LIVRO DE CAVALGAR, http://www.geocities.com/Athens/Academy/9062/duarte/index.htm

Thimm, Carl A, A complete bibliography of fencing & duelling, as practised by all European nations from the middle ages to the present day. London and New York, John Lane, 1896, facsimile 1986

Wierschin, Martin, Meister Johann Liechtenauers Kunst des Fechtens. München, Beck, 1965.

[1] "Il Joignit heureusement l'exercise des armes la connoissance des letres e sciences." Scevole & Louis de Saincte-Marthe, His-

---

Notes

toire généalogique de la Maison de France, (Paris 1617), Book 42, chapter 5.

[2] Rui de Pina, Crónica D'El-Rei D. Duarte, ed. of Alfredo Coelho de Magalhães, Port, Portuguese Renaissance, 1914, pp. 69-71, 68-82.

[3] Sydney Anglo, 'Jousting—the Earliest Treatises', Livrustkammaren. Journal of the Royal Armoury (1991-1992), pg. 3

[4] Graziela Skonieczny Santos , , DOM DUARTE E O LIVRO DE CAVALGAR http://www.geocities.com/Athens/Academy/9062/duarte/index.htm, pg. 2

[5] Carl A Thimm, A complete bibliography of fencing & duelling, as practised by all European nations from the middle ages to the present day. By Carl A. Thimm. With a classified index, in chronological order, according to languages (alphabetically arranged). Illustrated with numerous portraits of ancient and modern masters of the art, title-pages & frontispieces of some of the earliest works. London and New York, John Lane, 1896, pg. 82

[6] Enrique de Leguina y Vidal, Bibliografia e Historica de la Esgrima Espanola, Madrid, Est. Tip. De Fortanent, 1904 & Martino Pub., Mansfield Center, CT, 2000, p. 59

[7] Leguina, pg.139

[8] José Almirante, Bibliografía militar de España, por José Almirante,Madrid, M. Tello, 1876., pg. 250x

[9] Diôgo Barbosa Machado, Biblioteca lusitana histórica, crítica e cronológica.(t.I. A.-E. 1741), 2. ed., Lisboa, 1930-35, pg. 700-705

[10] Nicolás Antonio, Bibliotheca Hispana vetus, Madrid : Visor, 1996. , book 20, chapter 5, pg. 288

[11] Duarte, King of Portugal, 1391-1438., Livro dos conselhos de el-Rei D. Duarte : (livro da cartuxa) / transcrição de João José Alves Dias , introdução de A.H. de Oliveira Marques e João José Alves Dias , revisão de A.H. de Oliveira Marques e Teresa F. Rodrigues., Ed. diplomática., Lisboa : Editorial Estampa, 1982, pg. 270

[12] Anglo, Sydney, "How to Win at Tournaments – The Techniques of Chivalric Combat", Antiquaries Journal, LXVIII, Part ii (1988), p. 248.

[13] Poem of the Pell, Cotton Library: Titus A, xxiii fol 6 and 7 (early 15th century)

[14] Anonymous, The King's Mirror (Speculum Regale – Konungs Skuggsjá) trans. by Laurence Marcellus Larson, Twayne Publishers, NY 1917, pp. 212-213

[15] BITAGAP/ MANID 1154.Duarte, King of Portugal, 1391-, Livro da Ensinança de Bem Cavalgar Toda Sela (Book of the instruction of all good saddle riding) [Variant title] Livro do Cavalgar, Arte de Domar os Cavalos (Book of riding, The Art of Taming Horses) : Bibliothèque Nationale, Paris, Fonds Portugais 5 , ff. 99-128, ca 1438, http://sunsite.berkeley.edu/Philobiblon/BITAGAP/1154.html

[16] Duarte, King of Portugal, Livro da ensinanca de bem cavalgar, por Joseph M. Piel. [Lisbon] : Impr. Nacional-Casa da Moeda, 1986.(pp. 113-117)

[17] Baldassarre, Castiglione, The book of the courtier [by] Baldesar Castiglione, translated and with an introduction by George Bull, Harmondsworth, Penguin, 1967. pg. x

[18] Luca Porzio, personal correspondence translating Fiore Furlan dei Liberi da Premariacco, Fior di Battaglia, Getty Museum 83.MR.183 Call Number: MS LUDWIG XV 13. fol. 22r.

[19] Anon., The King's Mirror, p. 211

TALHOFFER'S SWORD AND DUELLING SHIELD AS A MODEL FOR RECONSTRUCTING EARLY MEDIEVAL SWORD AND SHIELD TECHNIQUES

By Stephen Hand and Paul Wagner

Figure 1: Talhoffer Plate 128
Both fencers have their shields in the Outside Ward. The left hand figure has his sword in the Pflug Ward, the right hand figure in the Ochs Ward.

Introduction

In the last decade, great advances have been made in the understanding of historical western weapon-play. The systematic study of historical fencing manuals has revealed the correct method of using a large number of historical European weapons. A notable exception has been what is seen by many as the quintessential medieval combination, sword and large shield.[1]

In fact, the combination of sword and shield became distinctly uncommon with the widespread introduction of plate armour in the 14th century. It is a source of some irritation that the fall in popularity of sword and shield corresponds with the rise in popularity of the fencing manual, our prime source for the reconstruction of historical western swordsmanship.

Sword and shield is the single most popular weapon combination amongst thousands of Early and High Medieval re-enactors.[2] These people often dismiss historical swordsmanship as being irrelevant to their chosen weapon or historical period. A credible reconstruction of Early Medieval sword and shield technique would go a long way towards dispelling this scepticism amongst re-enactors This could have many benefits for students of historical swordsmanship, not least of which would be the possibility of making the modern world's most visible manifestation of historical swordsmanship a lot more historically accurate.

No surviving manual tells us how a Viking or a Crusader used his shield. We do, however, have a large body of iconic evidence. Unfortunately, we have no way of telling how accurate individual illustrations of medieval combat are. In the absence of a firm idea of how shields were actually used we can pick up a few basic stances, but really, no more. What we need to put this iconic evidence into perspective is a fencing treatise on sword and large shield. But no treatise or fechtbuch exists for sword and shield; or does it?

One of the features of many German *fechtbucher* of the 14th and 15th centuries is a section on judicial duelling. German judicial duels were fought with a range of weapons, often alongside enormous spiked shields. The unusual nature of these shields has prevented historical fencing researchers from seeing the obvious. That is, that these *fechtbucher* contain almost our only detailed commentary on fighting with sword and large shield[3].

The most detailed section on sword and duelling shield is found in Talhoffer's Fechtbuch of 1467. The section on sword and shield includes 23 plates. These plates and their accompanying text form the core of this paper. Talhoffer's Fechtbuch was recently translated by Mark Rector[4] and Mark's translation is used throughout. The illustrations from this edition are used by kind permission of Lionel Leventhal, the publisher.

Once Talhoffer's techniques have been analyzed, they will be compared with other evidence for European sword and shield use, notably the iconic record.

A Note on Shields, Targets and Bucklers
Although no surviving manuals exist telling us how medieval shields were used, the same can not be said of the buckler, a small shield held by a single handle. MS I.33[5], currently the oldest known fencing treatise describes combat with sword and buckler. It is the most complete work on the sword and buckler. The authors have worked extensively with I.33 and consider it to contain a superb and effective system. However, they also consider the large shields of the Early and High Middle Ages to be a distinct weapon. Anyone who does not believe this should attempt the techniques described in MS I.33 with a large round, kite or heater shield. There are many techniques that are simply physically impossible with larger shields[6]. The central tenet of I.33 (that the arm must be covered in attack) is still valid when using larger shields. However, covering the sword arm with the buckler exposes the rest of the body, something which is not true with large shields. There are some instances where techniques and principles drawn from I.33 may provide possible solutions to situations not covered by Talhoffer (for example, an attack to the lower legs – not really an issue with Talhoffer's duelling shields). However, such speculation is beyond the scope of this paper, and in general I.33 is not seen as a valid model for large shield use.

The Target, a medium sized shield held on the arm by straps (enarmes), shares (in the opinion of the authors) some of the characteristics of the buckler and some of the large shield. Therefore examples of target use from fencing manuals and the iconic record will be included in the section comparing Talhoffer's shield use with that shown in other sources.

Moving to large shields, the closest shields in terms of form and function to those shown in Talhoffer are undoubtedly the large oval centre grip shields used in ancient times (see Figures 28 and 29). Not quite so closely related, but more important because of the many thousands of Early Medieval Re-enactors around the world are the large round centre grip shields used by Vikings and Saxons. This is the style of shield used by the authors in the photo reconstructions at figures 5 to 14. Shields held onto the arm with straps, such as the kite and large heater shields of the 11th-13th centuries are less closely related to Talhoffer's shields. The straps limit how freely the shield can be rotated, though as shown below, there is considerable evidence of strapped shields being used according to the same basic principles as Talhoffer's duelling shields, even

if the mechanics of individual techniques must of necessity be somewhat different.

The Techniques
All of the techniques described by Talhoffer for use with sword and duelling shield are, of course, practical with that weapon combination. However, the purpose of this paper is not to reconstruct Talhoffer's style of sword and duelling shield (in which few people are interested), but rather to use that as a basis for reconstructing Early and High Medieval sword and large shield (in which many people are interested). Therefore, only those techniques found to be practical in fencing with Early and High Medieval swords and shields[7] will be discussed. Notably, those techniques shown in plates 140, 149 and 150[8] would only be possible with a shield with an elongate handle that can be held in both hands. Other techniques which re-use already established principles have also been omitted (For example the technique in plate 148 where the shield has been discarded by one fencer. The concept that the shield can be discarded in mid-fight has already been established in plates 136 and 137, which will be discussed below).

It should also be noted that Talhoffer's techniques are for single combat, specifically judicial duels. Some of them would in the author's opinion, be almost suicidal in a shield wall or equivalent. This will be discussed further in the section below, comparing Talhoffer with the iconic evidence for Early and High Medieval sword and shield combat.

Stances
Talhoffer illustrates two basic shield wards which are combined with two different sword positions. He does not name any of these wards. Unlike sword and buckler, the sword and shield are moved independently and hence the most useful system of nomenclature seems to be one which treats the sword and shield separately.

The first of Talhoffer's shield wards has been christened the Outside Ward after Zachary Wylde's *outside guard* for backsword, broadsword and quarterstaff[9]. The ward is so-named because it protects the outside line. In fencing the outside line is the line outside the weapon, to the right of the weapon for a right hander and to the left of the weapon for a left hander. As the shield is held by a right-hander in the left hand, the outside line is to the left of the shield and the Outside Ward is that ward which protects against attacks coming from the left . Talhoffer's first sword and shield plate shows both combatants in the Outside Ward. The shields are held to the left of the body, angled inwards at approximately a 30 degree angle and are engaged. The engagement of the shields closes each fencer's outside line. Neither fencer may strike the other from this position without moving his shield. If the shields are not held engaged, the inside line is vulnerable. Talhoffer illustrates two examples of a fencer exploiting the faulty Outside Ward of his opponent, and these will be discussed below. Note that the legs of both fencers are outside the line of their shields. This may be to brace the shield and prevent it being rotated by pressure against the engagement. However, the legs of the combatants in Talhoffer's Plate 104, the first plate of the section on shield and wooden mace, are inside the line of their shields (as is the leg of the man in figure 32) so the significance of these leg positions is uncertain (and may indeed be irrelevant when using shields which do not extend to the ground).

The second shield ward shown by Talhoffer has been named the Inside Ward, again after the ward used by Zachary Wylde for backsword, broadsword and quarterstaff[10]. The Inside Ward unsurprisingly protects the inside line, recalling that for a right handed person this is the line to the right of their shield. This ward is shown in figure 2. At no point does Talhoffer illustrate shields engaged in this ward, but he does describe several instances where a failure to engage leaves one fencer open to an attack by his opponent.

The two sword wards shown by Talhoffer are single handed versions of the *Ochs* (Ox) and *Pflug* (Plow) wards of longsword play.[11] These are shown in figure 1, respectively by the fencers on the right and left. In experimentation by the authors with the shorter, broader swords used in the Early Medieval period it was found that more cutting orientated wards were also useful. These included *vom Dach*[12] (Silver's *Open Ward* and Marozzo's *Guardia Alta*),[13] *Nebenhut*[14] (Fiore de Liberi's *Posta di Coda lunga distesa*),[15] *Zornhut*[16] as well as wards only seen in Early Medieval iconography. These other wards will be discussed in more detail below.

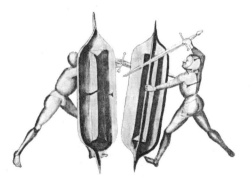

Fig. 2: Talhoffer Plate 130: *The fencer on the left has his shield in the Inside Ward. The fencer on the right is in a faulty ward, not covering his inside line and is being struck.*

Basic Principles
Opening and Closing the line of attack
Because the two shield wards each cover a line of attack, combat with Talhoffer's duelling shields revolves around closing a line of attack while opening a line of attack against the opposing fencer. This is achieved by changing the shield from one ward to the other. From the basic engaged stance shown in figure 1, either fencer can step forward, turning their shield from the

Fig. 3
Talhoffer Plate 131

Outside to the Inside Wards. As can be seen in the figure below, the rotation of the shield covers the inside line of the attacking fencer. As the shield has been rotated, the opposing sword and shield are bound out to the attacker's right leaving the defender completely open in his inside line. In this instance the attacker thrusts, but roversi (cuts from left to right)—are also effective.

Fig. 4
Talhoffer Plate 144

A similar attack using a cut is shown in Plate 144. The attacker has turned his shield into the Inside Ward, but has not attempted to bind his opponent's sword or shield. Instead he has cut downwards with an Oberhau (a cut from above) onto his opponent's wrist, cutting off his hand.

This rotation of the shield from the outside to the inside line can also be used as a defence, although Talhoffer does not use it in that way (although see the discussion of Di Grassi's sword and round target below). If a fencer refuses to engage shields in the Outside Ward he may attack to the unprotected right side, or inside line. The defender changes his shield into the Inside Ward, binding the attacker's sword away to his right and closing his inside line. Simultaneously he may attack to the head or right side of the body with a cut or thrust. Against a trained opponent the opportunity to use this defence should not arise (which is probably why Talhoffer doesn't mention it), but against those unfamiliar with Talhoffer's style it is extremely effective and therefore worthy of mention.

Fig. 8: *Paul is in Outside Ward. Stephen is in Inside Ward*

Fig. 5: *The authors are in Outside Ward, not engaged.*

Fig.9: *Stephen attacks Paul's exposed inside line.*

Fig. 6: *Paul thrusts to Stephen's inside line.*

Fig. 10 : *Paul responds by changing to Inside Ward and counterthrusting.*

Fig. 7: *Stephen responds by changing to the Inside Ward and counterthrusting.*

Fig. 11 : *From the position in figure 8 Paul attacks Stephen's exposed outside line.*

Fig. 12: *Stephen changes his shield to Outside Ward and cuts to the back of Paul's head.*

Fig. 13: *The authors are both in Inside Ward, not engaged*

Fig. 14: *Paul attacks by changing his ward and opening Stephen's outside line.*

Talhoffer does not mention commencing in the Inside Ward but it is an obvious extrapolation from the techniques he does show (also see the discussion of Di Grassi's sword and target, below). If one combatant is in the Inside Ward and the other is in the Outside Ward, several possibilities arise. Either combatant can allow his opponent to threaten his exposed line, drawing an attack to that line. He may then pass forward, changing his shield into the opposite ward, vigorously striking his opponent's shield aside and attacking with the sword to the exposed side or back.

If both combatants are in Inside Ward they may engage shields, though with the shields across the body, this brings them closer together than an engagement in

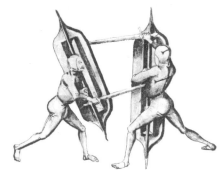

Fig. 15: Talhoffer Plate 133

Outside Ward. It is therefore more likely that if both combatants are in Inside Ward, they will not be engaged . Just as attacks and defences can be made from Outside Ward by changing the ward and opening the inside line to attack, so from Inside Ward attacks and defences can be made by changing the ward and opening the outside line to attack.

Talhoffer does not show the Inside Ward being used as a ward to lie in. It would appear that to avoid mismatched wards and the absence of shield engagement, which results when both combatants are in Inside Ward, Outside Ward was the standard ward. If this is true then we would expect to see the Outside Ward depicted far more often in the iconic record. As stated below this is indeed what is found.

Techniques to avoid being shield bound
Once the shield has been rotated into the opposite ward and the opposing sword and shield has been bound, the fight is effectively over. Therefore counters exist to prevent this from happening.

An attack made by rotating the shield into the Inside Ward is only effective if it can close the inside line by binding the defender's sword and shield across to the right. Therefore Talhoffer's response to such an attack is to draw back sword and shield, so that they cannot be

Fig. 16: Talhoffer Plate 146
The fencer on the left's inside line and the fencer on the right's outside line are both open and the faster attack is successful.

bound. As the attacker turns his shield into the Inside Ward, he exposes his left side as shown in figure 15. The caption to this plate reads,

"The combatant on the right tries to thrust behind his opponent's shield. The combatant on the left draws his shield back, avoiding the attack, and counters with a thrust from below."[17]

Talhoffer shows a response to this defence. The attacker can throw his shield at the defender once he realises that his shield bind has been unsuccessful. Talhoffer writes,

"Both combatants stand unprotected. The combatant on the right can throw his shield at his opponent to force him away."[18]

So, rather than relying on out thrusting your opponent in close distance you can use your now useless shield as a missile. In the next plate Talhoffer shows the result of the shield throw.

"The combatant on the right throws his shield at his opponent and shoves him away, forcing him to crouch, so he may hew him upon his head and back."[19]

If the attacker cuts to the inside line while changing his shield to the Inside Ward, the defender can respond by simultaneously changing his shield into the Inside Ward. The defender must draw his shield back as he changes his ward, to avoid his shield being bound by that of the attacker. The attacker's shield pivots around, meeting no resistance while the defender's shield blocks the attacker's cut. There will now be a gap between the two shields. the defender can now cut down into this gap with an Oberhau to the attacker's head. Talhoffer writes,

"The combatant on the left cuts closely between the two shields, striking his opponent on the head. 'I tried to cut crosswise and am undone!' "[20]

Fig. 17: Talhoffer Plate 141

With shields smaller than Talhoffer's the defender can simply cut over the shields, not even waiting until the attacker has completed his action.

Another defence against the shield bind is to interpose the sword between the shields, to prevent the shield being pivoted. Talhoffer's caption to the plate below reads,

"The combatant on the left is going to pivot his shield and cut at his opponent. However, the combatant on the right interposes his sword between the shields and stands just as strongly."[21]

Fig. 18: Talhoffer Plate 129

The key to this technique is to brace the sword with the edge of the shield. The effect of this is to upset the balance of the attacker, giving the initiative to the defender.

It was stated above that if a shield bind is successful, the fight is effectively over. The exception to this is an interesting technique that seems to run contrary to the logical use of the shield. It involves throwing the shield away. If the shield is bound, but not the sword then the defender can obviously parry the incoming attack with his sword. If the defender's shield is still bound then it is of no use to him, so he may simply discard it. This frees his left hand to pull aside the attacker's shield. The defender then ripostes, striking the attacker.

Fig. 19: Talhoffer Plate 136
The figure on the left has warded his opponent's thrust, discarded his shield and is pulling his opponent's shield aside in preparation for a cut to the head.

However, there is a twist to this technique. As the combatant on the right feels his shield being gripped, he can discard it and use his left hand to grip the elbow of the combatant on the left. Talhoffer writes,

> "This, however, is how the fight ends: the combatant on the right drops his shield and grasps his opponent by the elbow, turns him around, and thrusts him through the neck."[22]

Obviously while a centre gripped shield can be easily discarded, this would not be an option available to someone using a strapped shield.

Additional Attacking Techniques

Talhoffer includes two additional attacking techniques to be used when both combatants are in Outside Ward. The first must be done when the shields are not engaged. The attacker passes forward, as if he intends to attack directly into the shield. He then kicks the bottom left corner of the defender's shield, causing it to pivot around into the Inside Ward. The attacker can then thrust the defender through the body. The counter to this is to simply draw back the shield so that the kick misses and cut the attacker's leg off.

Fig. 20: Talhoffer Plate 134

If one combatant holds his shield too open while engaging in the outside ward, his opponent can thrust at him with a Punta Riversa (a thrust from the left). The attacker brings his sword to the left of his own shield and thrusts between his opponent's sword and shield. Because the defender's arm is not extended, the attacker can gain opposition against his blade, the distance between the target and the defender's blade being very small.

Summary of Techniques

What are the key points in Talhoffer's style? Firstly the shield is used to close a potential line of attack, usually the outside line. This is done by the shield being interposed between the defender's body and the attacker's weapon. Opponent's shields can be engaged in exactly the same manner as swords. Attacks are made by binding with the shield, closing your line of attack while opening the opponent's same line. For

Fig. 21: Talhoffer Plate 145

example rotating the shield from Outside Ward into Inside Ward closes your inside line and opens your opponent's (as for example in figures 3 and 4). The final basic principle is that the shield may be discarded if it is bound, although obviously this last option is not available to those using large shields held on the arm with straps.

Comparison with Other Sources
Other Fencing Treatises

Talhoffer's techniques are all very well, but what evidence exists to suggest that they were used with anything other than German duelling shields? The reason that we are examining Talhoffer in the first place is because there aren't any fencing manuals describing early medieval sword and shield combat. There are, however, later manuals which describe sword and shield. One of these is Giacomo Di Grassi's *Ragione Di Adoprar* of 1570, translated into English in 1594 as *Giacomo Di Grassi his true Arte of Defence*[23].

Di Grassi illustrates one basic ward with sword and round target (spada et rotella[24]) which bears a striking resemblance to the Outside Ward (see figure 1). The shield is held to the left of the body and is angled inwards at approximately 30 degrees.

Di Grassi describes this stance in incredible detail. The key points of his description are given below,

Fig. 22: Di Grassi (1570) p.79

"Of the maner how to holde the round Target

If a man woulde so beare the rounde Target, that it may couer the whole bodie, and yet nothing hinder him from seeing his enimie, which is a matter of great importance, it is requisite, that he beare it towardes the enimie, not with the conuexe or outward parte thereof,...Therefore, if he would holde the said Target, that it may well defend all that part of the bodie, which is from the knee vpwardes, and that he maie see his enemie, it is requisite that he bear his arm, if not right, yet at least bowed so little, that in the elbowe there be framed so blunt an angle or corner, that his eyebeames passing neere that part of the circumference of the Target, which is neere his hande, may see his enemie from the head to the foot. And by holding the saide conuexe parte in this manner, it shall warde all the left side, and the circumference neere the hande shall with the least motion defend the right side, the head and the thighes."[25]

All of which is a convolute way of telling the reader to hold the target as in the illustration.

As well as holding his shield in the Outside Ward, Di Grassi describes, both offensive and defensive binds, similar to those described above. An offensive bind made in conjunction with a thrust from the high ward (the same as Talhoffer's Ochs – see above) is described below.

"That which remaineth to be done, is to thrust forcibly with the sworde: and when one perceiueth, that the point therof is entred within the circumference of the enimies Target, it is necessary that he encrease a left pace, and with the circumference of his owne Target, to beat off the enimies sworde and Target, to the end, it suffer the thrust so giuen of force to enter in. And (hauing so beaten and entred) to continue on the thrust in the straight lyne, with the encrease of a pace of the right foote."[26]

As the thrust passes by the opponent's shield rim the attacker makes a pass forward with his left foot, beating his opponent's sword and shield away to his right.

A very similar technique is described by Agrippa.

"If O wants to wound C, he could do a feint to the face, advancing the right foot behind the left, to cause him to move, lowering the tip and moving to the right of the enemy, to attack C low, and putting the shield into his head, but if C should be a wary person, he wouldn't move at the feint with the shield, but at the same time he'll thrust at the right shoulder of the foe, retiring with a reverso in guard of O, from where he could go the grapple shown in T and Q in two ways. The first will go with the right foot behind the left, and with a feinted mandritto to the legs of the enemy, so that he parries and also tries a roverso the the legs, and at the same time turning the sword inside, of true edge and continuing with the right foot and passing with the left foot, so he'll come to grapple. The other way will be used if, being unable to turn the sword inside because of the speed of the part, or because of the size of the weapon, he'll lower the guard of the sword with the tip up, closing with the right foot and following with the left foot; and if he wouldn't like to close, he could, before finishing the cutting feint, turn the hand downside up, covering with the shield **the line** (authors' emphasis) to his own right knee for fear of the adversary's reverso, and closing with the point he'll finish the play."[27]

Note that the target does not pass completely into the Inside Ward. Because the target is held on the arm with straps, the rim or "circumference" as Di Grassi puts it is used to close the inside line rather than the face of the shield (as used by Talhoffer). Although the principle of closing the line is identical with duelling shield or target, the manner in which this is carried out is notably different between the different styles of shield. This is an important point to remember in any reconstruction with kite or heater shields.

Talhoffer did not describe the use of the same bind as a defence, but Di Grassi does.

"*The defence of the high warde at sword & round Target:* For the defending of the thrust of the high warde, it is most sure standing at the

Fig. 23:
Agrippa (1553)
Chapter XXI.
A bind with the target.

lowe warde, and to endeuour to ouercome the enimie, by the same skill by the which he himselfe would obtain the victorie. In the very same time, that he delivereth his thrust, a man must suddenly encrease a slope pace with the lefte foote, beating off the enemies Target with his owne, and driuing of a thrust perforce with the increase of a pace of the right foote. And with this manner of defence being done with such nimblenesse as is required, hee doth also safely strike the enimie, who cannot strike him againe, because, by meanes of the saide slope pace he is carried out of the lyne in the which the enimie pretended to strike."[28]

As the attacker turns his shield to close the inside line and beat the defender's shield aside, the defender takes a slope pace forward and left with his left foot, taking himself off the line of the attack and turning his shield to close the inside line (although as described above almost certainly not completely into an Inside Ward). This beats the attacker's shield out to the defender's right, opening the attacker up to a thrust.

Other Italian masters illustrate similar wards. Marozzo shows a ward very similar to Di Grassi, the only difference being the fact that he has his weight a lot further forward (Fig. 24). However, Marozzo also shows both the target and a larger shield in Medium Ward[29], indicating that his style of shield use is not identical to Talhoffer's. Capo Ferro shows the rotella, or round target, covering the outside line in both his illustrations of sword and rotella (Fig. 25).
The Scottish fencer McBane also illustrates and describes the Outside Ward. He states,

"This Target is of great use to those who rightly understand it, but to unexperienced People is often

Fig. 25: Capo Ferro 1610 Plate 42

very Fatal, by blinding themselves with it, for want of rightly understanding it. Therefore who has mind to use it must take care to have it upon an Edge, so as to Cover his Left-side from which is a defence against Bal? *(rest of word obscured)* any weapon."[30]

The presence of Talhoffer's wards, and in some cases, his techniques in Marozzo, Agrippa, Di Grassi, Capo Ferro and McBane illustrate that the stances and techniques described by Talhoffer were not restricted to combat with elaborate duelling shields. However, it still does not demonstrate that Early and High Medieval shields were used in this manner.

Pre 15th Century Pictorial Evidence
There exist a large number of illustrations, carvings etc. showing warriors fighting on foot with sword and large shield. If the extrapolation of Talhoffer's techniques back to earlier shield use is valid, then we might expect to see Talhoffer's Outside and Inside Wards illustrated, particularly in Early and High Medieval sources.

While Talhoffer's wards are indeed illustrated, by far the most common ward shown has the shield held close to the body with the face of the shield towards the opponent (fig. 27). In keeping with the use of Wylde's

Fig. 24: Marozzo 1536 p.29V

Fig. 26: McBane 1728 Illustration following page 64

terminolgy of Outside and Inside Wards it is proposed that this ward be called the Medium Ward. There is a very good reason for using this ward. While Talhoffer's wards may be excellent in single combat, they uncover the body unnecessarily in mass combat where the majority of threats come from combatants other than the one immediately in front of you. In this situation a passive defence is likely to be more successful than an active defence.

The problem with Medium Ward is that it is impossible to attack from it without uncovering the sword arm. One way around this is to move the shield into Outside or Inside Ward as an attack is made. However, Medium Ward is a very limited ward, and experience shows that two vaguely competent fighters in Medium Ward can bash away at each other in relative safety (at least until their arms tire). It is unsurprising that Medium Ward is the most common ward shown in medieval iconography, because battle scenes are far more commonly depicted than single combat.

One of the earliest depictions of Talhoffer's wards is that of a Celtic warrior from 6th century BC Slovenia. Another Celtic warrior is shown in a carving from Osuna, Spain dated to around 300BC. The large La Tene era Celtic shield is perhaps the closest battlefield equivalent to Talhoffer's great duelling shields, so it is unsurpring that it should be held similarly.
While it may be argued that these depictions are the result of artistic license, the following two figures show that artists were happy to show different figures using different wards. In these Early Medieval depictions, both Medium and Outside Wards are shown.

Illustrations of shields being used in single combat become more common from 1100. In the following illustrations from the early to mid twelfth century the combatants are all in Outside Ward, regardless of whether they are carrying kite or round shields.
The appearance of the Outside Ward by itself doesn't provide strong evidence that people were fighting in Talhoffer's style, by for example, pivoting the shield into

Fig. 28: *Celtic warrior with axe, javelins and shield in Outside Ward from 6th century BC Slovenia*

Fig. 29:
Celtic warrior in Outside Ward, from Osuna, Spain c.300 BC.

Fig. 30
Animal-headed Pictish gods battle in Medium and Outside Ward. Class II stone at Murthly, Perthshire, 7th century

Fig. 27: *Two 11th century English warriors in the "shield wall" style Medium Ward, from Cotton MS Cleopatra C.vii fl8v*

Fig. 31: *Northumbrian warriors advance on "Egil the archer" on the carved whalebone Franks Casket, 8th century*

Inside Ward to close the line of attack. Figure 34, also from 12th century France distinctly shows one combatant (the figure on the left) holding his shield in the Inside Ward. However, the two combatants are shown using clubs, and this perhaps represents some form of non-

Fig. 34: *12th century Carved Capital, in situ church, St Pierre de I'le, County of Saintonge, France*

Fig. 32: *A Norman Goliath receives a slingstone in the forehead, from the St Etienne Bible, AD1109-11 (Bib. Munic., Dijon, Ms. 168, f.5R, France)*

Fig. 35: *Judicial combat in a late 12th century French manuscript (Bib. Munic., Ms. 210, F4V, Avranches France)*

Fig. 33: *Two foot soldiers c. 1130-40. Carved Reliefs, in situ exterior of Abbey church, Andlau, France*

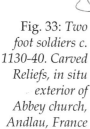

Fig. 36: *Manuscript drawing, northern France late 12th century. (Bib. Munic., Ms. 12/II f.62V, St Omer France)*

lethal competition, or judicial duel[31]. Figures 34-37 show remarkably similar combats with shield and mace or pick between unarmoured combatants. The similarity between the engagement of the shields in figure 35 and that shown by Talhoffer (illustrated here in figure 1) is striking. One item worthy of note is the position in which almost all the figures (for example, both men in figures 35 and 37) are holding their maces (the position of the left hand figure's sword in figure 33 is also in this ward). This is a position characteristic of medieval iconography and represents a ward not (to the authors' knowledge) shown in any fencing manual or fechtbuch. Based on experimentation, this ward seems to perform the same role as *vom Dach* (from the roof) (or vom Tag , Ringeck or Meyer are sources) enabling powerful blows to be struck to the upper body and in particular under the shield to the left side of the opponent. Raising the arm forms an *Ochs Ward*, as shown by the right hand combatant in figure 1, protecting the head and allowing a thrust.

A remarkably similar scene is depicted on a late 12th century cathedral door in Sicily. Figure 38 shows two figures fighting with targets in the Outside Ward. The right hand figure seems to be striking between the shields as is the left hand combatant in figure 17.

Fig. 37: *13th century judicial combat from Chertsy abbey. The left figure is in Inside ward, and the right figure appears to be left-handed and in Outside ward.*

Throughout the 12th and 13th centuries the Outside and Inside Wards continue to appear in iconography. Figures 39 and 40 show combatants in the Outside Ward while figure 41 shows the Inside Ward. Figure 42 is interesting. The figure on the left has changed his shield into Inside Ward, deflecting the point of his opponent's sword outside the line. While the shields may be drawn in this way to show off both coats of arms, this does not mean that the artist ignored reality to achieve his end. In fact the deflection of the rightmost figure's sword suggests that the artist was trying to justify showing the figure on the left in Inside Ward.

Fig. 38: *Late 12th Century panel from the bronze doors of Trani Cathedral in Sicily*

The following illustration, from the early 14th century, shows a similar action. The figure on the right, a left hander, has changed his shield into the Inside Ward, deflecting the axe cut out to his left. His sword guard is more reminiscent of Talhoffer than earlier illustrations. This is perhaps the clearest parallel to Talhoffer and the strongest evidence that a combat style similar to

Fig. 39: *Two knights from the Eneid of Heinrich von Veldeke c. 1145-1210. (Deutsche Staatsbib. Ms. Germ 20232, f.46V, Berlin Germany)*

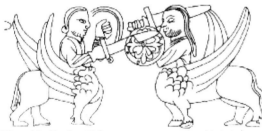

Fig. 40: *Early 13th century carved relief, in situ Cathedral, Freiburg im Breisgau, Germany*

Fig. 41: *Foot soldiers in Inside Ward. (Die Manessesche Liederhandschrift, 1300-1315 43V, Universitätsbibliothek Heidelberg, Germany)*

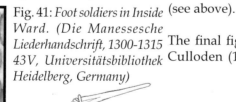

Fig. 42: *Knights fighting from a 13th century French manuscript. (The Romance of Lancelot, Deulofeu collection, Puigcerda, Gerona, Spain)*

that shown by Talhoffer was in use much earlier. This illustration is also very close to the parry with the target from McBane shown at figure 26. The repetition of such an unusual iconic combination would indicate historical continuity.

The next figure, from the early 14th century shows two-hands being used on the sword, indicating that the shield is beginning to be considered less important defensively. Figure 45 shows Italian infantrymen, again using Outside Ward. Large oval shields are used to close the outside line.

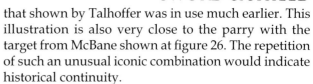

Fig. 43: *English Manuscript, early 14th century (British Library, Ms. Roy. 16.G.VI, f.172, London, England)*

By 1340 shields were beginning to fall out of favour and so depictions of them become harder to find. However, with illustrations being, in general, more lifelike, the proportion of combatants shown in wards similar to Talhoffer's increases. In figure 46, a 17th

Fig. 44: *A wolf-crested knight takes two hands to his sword against an opponent in Outside Ward (Die Mansessche Leiderhandschrift, 1300-1315 321V, Universitätsbibliothek Heidelberg, Germany)*

century depiction of Roman soldiers fighting we see an action very much like that described by Di Grassi (see above).

The final figure shows highlanders at the battle of Culloden (1745). The rightmost highlander can be

Fig. 45: *Italian Infantrymen in battle c. 1340 ('Battles of Guelphs and Ghibellines', wall painting, in situ Castle of Sabbionara, Avio, Italy)*

Fig. 46: *Roman troops practicing according to Johann Jacobi von Walhausen in* Romanische Kriegskunst, *Frankfurt-am-Main. 1616*

clearly seen deflecting the bayonet thrust to his armpit with an Inside Ward.

The illustrations shown above demonstrate that Talhoffer's Outside and Inside Wards appear in Medieval Art as do some of his techniques. As discussed in the section on Talhoffer's techniques above, the Outside Ward is far more commonly depicted than the Inside. This is thought to be because the Outside Ward is a far more practical Ward to engage an opponent from. Inside Ward is primarily a ward that is adopted during the course of a technique, not a ward that one lies in for any period of time.

Fig. 47: *Detail of charging Highlanders from Laurie and Whittle's painting "The Battle of Culloden", 1747.*

Conclusions

Throughout this paper it has been argued that Talhoffer's sword and duelling shield section provides a basis for the reconstruction of early medieval sword and shield technique. Of course in the absence of an early medieval sword and shield fencing manual this is almost impossible to prove. However, if such a manual existed there would be no need to extrapolate from Talhoffer (or indeed from modern experimentation as is commonly done by re-enactors) in the first place. At some point we must either accept an extrapolation as the basis for modern sword and shield play or cease fencing with sword and shield altogether. The latter is clearly not going to happen which leaves the only question as "is the extrapolation from Talhoffer sufficiently accurate and effective to supplant those styles developed by modern sword and shield fencers over the last quarter century?". The authors believe that the answer to this question is an emphatic yes.

With a few obvious exceptions Talhoffer's style does work with Early and High Medieval large shields. The sword and target sections of later manuals describe similar stances and techniques, including attack and defence by closure of the line. There are depictions of earlier medieval combat that show Talhoffer's wards, and even some of his techniques. It would seem that at very least, there was a broad similarity between Talhoffer's style of sword and shield and that used in Early and High Medieval Europe. This is more than can be said for the styles made up and used by most early medieval re-enactors (including, until recently, the authors). The authors feel that the vast gulf between the style shown here and the style adopted by practically every modern experimenter demonstrates the weakness of modern experimentation as an approach to reconstructing martial arts for which we have no documented information.

Perhaps most importantly for some people, the style is brutally effective in a modern re-enactment or historical fencing environment. In the absence of any specific evidence for how early medieval shields were used it is felt that Talhoffer's style forms a sound basis for any reconstruction.

Afterword

There are 47 figures in this paper, a number the authors thought was quite enough. However, our continued research (and the help of our excellent reviewers) has revealed many additional illustrations that support our thesis. Rather than adding additional figures to an already heavily illustrated paper we have decided to publish this material on a website (either on the Stoccata School of Defence website at http://www.stoccata.org or at a site linked from that site). In this way additional material can be constantly added.

Acknowledgements
This paper would have been impossible without Mark Rector's excellent translation of Talhoffer's Fechtbuch, published as *Medieval Combat*. The authors are indebted to Lionel Leventhal of Greenhill Books for permission to use images from *Medieval Combat*. Steve Hick, Greg Mele, Dr Ray Smith and Matt Easton are to be thanked for their thoughtful reviews of this paper. All provided excellent comments that have resulted in significant improvements to the finished product.

Bibliography
Agrippa, Camillo. Trattato di Scientia d'Arme. Roma, 1553
Anonymous. MS I.33. South German sword and buckler manual held in the Royal Armouries at Leeds c.1300
Capo Ferro, Ridolfo. *Gran Simvlacro Dell'Arte, E dell'vso Della Scherma*. Siena 1610
Di Grassi, Giacomo. *Ragione Di Adoprar Sicvramente L'Arme si da Offesa, Come da Difesa*. Venetia 1570
Di Grassi, Giacomo. *His true Arte of Defence*. Translated by I.G. Gentleman, London 1594
Dei Liberi, Fiore. *Flos Duellatorum*. Milan 1409
Galas, S. Matthew. *Kindred Spirits: The Art of the Sword in Germany and Japan*. in *The Journal of Asian Martial Arts* (Vol.6 No.3, 1997)
McBane, Donald. *The Expert Sword-Man's Companion*. Glasgow 1728
Manciolino, Antonio. *Opera Nova*. Bologna 1531
Marozzo, Achille. *Opera Nova*, Modena, 1536
Nicolle, David. Arms and Armour of the Crusading Era 1050-1350. London 1999
Silver, George. *Bref Instructions Upo my Pradoxes of Defence*, Unpublished MSS Sloane 376. British Library c. 1605
Talhoffer, Hans. *Medieval Combat: A Fifteenth-Century Illustrated Manual of Swordfighting and Close-Quarter Combat*. Translated and Edited by Mark Rector. London. 2000
Wallhausen, Johann Jacobi von. *Romanische Kriegskunst*. Frankfurt-am-Main 1616
Wylde, Zachary . *The English Master of Defence: or The Gentleman's Al-a-mode Accomplishment*. York, 1711

Notes

[1] As opposed to sword and buckler for which we have a number of excellent sources (see the note on shields, targets and bucklers).

[2] The Early Medieval period is usually regarded as being up to 1100, the 12th and 13th centuries are High Medieval. Dr Ray Smith, Adjunct Professor of History, Northern Virginia Community College, pers. comm. June 18th 2001

[3] A number of 16th and 17th century Italian manuals contain short sections on sword and target (a medium sized shield held on the arm with straps). These include Manciolino (1531), Marozzo (1536), Di Grassi (1570, 1594) and Capo Ferro (1610).

[4] Hans Talhoffer, *Medieval Combat: A Fifteenth-Century Illustrated Manual of Swordfighting and Close-Quarter Combat*. Translated and Edited by Mark Rector. London. 2000

[5] An anonymous south German sword and buckler manual held in the Royal Armouries at Leeds, dating to c.1300

[6] For example the grip shown in the lower illustration on plate 8.

[7] Specifically large round Viking shields, Norman kite shields and high medieval heater shields.

[8] Hans Talhoffer, *Medieval Combat: A Fifteenth-Century Illustrated Manual of Swordfighting and Close-Quarter Combat*. Translated and Edited by Mark Rector. London. 2000

[9] Zachary Wylde, *The English Master of Defence: or The Gentleman's Al-a-mode Accomplishment*. York, 1711. Wylde's section on back and broad sword starts on page 22 and his staff section starts on page 32. The guards are the first things discussed in each section.

[10] Ibid

[11] S. Matthew Galas, *Kindred Spirits: The Art of the Sword in Germany and Japan*. in *The Journal of Asian Martial Arts* (Vol.6 No.3, 1997) pp. 30-32

[12] Joachim Meyer, Gründtliche Beschreibung der freyen Ritterlichen und Adelichen kunst des Fechtens... Strasbourg 1570, fol. 6V

[13] George Silver, *Bref Instructions Upo my Pradoxes of Defence*, Unpublished MSS Sloane 376 British Library c. 1605 p. 8R, Achille Marozzo, *Opera Nova*, Bologna, 1536. *Guardia Alta* literally means High Guard (author's translation). It is illustrated at plate 34V. The arm and blade are held vertically above the head.

[14] Joachim Meyer, *Gründtliche Beschreibung der freyen Ritterlichen und Adelichen kunst des Fechtens...* Strasbourg 1570, fol. 8R. See note 15 for a description.

[15] Fiore de Liberi, *Flos Duellatorum*. 1409 Carta 19A Figure 158. The name translates as Position of the long, stretched tail (author's translation). In both Nebenhut and this posta the blade is held on the right side of the body, stretched out behind the fencer.

[16] Joachim Meyer, *Gründtliche Beschreibung der freyen Ritterlichen und Adelichen kunst des Fechtens...* Strasbourg 1570, fol. 8R, Zornhut: fol. 7V, The blade slopes down the back.

[17] Hans Talhoffer, *Medieval Combat: A Fifteenth-Century Illustrated Manual of Swordfighting and Close-Quarter Combat.* Translated and Edited by Mark Rector. London. 2000. Plate 133. The original text reads "So zuckt ich mynem Schilt und Tryt usz Sinen treffen damit So tun ich Im sin Stuck Brechen. – Ich hon wöllen geschrenckt Stechen hinder Sinen Schilt."

[18] Ibid. Plate 146. The original text reads "Hie stant wir bayd blos. – Aver der mag den schilt wol hinyn werffen und In von Im stossen."

[19] Ibid. Plate 147. The original text reads "Da hatt er In von Im gestossen vom wurff und vom stosz musz er Sich bucken des how Ich In In Kopff und In Rucken."

[20] Ibid. Plate 141. The original text reads "Da bin Ich zwüschen Schilt und Swert gedrungen, das ich dir zum houpt bin komen. –Als Ich hon gehowen geschrenckt Da Ist mir mysse lungen."

[21] Ibid. Plate 129. The original text reads "Der wyl den Schilt wenden und howen. – So bringt er Sin schwert swüschen die schilt und versucht wie starck er Stand."

[22] Ibid. Plate 137. The original text reads "Hie Ist aber ain end. – So latt aver der sinen schilt och Fallen und ergryfft In by den Elbogen und Stoszt Schwert durch In."

[23] Giacomo Di Grassi. *His true Arte of Defence*. Translated by I.G. Gentleman, London 1594

[24] Giacomo Di Grassi. *Ragione Di Adoprar Sicuramente L'Arme si da Offesa, Come da Difesa.* Venetia 1570

[25] Giacomo Di Grassi. *His true Arte of Defence.* Translated by I.G. Gentleman, London 1594 pp.50V-51R

[26] Ibid. p.51V

[27] Camillo Agrippa. Trattato Di Scienta d'Arme. Roma 1553 Chapter XXI (there are no page numbers) Translation by Luca Porzio. The original text reads, "Volendo O. ferir C. potra' farli una finta uiso, crescendo col pie dritto appresso il manco, per farlo mouere, abassando la punta & contrapassando à mandritta del nemico, per in vestir lo sotto di C. & mettendosila rotella per testa, ma se C. fosse persona accorta, non si mouerebbe à la finta con la rotella, anzi in quel tempo spingerebbe la punta de la spada ne la spalla diritta de l'Auersario, ritirandosi con un riuerso in Guardia di O. per due vie. L'una se andara' col pie dritto apresso il máco, con un'mandritto finto à la volta de le gambe de l'auersario, per che venghi à parare accompagnato, per darli un'riuerso à le gábe, & in quel tempo voltar la spada in drento, di dritto filo, & seguitar col pie dritto, & passar' col pie manco. cosi stringeria à la presa. L'altra via sarà, se non potendo voltar' la spada in dentro per la prestezza de la parte, ouero per la grauezza de l'arma, abbasara'li fornimenti de la spada con la punta in su, stringendo col pie dritto, & seguitando di pie manco: & quando non volesse andare à la presa, prima, che fini sce la finta di taglio, potra' voltar' la mano di sotto in su, coprendosicon la rotella il ginocchio dritto per timor' del riuerso de l'auersario, & stringendo di punta, finira' la botta."

[28] Giacomo Di Grassi. *His true Arte of Defence.* Translated by I.G. Gentleman, London 1594 p.52R

[29] Achille Marozzo. *Opera Nova.* Modena, 1536. A large shield is shown in Medium Ward on page 50V and a target on page 52R.

[30] Donald McBane. *The Expert Sword-Man's Companion.* Glasgow 1728 p.66

[31] Compare figures 32-35 with Talhoffer's plates showing combat accoding to Frankish law with mace and shield (plates 104-126 of the 1467 edition)

RECONSTRUCTING THE USE OF
MEDIEVAL & RENAISSANCE HUNGARIAN SABRES

By Russell Mitchell

Introduction

There are two weapons that are deeply embedded in the Hungarian culture, to the point that they can be described as "cultural weapons," similar to the *katana* in Japan. These two weapons are the *fokos* (pronounce the s as in "sugar."), which is a long-handled axe with a light head, and the sabre. Both of these two weapons were used by the Hungarians from at least the time of their movement into the Carpathian Basin in the late ninth and early tenth century, up until their demise as a status and/or "carry weapon" in World War One.[1] Of the two weapons, the *fokos* plays a more active role in modern times, retaining a role in ritual, and, increasingly rarely, in rural home defense, but its taxonomy is worthy of its own book. The sabre is far more significant for European history at large, and therefore this paper will devote itself exclusively to the latter weapon. Although anyone might carry a *fokos* made by one's village smith, the sabre required specialist smiths to make, and was carried exclusively by warriors.[2] Given that the sabre was also used continuously for at least twelve centuries, there is a great interest in its use, both in modern sport and regarding its role throughout Hungarian history.

On the other hand, I am presenting material on the Hungarian sabre, as one of two surviving practitioners of a living tradition, which happens to be Hungarian. On the other, in terms of weapons and their development in the Middle Ages and Renaissance, Hungary presents a unique environment. Hungary is sometimes referred to as a land "between East and West," and for good reason. The Carpathian Basin is a natural crossroads on the European peninsula, and Hungarian rulers were required to deal politically and militarily with Central European and Mediterranean societies, the Normans, the Byzantine Empire, the Russian Principalities, as well as various Kipchak Turkic and Alanian groups, and, unfortunately for the Hungarians, the Mongols. For example, Muslim soldiers were extensively used in Hungarian armies during the rule of the Arpadian dynasty during the twelfth and thirteenth centuries

(but particularly in the twelfth). During the reign of Sigismund of Luxemburg in the early-mid 15th century, while Hungary fought the Ottoman Turks, it was also involved in negotiating political alliances with the Golden Horde, and with the Khwarazmians in Persia. Hungarian weaponry reflected this mix of cultures, and the traditional steppe weapons that are indigenous to it existed alongside the full range of Western and Central European military equipment for the length of the Middle Ages and Renaissance. Through all of that time, the "basic lines" of the typical Hungarian sabre did not change.

One of the problems faced by historical re-enactors and martial artists in Hungary is that, unlike the recent flood of manuscripts covering the dominant weapons of Western Europe, there is a severe lack of similar works for Central and Southeastern Europe, particularly regarding the sabre as it was used in a military context, rather than its use in 19th-century dueling and military sport-fencing. Unfortunately for scholars in this region, very few manuscripts have survived in Hungary from the medieval and renaissance periods, perhaps as little as 1% of what survived in Western Europe. The Hungarian royal libraries were lost in the looting and occupation of Buda by the Ottomans. What survived the devastation of the Turkish Wars was similarly lost during two World Wars and a Stalinist occupation.

There are some bright points emerging for scholars seeking to better understand the earlier use of the sabre, however, insofar as some recently-uncovered manuscripts do cover weapons that are very close to the sabre, particularly the *messer* and *dussack*. The recent "rediscovery" of the Goliath and Gladiatoria fight books is somewhat helpful in this respect, with tantalizing clues concerning a specific form of footman's shield coupled with a messer.[3] The fencing manual of Paulus Hector Mair depicts the use of what is clearly a stirrup-hilted sabre, yet calls it a *dussack*, and the Codex Wallerstein (Vom Bauman's Fechtbuch," Cod. 1.6.4.2

Universitätsbibliothek Augsburg) also contains very practical material for the *messer* that is relevant to this study.[4] But while the messer and dussack have some applicability to understanding the sabre (after all, they are both single-handed, curved blades), there are several notable distinctions between the traditional Hungarian sabre and these weapons. The first, and most notable from the fighter's perspective, is the presence of a raised false edge. The second difference between them is a notable difference in curve geometry.

Sabre Typology/Morphology

In order to distinguish the use of the sabre from the messer and dussack, we need to take a step back and determine what exactly we are talking about when we discuss the sabre. The medieval and Renaissance sabre[5], with one theoretical exception which will be addressed shortly, was largely absent from Western Europe, only coming into common use in the early eighteenth century after its introduction to France via the Bercsényi Regiment.[6] Therefore, in order to say anything meaningful about the sabre, which came in a variety of forms, we need to come to a classificatory strategy that will enable us to place the sabre into the broader context of medieval edged weapons.

In order to describe and classify the sabre, we need to take yet another step backwards into "background work," and either unravel or dodge a question that has plagued arms historians for some time: should swords, and particularly sabres, be classified according to the design of the blade, or of the hilt? I intend to sidestep the matter and propose an entirely new system of classification, which, while it might seem unnecessarily broad at first, will nevertheless be tied directly to the weapon's *actual function when being used by one man to kill another*. It is now well-established, via the work of Oakeshott and others, that straight swords should be classified by their blade structure, with the hilt construction an important but largely secondary feature.[7] Historians of the sabre pay lip service to this idea, but the reality of their writings mostly centers around the hilt design.[8] There are good reasons for this, especially when armory catalogues consist of an almost endless parade of pretty hilts. There are bewildering arrays of hilt types for sabres, some of which, such as baskets, thumb loops, and "anatomic handles," make a dramatic difference in the handling of the weapon. While one can make the argument that a choice between a wheel or brazil-nut pommel is a matter of aesthetics, such a choice would make a significant difference in the handling of a sabre. For a sabre, all aspects of the hilt design are critical to the weapon's use.

After all of that, I am going to classify the sabre *first* on neither the construction of the hilt nor the blade,

but rather on the position of the blade relative to the wielder's hand, which will be explained shortly. Observe, if you will, the following two photographs, taken during shooting for an educational program in Budapest. In the first image, as I stand on the right, the attacker cuts at my head with a replica of a Tatar sabre. Were this a strong, angry cut such as one would encounter on a battlefield, there could be no possible disagreement: I would be dead, and nothing I could do would save me. Now observe the second photo, where the Tatar sabre has been replaced by a *kilij* (in a form that, with potential variations in hilt design, could have been used by Ottoman, Seljuk, Serb, or Byzantine troops). In this case, were it a real cut, I would *almost certainly be dead*, though it is remotely conceivable that a last-second flinch or strategically-placed banana peel might suffice to save my life. The important thing that the reader does not yet know about these pictures is that the only difference between them is the weapon in question. Neither of us have actually moved, and a third party has actually replaced the Tatar weapon with the Ottoman one while the man on the left held his arm as still as possible. That inch, or perhaps inch and a half between the blade and my forehead, through

Fig. 1: *A cut to the forehead with a Tatar sabre.*

Fig. 2: *An identical cut with the Ottoman Kilij*

which trees in the background can be seen clearly, is the difference between life and death, of a certain mortal wound and the possibility, however remote, of receiving only a light one. That inch is the distance between an attacker who is slightly closer than he would prefer to be, and an attacker who is slightly too far away. Of such distances is fencing made.

Consider the following table, which gives a basic (and by no means complete) comparison of sabres and sabre-like weapons.[9] As one progresses from the left, the first group, beginning with the shamshir (#1) and ending with the late Avar sabre (#6), curve back from the hand, back over the forearm, and in the case of the shamshir, even back over the elbow. This means that it controls space between the hand and the body. The stronger the curve in question, the more three-dimensional space it controls, and the higher the moment of rotation of the blade.[10] The shashqa (#2) depicted is out of period, but is included for comparative purposes because there are a number of sabre finds which do have this general curve, and also because it is the curve type which one commonly sees on early-modern and modern cavalry sabres.

The third category includes roughly 80% of all Hungarian and Tatar sabres, a distinct branch of Polish sabre, and all Turkic so-called "pistol-grip" sabres -- if one were to go to a far extreme beyond what can reasonably be called a sabre, it would also include weapons such as the Conyers falchion, yataghan, and Ethiopian *shotel*. These weapons place the curve of the weapon in front of the hand. This allows for strong draw cuts and slashing cuts, though these weapons do not slash with anywhere near the proficiency of the first category of sabres. It also, by placing the curve in front of the hand, enables the same kind of shearing and splitting cuts that a straight sword or axe makes. These sabres are designed for fighting in a heavily-armored environment (though it is still extremely unlikely that they could do more than lightly dent any sort of plate armor). All of the "pistol grip" or "canted handle" sabres have an additional advantage. They often have a very mild curve, which, in conjunction with the angle of the hilt, results in a curved weapon that nonetheless has its point aligned in parallel to the hand. This makes them excellent thrusting weapons, particularly for stop-thrusts. In spite of their wide, cutting blades, the hilt angle places the point in a position relative to the hand that allows thrusts to performed just as easily as if one were wielding an estoc or rapier.

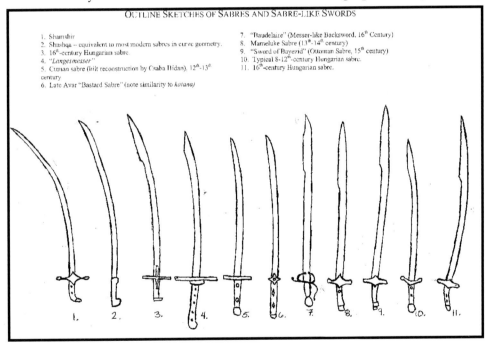

OUTLINE SKETCHES OF SABRES AND SABRE-LIKE SWORDS

1. Shamshir
2. Shashqa -- equivalent to most modern sabres in curve geometry.
3. 16th-century Hungarian sabre.
4. "Langesmesser"
5. Cuman sabre (hilt reconstruction by Csaba Hidan), 12th-13th century
6. Late Avar "Bastard Sabre" (note similarity to *katana*)

7. "Baudelaire" (Messer-like Backsword, 16th Century)
8. Mameluke Sabre (13th-14th century)
9. "Sword of Bayezid" (Ottoman Sabre, 15th century)
10. Typical 8-12th-century Hungarian sabre.
11. 16th-century Hungarian sabre.

1.   2.   3.   4.   5.   6.   7.   8.   9.   10.   11.

Another significant feature of these sabres is that, in spite of their curve, the cant of the handle keeps the entire weapon close to the centerline of the hand, giving these sabres a very low moment of rotation. In layman's terms, if you have a "standard" Hungarian sabre, it will change the alignment of its primary edge much more quickly than will a shamshir, with its wide, sweeping curve. Both of them will rotate more

Next, dividing the two types of sabres, comes the one sword on the chart, a "Baudelaire. (#7)" In terms of basic blade geometry, it is the equivalent to straight swords, estocs, Thorpe-type falchions, etcetera,[11] where the blade extends in an essentially two-dimensional ray from the hand. In this case, the sword controls an area directly around the blade, and any rotation of the blade is only relevant insofar as one presents the weapon's edge or flat to an opponent or incoming blow.

slowly than will a straight sword, which will, outside of moulinets and certain longsword parries, generally have little reason to do so (though it must be kept in mind that the moulinet is an essential part of Western swordplay). This explains in great part why the shamshir was held in such low regards by westerners: it is designed for a style of swordplay that uses many obliquely-angled thrusts, alien to most Western European swordplay (examples to follow later in the text), and is very clumsy when one is performing the moulinets which form such a foundation for much of Western Europe's sabre practice.

So we have three basic categories for swords that renders various weapons with curved blades intelligible on a comparative basis. The first is that group of swords which has a *trailing blade*, meaning that as the blade moves through space in a cut, the center of percussion (the part with which, optimally, you strike) of the weapon trails behind the position of the hand. The second category is what we might call "true swords." These weapons have *aligned blades*, meaning that the blade moves in exact alignment with the hand while cutting. And the last group is that of those sabres derived from the Hungarians, and from the Kipchak Turkic peoples, which are constructed with a *leading blade*. I strongly suggest "blade" be used here instead of "edge" in order to avoid any association of the classification with the primary cutting edge and the false edge of the weapon: "leading and following edges" is an instant recipe for confusion.

Besides cutting or thrusting, why is the curve of a weapon important? Unfortunately, by focusing not on *how* various sabre-like weapons are curved (i.e., what type of curve the weapon has: circular, hooked, etc.), but instead on *how much* they are curved, scholars researching these weapons have missed out on something very important: the type of curve of a weapon is not only important for how well it performs a drawing or slashing cut, but also for which of the various guards one would adopt with the weapon, and through which the weapon would flow while fighting. A sabre such as #3, with a hooking curve, will behave entirely differently in the hand than will the shamshir (#1), even if the total degree of curve is equal.[12] The Mameluke sabre (#8), which is essentially a straight weapon with a curved handle, will behave much like a short-sword, whereas the next three sabres (#s 9-11), each with subtly different curves, will not. All of the guards for the straight sword that have a direct defensive value – Fiore di Liberi's Posta Longa and Posta Frontale, for example, as opposed to the Posta de Dona, which has a strong, but indirect defensive value[13] -- place a line, a wall of sorts, between the opponent and one part of the wielder's body. It may be a line on an angle, but it is still a line. In relationship to a curved weapon, the guard is relatively less complex. This is very good if your system of fencing takes it into account, and disastrous if it doesn't. For example, Silver's True Guardant[14] is, to the best of my knowledge, never depicted in any medieval or early renaissance manual. There's a reason for this: Silver's method is designed for a sword that has an enclosed hilt to protect the hand. Without that enclosed hilt, the hand is extremely vulnerable[15] – similar positions such as one would find in Sutor and Meyer's dussack

manuals tend to have the blade placed with the point forward, thereby protecting the hand. (Of course, a well-trained fighter may simply present the hand as an inviting target).

Fig. 4: *The position of the point in the "Ochs" protects the fighter's entire right side.*

A fighter who is sensitive to his weapon, however, can angle a curved blade used in a vulnerable guard, such as the middle guard or one of the forehand wards, in order to shut down that line of attack and seal away his hand -- and depending on the degree of curve, even his forearm – from his opponent. "The ability of the sabre to "lock out" targets from the opponent using its curve is a significant feature of the weapon: the sabre was often used by troops who were horse archers, and were therefore less likely to carry a shield or buckler. It was quite likely that a fighter with a sabre, therefore, would end up fighting against an opponent with a sword and shield. Unless he was equipped with the same, or even a short-hafted axe as

Fig. 5: *This guard allows a direct cut to the hand and forearm.*

Fig. 6: *With only a slight rotation of the wrist or elbow, the curve of the sabre protects the hand and forearm.[17]*

a parrying weapon[16], he would find himself at a serious disadvantage unless he was highly skilled at using the sabre's curve to defend his body.

Only after classifying sabres based on the position of the blade relative to the hand of its wielder does it make sense to examine hilt designs. To begin with, the "canted handle" or "pistol grip" of the sabre begins to make sense: it allows the wielder to have a sabre with a strong curve, such as #11, while, at the same time, also having the weapon's point in parallel alignment to the hand, which makes thrusting much simpler. The complex shell and basket guards of Western European sabres show little difference from those used on swords of the period, which suggests that their use would also be similar.[18] The weapons from Central and Eastern Europe, the Ottoman Empire, and Persia show various knobs, bumps, and bends to the handles. These serve the purpose of maximizing the leverage which can be applied to the cut, as well as providing lateral support for maneuvering the weapons quickly. On the Mameluke sabre(#8), such a design was already present in the 14th century, and the bent handle depicted is present on sabres dating back to the Khazar Khaganate.[19] This leverage is very important with weapons such as the *kilij*, which have no thrusting tip, but whose strongly curved hatchet tip, in conjunction with its knobbed handle, can actually hook an opponent's crossguard and lever it from his grip. We can see that various sabres with oversized handles, such as the messer, late Avar sabre, or "sword-hilted sabres" (as will soon be shown) allow for either an extra hand to be put on the weapon for additional power, or for easier employment of binding actions with the hilt (as is done in Von Bauman's *Fechtbuch*).

Technique Reconstruction

Now that we have gone through all of that, allow me to show why it is necessary knowledge if one is going to attempt to reconstruct the use of the sabre, and to see in what ways its use may have differed from the messer and dussack manuals which have come down to us. Johannes Lichtenauer, the "grandfather" of the so-called German School of medieval swordsmanship was said to have traveled extensively in Central Europe.[20] His false edge-cuts, designed to wind around and behind an opponent's blade are essentially unique to his school of swordplay, having no explicit parallel in the Bolognese school and certainly none in the later survivals from the English, Italian, and Spanish schools of fencing. They are considered valuable only for unarmored fighting, or at best for harassing strikes while in armor. These cuts are, at the same time, the characteristic technique of Hungarian sabre play[21], and, as will be seen below, they differentiate the sabre unequivocally from the messer. In the following techniques, I have taken the dictum of "what can be done with the sabre," and used that to determine *what it is likely that fighters did with the sabre.*

The following seven techniques are for the Hungarian sabre. They differ in period, and in application depending on what type of sabre is used. The techniques which will be shown are derived from study with the experimental archaeology group of Csaba Hidán, who teaches at the Calvinist University in Budapest. His grandfather was one of the last hussar drillmasters, and taught the sabre extensively. In addition, Prof. Hidán grew up in Transylvania, where sabre play is still a fairly common pastime with older boys in the more remote villages. Prof. Hidán has taken the sabre play which he was taught, and has attempted to use it in his recreation of the daily life of the warriors of the ancient Hungarians and steppe peoples who were its allies and neighbors. Techniques 1-4 are derived either directly from hussar drill(1-3), or have emerged from continuous experimentation and sparring under armored and/or bucklered conditions (#4). The last three techniques, #s 5-7, are derived from a sabre manual which was apparently published in 1830 as an attempt to preserve older methods of fighting with a shamshir-like sabre which was popular at the time. It apparently only survives in photocopy form. Professor Hidán has seen it only once, and is in the process of obtaining permission to take a copy of it from its owner.[22]

Fig. 7: *Right Protect, as done from horseback.*

Technique #1 is the standard, almost primordial Hungarian technique for use while mounted. It can be depicted either as a strike-and-cut, or as a brushing parry-and-cut. I am going to depict the latter, because it will help to give some clue as to how modern sabre play came about.[23] In this image I am warding a blow, with my legs spread out as if I were riding a horse. This is the position that Angelo, in his *Hungarian and Highland Broadsword*, depicts as "Right Protect."[24] From here, however, all similarity with Angelo ends abruptly. As I pass by my opponent, as we would surely pass each other on charging horses, I flip over my wrist and decapitate him with the false edge. Great power is not needed for this cut, since the power for it comes from the mass and speed of the horse. If the technique had been done from the attack, as that attack was parried the following false-edge cut would likely be thrown lower, under the opponent's hand, either to disembowel the opponent, cut his reins, injure his horse, or a combination of the three.

Fig. 8: *False edge cut in passing.*

Fig. 9: *The opening attack has been parried at the ricasso.*

Technique #2 is a winding cut performed on the attack.

In this case, my opponent has parried with his edge at the ricasso, probably in preparation for a direct riposte. As it becomes evident that the attack has been negated, the attacker turns over his wrist, bringing the false edge of the sabre behind the sword, and then cuts out the defender's wrist arteries, thumb, and/or any fingers that present themselves.

Fig. 10: *Winding around the blade with the false edge.*

Fig. 11: *The false edge cut against the wrist and hand.*

The same technique applied from a different angle shows how a winding cut such as this can be performed from a displacement. In this case, a parry with the sabre is made according to Durer's fight book on the messer.[25] After the parry, the sabre flips under as the defender drops his elbow, and again cuts out his opponent's wrist, this time from the other side.

Fig. 12: *The incoming attack is parried.*

In these cases, the winding cuts are essentially ways for the fighter to inflict a small wound on his opponent while otherwise withdrawing his weapon, making it capable of inflicting a wound while, as Silver puts it, "lying spent." These cuts would have little to no value against an armored gauntlet, but against an opponent with little or no hand protection (and there is a plethora of images from the medieval and renaissance periods showing just that), these techniques could inflict either a fight-stopping blow, or else open up the opponent for the *coup de grace*, with relatively little risk to the wielder.

Fig. 13: *False edge cut attacking the opposite side of the wrist.*

Technique #3 involves rotation of the sabre blade from the elbow and/or wrist in order to make an effective thrust. In the following image, the defender blocks with a buckler. Rather than withdraw the blow to launch another one, the sabre wielder takes advantage of the blade's curve and slides around the buckler in order to thrust, even as the defender raises it in an attempt to ward off the strike.[26]

Fig. 14: *On having his attack blocked with a buckler…*

Fig. 15: *The sabrist winds his weapon's point into his opponent.*

The same technique applied on a horizontal plane is depicted in order to illustrate why Angelo's *Broadsword* is only effective on foot if one is ignoring the fact that the sabre one is holding is a curved weapon.

Fig. 16: *Left Protect according to Angelo – a typical Western European sabre parry.*

In this case, the defender has responded with "Left Protect."[27] The attacker, in order to circumvent it, merely covers his opponent's hand or blade as a precaution while reversing the wrist, which positions the sabre blade for a stab to the throat. The covering hand is usually unnecessary given the speed of the stab.

Fig. 17: *The blade curve allows it to bypass many parries in order to continue an attack.*

Technique #4: Direct cuts with the false edge generally correspond to cuts with the "short edge" from Lichtenauer/Ringeck, with the understanding that the distances and angles involved are changed because of the sabre's inferior reach and blade curve. For example, it is trivially easy to throw the equivalent to a *krumphau* against the opponent's cutting hand or wrist (where the wrist is turned over to hit the opponent's striking arms or hands. With a longsword, the blow can either follow or intercept the opponent's movement, whereas the lesser reach of the sabre largely restricts it to intercepting strikes). This must be done with appropriate footwork, usually a slight shift backwards or a pass to the side.

Fig: 18: *A "sabre* krumphau.*"*

The *krumphau* equivalent is an example of a direct cut with the false edge. It can be applied in ways that are not available to a straight sword. For example, in this image, as the opponent attempts to control the fighting space with his buckler, the sabre wielder makes the exact same cut, directed into the buckler-holding arm. Such a cut might also be thrown at the foot or ankle if one's opponent has sealed away the angles required more direct primary-edge cuts via an opposing weapon or bind.[28]

The next techniques are also completely impractical with a straight sword, and give an idea of the extent to which the curve of a sabre can be exploited in a lightly armored environment. These techniques are derived from a sabre manual that is, by hearsay, a Hungarian manual from the early 19th century.[29] Technique #5,

Fig. 19: *The sabre's curve allows the possibility of bypassing the opponent's weapons.*

Fig. 22: *The attack is parried on a buckler.*

Fig. 20: *Basic defense against a strike while charging.*

Fig. 23: *Because of the sabre's curve, it can be used to thrust on unusual angles.*

the first thrust illustrated in this series, is to be done when crowds of men are charging each other.

Beginning from a parry as one's opponent cuts at one's head, which can be done either with the sabre blade or with a buckler, one simply drops the weapon down over the shoulder in order to stab the opponent in the bladder or groin. This is a more practical technique

Fig. 21: *By dropping the shoulder, the weapon's curve is exploited to create unusual openings.*

than it may seem at first glance, since one is then in a much better position to face a second or third man than if one were still bound up with the first opponent.

Technique #6: the next thrust is done from a buckler parry, where one thrusts along the outside of the buckler into the opponent's neck. I have intentionally raised the sabre up onto a vertical plane here so that it may be seen more easily: the actual technique is entirely horizontal.

Technique #7: the same principal holds true for the vertical plane. By sidestepping and thrusting from below, or from above just as the fight gets into cutting range, the enemy's buckler may be bypassed completely. The thrust from below is far easier to complete, whereas experimentation has shown that the thrust from above, while feasible, tends to work best as a feint prior to a leg cut or after the opponent's attempt to bind with the buckler, since it's otherwise easily visible during most of its movement. It is worth noting that Hungarian hussar sabre practice specifically forbids thrusting with the knuckles turned up (as in the Spadroon guard), because it leaves the entire weapon side, from the elbow to the ribs, open for a counter-attack: it instead emphasizes thrusting with the palm straight up or straight down, with the palm-up position the preferred one. Thrusts performed on the horizontal plane with a rotation of the palm from the up or down position to its opposite routinely slip past bucklers and attempts to make a "cross" with the blade, because a small turn of the wrist, combined with the blade's curve, produces a large displacement of the weapon, which allows it to bypass the defense on its way into the target.

Fig. 24: *A thrust from below.*

Fig. 25: *The same technique on a different angle.*

The interesting part of all of these techniques is when we move away from the "what could be done" and into the "what did these fighters probably do?" A skilled swordsman, looking these techniques over, will probably have seen that the winding attacks and the direct false-edge cuts looked like they were practicable in terms of distance, whereas the various oddly-angled thrusts at the end, techniques #5 and #6, don't look quite right. There's a very good reason for that. The sabre that is used in the images has enough curve that it can perform the illustrated techniques. However, it is not really sufficiently curved to make these thrusts easy. Sabres 2 and 3, the shashqa and the 16th-century hussar's weapon, would be much better blades for the job. Sabre #11 would probably work well for all of the techniques shown – except for the groin thrust, because this sabre's blade is placed so far in front of the hand that it would miss the opponent entirely. The hussar's blade, with its strong hooking curve, would work very well for thrusting around opposition, but would very likely turn slowly in the hand, making direct false-edge cuts awkward. The shamshir, of all of these sabres, is best suited for the circular thrusts – the techniques are, in fact, intended for it., and the shamshir is almost always paired with a small, round buckler. By the same token, the shamshir would be all but useless for attempting the winding techniques: it has no false edge

at all for cutting, and rotates so slowly in the hand that any skilled opponent can counter the technique.

Conclusion

It is obvious that many of these techniques would be useless against 14th-16th century opponents in full armor, unless the thrusts were performed perfectly. It is no surprise, therefore, in the Hungarian martial context "between East and West," with the Holy Roman Empire and Italy on one side, and the Golden Horde and Ottoman Empire on the other, that the weapons shown in the outline sketches (or their close historical equivalents) existed alongside the full range of Western European arms and armor. The sabre was to the Hungarian and Pole what the *katana* was to the Japanese: although other weapons were used with great, and often greater, effectiveness, this is their "cultural weapon." In Budapest, the sabre is the gift presented to prominent ministers and awarded to poets. Until such a time as a period manual is found, we can only attempt to do it justice with continued experimentation.

Manuscript Sources
Codex Wallerstein/"Vom Baumans Fechtbuch," Cod. 1.6.4.2 University Library of Augsburg. 15th century, dating problematic.

"Gladiatoria," Jagiellonian University Library, Cracow, Ms. Germ. Quart. 16 Num 5878. Early 16th century.

"*Goliath,*" Jagiellonian University Library, Cracow, Ms. Germ. Quart. 2020 Num 5879. 15th century.

Mair, Paulus Hector. Untitled Fechtbuch. Codex Vindobonensis 10825, Austrian National Library. Early 17th century, but after 1620 (cited manuscript is a modified copy of the original text of 1620).

Primary Sources
Dornhoffer, Friedrich. *Albrecht Dürer's Fechtbuch* (Jahrbuch der Kunsthistorischen Sammlungen des Allerhochsten Kaiserhauses, XXVII/6) Vienna: F. Tempsky, Leipzig: G. Freytag, 1910. [Facsimile edition of a fencing and wrestling manuscript illustrated by Albrecht Dürer, with extensive commentary].

Angelo, Henry. *Hungarian and Highland Broadsword.* London: , 1798

Hungarian National Museum. *The Ancient Hungarians: Exhibition Catalogue,* ed. István Fodor, László Révész, Mária Wolf, Ibolya M. Nepper. Budapest: Hungarian National Museum, 1996.

Novati, Francesco. *If Fior di Battaglia di Maestro Fiore dei Liberi da Premariacco.* [Facsimile edition of Fiore dei

Liberi with extensive commentary]. Bergamo: Istituto
Italiano D'Arti Grafiche, 1902.

Silver, George. *Brief Instructions Upon My Paradoxes of
Defence*. 1599. Edited and transcribed by Steve Hick.
From British Library, Sloan MS. No. 376.

Silver, George. *Paradoxes of Defence*, [...], London,
Printed [by Richard Field, alias de Campo] for Edward
Blount, 1599 K.U.Leuven, Universiteitsbibliotheek, 4A
1307.

Secondary Literature

Oakeshott, Ewart, *Records of the Medieval Sword*. Woodbridge: The Boydell Press, 1991.

Oakeshott, Ewart. *European Weapons and Armour: From
the Renaissance to the Industrial Revolution*. Woodbridge:
The Boydell Press, 1980.

Tóth, Zoltán. *"Attila's Schwert": Studie "Uber die Herkunft
des sogenannten Säbels Karls des Grossen in Wien*. Budapest: Hungarian Academy of Sciences, 1930

Zabłocki, Wojciech. *Cięcia Prawdziwą Szablą*. Warsaw:
Institute for Sports and Tourism, 1989.

Notes

[1] *The Ancient Hungarians: Exhibition Catalogue* [of the Hungarian National Museum], ed. István Fodor, László Révész, Mária Wolf, Ibolya M. Nepper. Hungarian National Museum: Budapest, 1996, pp. 87, 96. Sabres were used by Hungarians early enough that archaeologists are able to determine which of them were made while the Hungarians were in the service of the Khazar Khaganate, and those made after their migration into "Europe" in the first third of the ninth century (pp. 87, 96 for hilt examples).
[2] *Ibid., pp. 43,46.*
[3] "Gladiatoria," Jagiellonian University Library, Cracow, MS. Germ. Quart. 16. Num. 5878. "Goliath," Jagiellonian University Library, Cracow, Ms. Germ. Quart. 2020, Num. 5879. A full image of the plate in question is available at the Acaedemy for European Medieval Martial Arts website: http://www.aemma.org/onlineResources/library_H.htm, Plate 113. The plate in question discusses fighting with the "Hungarian shield."
[4] For Paulus Hector Mair's fechtbuch, I have access only to the copy contained in the Codex Vindobonensis 10825, Austrian National Library. This appears to have be a copy of the original work, adding text in German. It is therefore possible that the original, earlier work depicts the *dussack* in its traditional form.
[5] Hereafter simply "medieval," both for convenience, and because in Eastern and Southeastern Europe, there never was a Renaissance, and history jumps from "medieval" to "early modern" or "Turkish Period." Although there was certainly a Renaissance in Hungary and Poland, where the sabre holds great sway as a cultural symbol, the peoples of Southeastern Europe, under the influence of Byzantium and the Greek Orthodox faith, never lost contact with the learning of the ancients in the first place.
[6] This regiment, in French the *1e Hussards, Regiment Bercheny*, were formed for the service of Louis XIV in 1720, under the command of Count Bercsényi, whose father was the primary commander of Ferenc Rakóczi II in the Rakóczi Independence Wars, fought against the Austrian Habsburgs. Both father and son were exiled after the revolution's failure, the son taking service to Louis XIV as mentioned, the father eventually moving to Turkey. The unit was originally composed of Hungarian troops, and formed the basic pattern upon which all French Hussar units were formed.
[7] Ewart Oakeshott. *Records of the Medieval Sword*. Woodbridge: The Boydell Press, 1991, pp. 2,3,11. Note that Oakeshott specifically distinguishes "type" of sword, drawn from blade silhouette, structure, and cross and hilt type, from sword "families," which are more relevant for the study of various hilt fashions.

[8] Wojciech Zabłocki. *Cięcia Prawdziwą Szablą*. Institute for Sports and Tourism: Warsaw, 1989. ISBN: 83-217-2601-1

[9] The sabres in this table are drawn from Zabłocki's excellent work, with certain exceptions. Those are #5, the Cuman sabre, reconstructed by Prof. Csaba Hidán, #6, the Late Avar "Bastard Sabre," referred to as the "Säbel von Székesfehérvár," in *"Attila's Schwert": Studie "Uber die Herkunft des sogenannten Säbels Karls des Grossen in Wien*. Zoltán Tóth. Budapest: Hungarian Academy of Sciences, 1930, p.42. The #10, "Typical 8-12th-century Hungarian sabre" is given as an agglomerate form, and may have a number of small variations, such as the length of the false edge, or the presence or absence of a fuller. It is also important to note that by citing a *shamshir*, I am using the word in its western connotation, i.e., to refer to a particular form of sabre, rather than how the word is used in modern Farsi, where it is interchangeable with the word "sword." Those drawn from Zabłocki are: #1, Shamshir, p. 319; #2, Shashqa, p. 329; #3, Hungarian sabre, p. 299; #4, Messer, p. 343; #7, Beaudelaire, p. 333; #8, Mameluke sabre, p. 267; #9, "Sword of Bayezid," p. 265; #11, Hungarian sabre, p. 291.

[10] In other words, the harder it is to rotate, for the same reason that a figure skater extends her legs when she wants to spin slowly, but pulls her feet close to her when she wants to revolve more quickly.

[11] There is considerable confusion regarding the falchion and its role vis-à-vis the "scimitar," longsax, and other single-edged weapons. While Thorpe-type falchions essentially are straight weapons that are the equivalent of backswords with a more complex tip, the Conyers type places the impact surface in front of the hand, and is therefore closer in function to an axe, yataghan, or falcata. The "standard" falchion, the only weapon indigenous to Western Europe that has ever had a strongly raised false edge, is very similar in most respects to a typical *kilij* except insofar as it tends to be more straight. It can surely be no coincidence therefore, that the **typical** falchion depicted became popular in the early 1200s, directly after the fall of Constantinople to Western crusaders, where they would have encountered numerous Seljuk and Byzantine fighters using similar weapons.

[12] Admittedly unlikely in this example, as one of the defining characteristics of the Persian Shamshir is its extreme curve.

[13] Francesco Novati. *Il Fior di Battaglia di Maestro Fiore dei Liberi da Premariacco* [Text commentary and facsimile edition of the manuscript]. Bergamo: Istituto Italiano D'Arti Grafiche, 1902. The Posta Longa and Posta Frontale are depicted in Carta 18b, first two quarters, and the Posta di Donna is shown on Carta 18B, third quarter.

[14] George Silver. *Bref Instructions Upon my Paradoxes of Defence* Unpublished MSS. c. 1605 (Sloane MS 376, British Library) Cap. 3, p. 8R: "Gardant fyght in gen'rall is of ii sorts, y' fyrst is true gardant fight …. to carry yo' hand & hylt aboue yo' hed w' yo' poynt doune to wards yo' left knee, w' yo' sword blade somewhat neer yo' bodye, not bearing out your poynt but rather declynyng in a lyttle towards yo' said knee"

[15] George Silver. *Paradoxes of Defence*, […], London, Printed [by Richard Field, alias de Campo] for Edward Blount, 1599 K.U.Leuven, Universiteitsbibliotheek, 4A 1307, p. 33. *"And what a goodly defence is a ftrong fingle hilt, when men are cluftering and hurling together, efpecially where varietie of weapons be, in their motions to defend the hand, head, face, and bodies, from blowes, that fhalbe giuen fometimes with Swordes, battell Axe, Halbardes, or blacke Billes, and fometimes men fhalbe fo neare together , that they fhall haue no fpace, fcarce to vfe the blades of their Swordes belowe their waftes, then their hilts (their handes being aloft) defendeth from the blowes, their handes, armes, heads, faces, and bodies…"*

Because of this text and the depiction of the hilt in the *Paradoxes* -- which curves down to protect the knuckles -- I believe that "single hilt" used here is to be understood in contrast to compound rapier hilts, rather than in contrast to a simple crosspiece.

[16] For example, in the border wars between the Turks and Hungarians in the 16th century, Hungarians who do not have some sort of shield are, almost without exception, shown with a short-hafted axe tucked into their belt. Such an axe was also standard equipment for Pechenegs and Cumans/Polovitsi. The Tatars sometimes used a hatchet, but also sometimes used a hooked mace that could be used for binding opponents as well. It is interesting that cultures that traditionally used the sabre, such as the Hungarians and Ottomans, also placed great value in the axe.

[17] This is trivially simple to demonstrate to a living person, and very difficult to render with any two-dimensional image. In the picture provided, even I find it difficult to believe that my arm would be protected, though I know it to be true: holding the weapon, I have no such doubts.

[18] Considerations of space preclude me from going into greater detail, but see Ewart Oakeshott. *European Weapons and Armour: From the Renaissance to the Industrial Revolution*. Woodbridge: The Boydell Press, 1980, pp. 151-91.

[19] See footnote #1.

[20] Johannes Lichtenauer was a mid-to-late-14th century German armsmaster, traced to both Swabia and Franconia. His style of swordsmanship began a tradition which dominated German fencing for two and a half centuries. Paulus Kal, a later master of the "Liechtenauer tradition," presented a brief biography of this grandmaster. Kal noted that Liechtenauer travelled extensively through the Holy Roman Empire and into Eastern Europe, where he studied fencing with

Virgily of Cracow, Lamprecht of Prague, and Andres of Liegnitz .

[21] I am not including the dueling sabre here for several of reasons. First, and most obvious, it has no raised false edge. Second, it is wielded in essentially the "modern" smallsword-influenced method, and third, it is such a lightweight weapon, meant for settling affairs of honor with a minimum of bloodshed, that such attacks with a dueling sabre are good only for harassment even on an unarmored opponent.

[22] Manuals such as this, which were almost always tied to the lower aristocracy in Hungary, were held in very poor esteem by the Soviets and the Communists who were in power until recently. Although this loosened up after the 1956 Revolution, before then it was appallingly strict, and made the loss of manuscripts such as this even more acute than it would have been after two world wars, and much knowledge was lost. In Ceaucescu's Transylvania, when Professor Hidán trained as a child, it could literally be one's death warrant if word got out that one practiced with old sabres. Professor Hidán learned from not only from his grandfather, but from half a dozen of his grandfather's peers, whose attitude towards technique was largely pragmatic, and encouraged inventing "good tricks." This attitude has been continued in his current practice in Budapest, and so the sense of what is a "legitimate technique" is not so dogmatic as in other arts.

[23] These techniques are shown with Rolf Kvamme. Kvamme is a skilled SCA fighter with an interest in period fighting manuals. However, his background is with a mass weapon, and his attacking distances reflect his lack of familiarity with a cutting blade. We therefore posed these shots, and I would like to thank him and Mike Catron for being kind enough to take pictures in the process. The sabre shown is a replica of a 15th-century Hungarian sabre, the "sword-hilted" type, which otherwise corresponds to sabres 9-11. It is, also, unfortunately, far too heavy, which also militated strongly for posed sequences.

[24] Henry Angelo. *Hungarian and Highland Broadsword*. Plate 7. Available for public download courtesy of Peter Valentine and the Historical Armed Combat Association (HACA): http://www.thehaca.com/masters.htm

[25] Sketches of Dürer's messer work are viewable, courtesy of the University of Michigan, at http://digital.lib.msu.edu/onlinecolls/colection.cfm?CID=7

[26] It is very important to understand that this "winding" of the sabre around the buckler occurs immediately upon the block, or even as the block occurs, if the attacking fighter sees it coming, *not* after stepping forward. If the opponent was within range for a cut, then the distance is already appropriate for the continuation of the attack within Silver's "time of the hand." The technique is shown with a step and a covering move toward the opponent's hand so that the audience is aware of the danger the opponent's blade presents during this continuation. Although the following attack, being a simple flick of the wrist, usually out-times a response, especially when the resulting thrust threatens the opponent's face, it's important to remember that the man with the buckler will be looking for his own opportunities to strike.

[27] Angelo, *Broadsword,*, Plate 6.

[28] These techniques raise a point of controversy, as it can easily be said that "this is just an SCA wrap shot." One of the reasons, in fact, that I am posing these sequences with an SCA man is that I originally visited him to double-check the difference between the direct false-edge cuts that we have been using with the sabre in Hungary, and the way that the SCA throws these blows with their rattan sparring swords (the SCA being entirely unknown in Hungary, unless perhaps on the new NATO bases). My conclusion is this: these techniques are feasible, given an appropriate fighting distance, with certain sabres, and at the same time, these techniques are not appropriate for use with straight swords, for a number of reasons. First, and foremost, they do not appear in any period manuals. Second, the fighting geometry and distance is wrong for a straight blade: attempting to do the same thing with a linear blade is an invitation to a thrust in the face, or to have one's forearm removed. Third, direct cutting with the false edge is only feasible with those weapons which have *raised* false edges, and even then only against opponents in light to no armor. This is because the raised false edge places more mass at the point of impact on the blade, whereas a traditional straight sword simply tapers too strongly to cut effectively this way. Our archaeological group in Budapest has made similar, though not identical, types of attacks with only one straight weapon, the mace, which, obviously, also has dramatic differences in weight distribution from a standard cruciform short-sword.

[29] Unfortunately, although I have a contact for where to find copies of this manual, in my past three trips to Hungary, I have been unable to track down the individual who is said to own it.

INSIDE, OUTSIDE, LEFT FOOT, RIGHT FOOT:
ASSUMPTIONS OF HANDEDNESS IN WEAPONS OF THE STAFF

By Paul Wagner

Introduction

As Sydney Anglo has pointed out, there is a great deal in common between poleaxe and quarterstaff combat[1]. Silver agreed, noting in his section on quarterstaff;

> " The like fight is to be used wt ye javelen, prtyson, halbard, black byll, battle Axe, gleve, half pyke, &c."[2]

and Di Grassi reasoned that;

> "Of the weapons of the Staffe, namely, the Bill, the Partisan, the Holbert, and the Javelin...I am of opinion, that all of them may be handled in manner after one waye."[3]

However, the terminology within the manuals dealing with these weapons is not consistent, and the techniques often rest upon conventions which even the Masters disagree on. It is important to understand these differences, as proceeding on a false assumption can lead to radical misinterpretations of the material.

Holding Staff Weapons

Even the most basic question, "How do you hold the weapon?" receives different answers from different sources. The further back the staff is held the more range, but the further up the shaft the more control you have. Di Grassi said they can be held in whatever way "shall be thought most commodious to the bearer" - some "who greatly regarding ease & little paine" hold it forward for balance, while others, "more strong of arme, but weaker of hart" hold it further back.[4] For quarterstaff, Swetnam preferred the later grip, with the rear hand at the very butt.[5] Silver, however, is clear that the front hand should be on the centre of balance, and gives a practical reason for it, in the overhand "thrust-single" with the butt.[6]

One thing Silver does not say, however, is which hand must be forward, sensibly describing his techniques in terms such as "lie you with your point down also, with your foremost hand low and your hind most hand high,"[7] or, when necessary to specify, describing the difference between and left and right hand grip.[8]

The need for Silver to specify this highlights the major problem of deciding which hand should be forward. All the masters assume you must be able to fight from both, as engagement or crossing of shafts is of the utmost importance to a secure fight - Swetnam said;

> "always standing crosse with your enemie, I meanie, if his right hand and foote be foremost, let yours be so likewise, and if his left-hand and foote be foremost, then make you your change and crosse with him also...Now, if your enemie doth assault you upon the contraie side, you must change both your foote and hand to crosse with him, as before."[9]

European polearm sources such as Agrippa, dei Liberi, Mair, Meyer, Sutor, Talhoffer and Vadi, all show matched, engaged stances (see Figure 1),[10] and di Grassi also instructed;

> "regarding alwaies to place himself with the contrarie foote before to that which the enemie shall set forth, that is to say: Yf the enemie be before with the left foote, then to stand with his right foote, or contrarie wise."[11]

The reason for doing so is explained by Swetnam;

> "It is necessary, that hee which useth the Staffe, should have use of both his hands alike, for thereby he may the better shift his staffe from hand to hand, whereby to lie crosse alwaies with your enemie, changing your hand and foote, as hee changeth for lying the one with right hand and foote for-most, and the other with the left, then he that striketh first, can not choose but endanger the others hand."[12]

Inside & Outside

This choice is not a simple question of left- or right-handedness. A review of the Masters and historical artwork confirms the modern experience that some people simply prefer their dominant hand forward, some back. This is most clearly shown in the confusion between Wylde's and Swetnam's definitions of the "inside" and "outside" lines.

For all practitioners, the "Low Ward" was the primary ward for weapons of the staff, with the rear hand low by the rear hip, the front arm extended, and the point of the weapon sloping upwards across your body, pointing at the enemy. Swetnam called this "the true guard for the Staffe," [13] and di Grassi said "there shall be framed (by my councel) no more than one ward,"[14] which was this one. For Swetnam, the Low Ward defined the staff fight - your "outside" is the side of your rear hand when you are in Low Ward, and your "inside" is the other. If your Low Ward is held correctly it secures the entire Outside line;

> "…alwaies have a care to keepe your stafe in his right place, that is to say, if your right hand and foote be foremost, then leave all your bodie open, so that your enemie can not endanger you on the out-side of your staffe, but if he will hit you, he must needed strike or thrust in the in-side of your stafe."[15]

or

> "if he proffer a thrust on the out-side of your Staffe: you neede not to feare nor offer to defend it, for there is no place in anie danger, but all is guarded."[16]

Fig. 1: *Some examples of polearm wards. Note that in all cases the stances are matched, allowing shafts to be crossed and engaged. top-left – Halberds in Sutor; top-right – Pollaxes in Fiore dei Liberi; lower-left – Shortstaff in Mair; lower-right – Longstaff in Meyer*

This makes intrinsic sense - if, for example, the right hand and right foot is forward, the staff sits defending all blows to the left-hand side, and logic would dictate that this is the "outside."If the front hand is taken away, the lines match the engagement of single sword or rapier in an "outside" guard, in this case a left-handed one.

Wylde, however, says;

> "...come to an inside Guard; the Butt end of your Staff then will be against your left Side, both your Arms being stiffly extended, the other Part of your Staff will cross your Opposer's Eyes: Lying on this manner, if your Opposer makes a Blow or Stroke to your left Ear or inside, you are then prepared with a true Guard."[17]

This is, of course, is the same ward as Swetnam's, but is defined as the exact opposite. Whereas Swetnam would seem to assume the dominant hand is likely to be at the rear, Wylde's assumption is that the dominant hand is forward. If the right hand and right foot is forward, the staff sits defending all blows to the left-hand side. If the rear hand is taken away, the line of the staff from the front hand then matches Wylde's "inside" or *Cart* guard of backsword and smallsword[18]. While these is some amount of twisted logic to this, the consequence is that the "natural" guard of the staff leaves the "outside" completely open.

Interestingly, there is a little of this confusion even in Swetnam. One of his two quarterstaff illustrations is of two figures facing each other in Low Ward. According to the text, they should be engaged, "standing crosse with your enemie."

Fig. 2: *Figures from Swetnam's "The Schoole of the Noble and Worthy Science of Defence", 1617. a) As originally published. The left-hand staff being behind the right-hand staff is clearly an error by the artist. b) Corrected by the author to conform with Swetnam's text, every other Master, and the generally accepted laws of the space-time continuum.*

Instead the picture shows the staffs both inside each other's line. Apart from the Escher-like perspective of this impossible situation, there is nothing to prevent either party from immediately striking the other. When redrawn with the right-hand staff in front of the left, the illustration then matches both the written text and the laws of physics. Swetnam himself makes a caveat about the illustrations, saying "...according to this Picture, yet regard chiefly the words rather then the Picture."[19] It would seem even the artist got confused as to which was the "outside" too (see Figure 2).

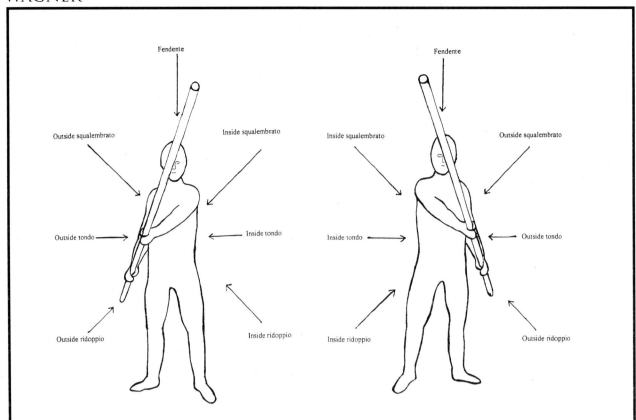

Fig. 3: *The ordering of blows according to Swetnam's definition of the Outside and Inside lines of the staff fight. The figure is in "Low Ward", and his staff secures his entire Outside line. a) "Right-handed" grip; b) "Left-handed" grip. The terms are necessarily an awkward mix of English and Italian (see note 26).*

The attempt by the English Masters to define the staff fight in terms of "Inside" or "Outside" lines was necessary because the need to be able to fight from either hand forward plays havoc with normal fencing terminology. A *mandritta*, for example, is by definition a blow delivered from your right side to your opponent's left side. If you hold your staff right-hand-forward, this remains a valid definition. However, on the whole English quarterstaff tended to be held with the controlling hand at the rear - Allinson-Winn wrote "…the butt of the staff, i.e. that end which is nearest the right hand of a right-handed man…",[20] the convention also shown by both MacCarthy and the Boy Scouts. The "natural" blow here would technically be a *roverso*, as it travels from your left and is aimed at your opponent's right side. This, of course, makes no practical sense. The only way of making the terminology hand-independent is to define it in terms of "Outside" and "Inside" - the natural blow could thus be described as an *outside squalembrato*, as it is delivered from your outside line into your opponent's outside line (see Figure 3).

Handedness in *La Jeu de la Hache*

Despite the legendary superiority of the English quarterstaff, the theoretical basis of all polearm combat is (unsurprisingly) fairly consistent across both Europe and Asia. Although the English developed a convention of left-hand-forward for staff weapons, in the European works, either with staff or the polearms of various sorts, there is no consistency as to which hand should naturally be forward. While the texts all recommend that the longsword be held with the right hand at the front[21], the pictures in Lebkommer, Meyer, Sutor, Pistofilo and Agrippa show staff weapons held left-hand forward, while Vadi, Di Grassi, Talhoffer and Fiore dei Liberi are primarily right-hand forward. This lack of uniformity becomes a major problem when looking at unillustrated manuals such as "Le Jeu de la Hache."

"Le Jeu de la Hache" is an anonymous 15th century Burgundian manual which deals specifically with armoured combat with a "poll-hammer" or *bec de faucon* (see Figure 4).[22] It describes most moves in terms of "left" and "right", and is also one of the few manuals to provide instructions on what to do if your opponent refuses to cross shafts, and insists on fighting "left handed," The author obviously assumes that the right-handed knight will hold the axe in a certain way, either left-hand forward (ie. left hand near the head of the axe) or right-hand forward. But which one? There are simply no overt instructions in the text that allow us to distinguish which hand is forward, different assumptions lead to different interpretations, and only careful consideration of the techniques themselves can provide an answer.

The first sequence in "Le Jeu de la Hache" reads;

> "When one would give you a swinging blow, right-hander to right-hander. If you have the croix in front, you can step forward with your left foot, receiving his blow, picking it up with the queue of your axe and - in a single movement - bear downward to make his axe fall to the ground. And from there, following up one foot after the other, you can give him a jab with the said queue, running it through the left hand, at the face: either there or wherever seems good to you. Or swing at his head." [23]

The first possibility is that the axe is held left-hand forward[24]. Under this assumption, the sequence has been interpreted as below;[25]

1) Agent:[26]
Left foot forward. Axe ready to deliver a Squalambrato mandritto[27] *or Tondo mandritto towards the head (i.e. a right-handed swing to the opponents left side).*

2) Patient Agent:
Left foot back, right foot forward, 3/4 stance, axe held in a high guard with the axe head forward, threatening a thrust towards face of opponent.

3) Agent:
Swing blow the blow, either squalembrato or tondo, making sure that you are aiming at the P.A.'s head.

4) Patient Agent:
Step forward with left foot and ward with shaft with an inside guard. This will take the motion of swinging a blow in opposition to the Agent's blow. When axes make contact on the shaft, push Agent's axe to ground and step forward with the right foot as you do so. Recover axe and thrust with the queue at the face as you continue stepping forwards or swing the axe head at agent as a ridoppio reverso aiming at the Agent's head.

Some objections might be raised to this interpretation. Firstly, the first attack described in the manuscript, "a swinging blow, right-hander to right-hander", could reasonably expected to be the most natural blow i.e. an "outside squalambrato." If the axe is held left-hand forward, this would be a blow towards the opponent's right side, not their left. Secondly, the Patient Agent's stance of left-hand-forward but "left foot back, right foot forward, axe held…head forward, threatening a thrust towards the face" is awkward; it is necessary in order to fulfil the movement instructions of the manual, and while there are some precedents in longsword technique,[28] such a "crossed" position is not shown in any other staff or pollaxe manual, and, as the author pointed out;

> "This seems quite strange as you feel like you are striking in opposition to your movement, ie stepping forward with the left foot while striking from the right hand side." [29]

The sequence seems also quite complicated, with a number of steps not contained within the original instructions, and the act of "bearing downward to make his axe fall to the ground" actually brings the Agent's staff up into an almost perfect hanging guard, allowing the very real possibility of him escaping unharmed.

If, however, we assume both grip their axes right-hand-forward, the fight proceeds long quite different lines:

1) Agent:
Stance: Right hand and right foot forward, in Low Ward

2) *Patient Agent:*
Stance: Right hand and right foot forward, in Low Ward

3) *Agent:*
Swings an Outside Squalambrato, the natural blow, at PA's left shoulder

4) *Patient Agent:*
Passes forward "with your left foot", crossing shafts and warding the blow on the demi-hache, then turns his shaft clockwise, turning his butt into A's face. This "picks up" or binds A's shaft and leaves the butt directly in A's face, ready to thrust.

On balance, this seems a much simpler interpretation, and exactly such a move is described in several quarterstaff sources. It also explains the instructions for the "jab with the said queue, running it through the left hand, at the face" - from the position described in (4), the Agent can grab the Patient Agent's left forearm stopping a two-handed thrust, but if the Patient Agent runs the shaft "through the left hand" he still strikes the Agent's face.

There is, however, a problem here, in that this interpretation does not deal with the instructions to "bear downward to make his axe fall to the ground" - the opponent's shaft is simply deflected. However, further comparison with other works offers one possibility. In Swetnam's section dealing with Welsh Hook, after describing how to "turn the butt" into the opponent's face, he provides a neat counter where;

> "you may fall away turning the edge or your Bill or Hooke towards his legge, and so by a drawing blow rake him over the shins, and keeping up the But-end of the Staffe for the defence of your owne head, and so you may fall out of his distance, and recover your guard before he can any way endanger you."[30]

In other words, the above sequence can be continued;

5) *Agent:*
As Patient Agent turns his butt, Agent steps or traverses right with rear foot, pulling butt up to his head and drawing croix over P.A.'s shins.

If, however, we follow the instructions of "Le Jeu de la Hache" to the letter, Swetnam's clever counter is neutralised[31];

4) *Patient Agent:*
Passes forward with the left foot, crossing shafts and warding the blow on the demi-hache, then turns his shaft clockwise and bears down on the Agent's shaft to force it to the ground. The Patient Agent can then thrust his butt into the Agent's face "running it through the left hand", or step back and deliver a fendentae at the Agent's head.

If this is correct, and "Le Jeu de la Hache" assumes a right-hand forward grip, as preferred by Talhoffer and Fiore dei Liberi, many of it's techniques would seem to become clearer and simpler. Any number of examples could be given, but as just one particularly clear sequence, here are the instructions dealing with what to do if your axe heads become entangled;

> "You can otherwise counter it by following up his tugging, stepping forward as he pulls. And from there, stepping with your left foot to his right side, hit him violently with the queue of your axe on his neck, knocking him over."[32]

Standing right-foot and right-hand forward, with heads entangled, the technique is to pass forward-and-left with the left foot (which will unentangle the heads), and striking the back of the opponent's head with the butt, which is held in the left hand. Again, this is simple and instantly recognisable from similar moves in other works, such as MacBane, who uses a feint to open up his opponent for a similar strike;

> "Dart your staff at his Face with your Left Hand, which he endeavours to stop, slide your Right Hand to your Left, and at full length hit him on the left side of his Head, which is scarce to be Defended"[33]

By comparison, standing left-hand forward, stepping to the left and hitting the opponent's neck with the butt would seem all but physically impossible.

Conclusion

In conclusion, there is no agreement, even among the Masters, as to where the dominant hand should be held in two-handed polearms. While it is recommended that practitioners must be able to fight from both stances, some sources use only one or the other for instruction purposes. Where this is not clearly stated or shown, such as in "Le Jeu de la Hache," different assumptions of handedness can lead to dramatically different interpretations of the material, and only by through analysing the entire work may its internal assumptions be clarified. In the absence of any clear instructions from the Master, it is therefore recommended that such assumptions not be made, and that all possibilities be explored.

Acknowledgements

Thanks to Rob Lovett for enlightening discussions on the subject, Ben Carpenter for being beaten regularly with quarterstaffs, and Steve Hand for his valuable pointers.

NOTES

1. Anglo, Sydney "Le Jeu de la Hache: A 15th century Treatise on the Technique of Chivalric Axe Combat", Archaeologia, CIX (1991) pp 113-128
2. Silver, George, "Brief Instructions upon my Paradoxes of Defence", ed. Matthey, Col. Cyril, 1898,
3. di Grassi, Giacomo, "His True Arte of Defence", 1594. Cap.14
4. di Grassi, Giacomo, "His True Arte of Defence", 1594. Cap.14, Pt.8
5. "Keep the point of your Stafffe right in your enemies face, holding one hand at the verie buttt end
of the Staffe, and the other a foote and a halfe distant, looking over your Staffe with both your
eies"; Swetnam, Joseph "The Schoole of the Noble and Worthy Science of Defence", 1617, p. 134
6. Silver, George, "Brief Instructions upon my Paradoxes of Defence", ed. Matthey, Col. Cyril, 1898, Cap.11 Pt.9. See also Brown, Terry, "English Martial Arts", 1997, p.156. It should also be noted that all English, and the majority of European, masters gripped the shaft with one-palm-up, one-palm-down. Although a few German manuals illustrate the both-palms-down (thumbs facing in) grip, the consequences of this are beyond the scope of this paper, and it is not considered relevant to the discussion of Le Jeu de la Hache (see also note 24)
7. Silver, George, "Brief Instructions upon my Paradoxes of

Defence", ed. Matthey, Col. Cyril, 1898, Cap.11 Pt.6
8. Eg. Silver, George, "Brief Instructions upon my Paradoxes of Defence", ed. Matthey, Col. Cyril, 1898, Cap. 11, Pt. 9 & 10
"If you play with your staff with your left hand before and your right hand back behind (etc)....
The like must you do if you play with your right hand before, & your left hand back behind, but if you need not to slide forth your left hand, because your right hand is in the right place on your staff already to use in that action."
9. Swetnam, Joseph "The Schoole of the Noble and Worthy Science of Defence", 1617, p.134
10. There are a few isolated exceptions to this general rule. For example, Talhoffer's 1467 fechtbuch contains two illustrations of mismatched hands, specifically tafel 88 and 99. Even here, however, they are greatly outnumbered by matched stances.
11. di Grassi, Giacomo, "His True Arte of Defence", 1594, Cap.14, Pt.3. Although this passage is confusing, "Yf the enemie be before with the left foote" he means your opponent's left foot is forward, and "stand with his right foote" his means put forward the foot opposite your opponent's right foot, ie your left foot.
12. Swetnam, Joseph "The Schoole of the Noble and Worthy Science of Defence", 1617. P.136
13. Swetnam, Joseph "The Schoole of the Noble and Worthy Science of Defence", 1617, P.134
14. di Grassi, Giacomo, "His True Arte of Defence", 1594, Cap.14, Pt.3
15. Swetnam, Joseph "The Schoole of the Noble and Worthy Science of Defence", 1617, p.136
16. Swetnam, Joseph "The Schoole of the Noble and Worthy Science of Defence", 1617, p.137
17. Wylde, Zachary "The English Master of Defence", 1711, p32
18. Wylde, Zachary "The English Master of Defence", 1711, p 12
19. Swetnam, Joseph "The Schoole of the Noble and Worthy Science of Defence", 1617, p.86
20. Allanson-Winn R. G. and C. Phillipps-Wolley "Broadsword and Singlestick with chapters on Quarterstaff, Bayonet, Shillalah, Walking-Stick, Umbrella and Other Weapons of Self Defence", 1890, p.7
21 Galas, S. Matthew, "Kindred Spirits: The Art of the Sword in Germany and Japan", in Journal of Asian Martial Arts, vol. 6, #3, (1997)
22. Anglo, Sydney "Le Jeu de la Hache: A 15th century Treatise on the Technique of Chivalric Axe Combat", Archaeologia, CIX (1991) pp 113-128. The identification of the weapon in question as a poll-hammer is made on the on the basis that the manuscript refers to the head of the weapon as containing, amongst other things, a hammer (mail), but at no point is there mention of a cutting edge or taillant.
23. "Le Jeu De La Hache", Point. 4
24. The interpretations here also assume the "front hand" is holding the head of the weapon. While holding the head back with a cutting weapon (eg bill, axe) does have virtue in some circumstances, "Le Jeu De La Hache" is specifically about poll-hammers. In the manuscript, butt strikes (ie those done with the rear hand) are always thrusts, usually done by running it through the hand to spike the opponent in the face, and blows are done "swinging", with the head forward. Any blow delivered with the rear hand (thumbs in) grip would

be much less powerful that with the front hand (thumbs out) grip. There does not appear to be any evidence that a reversed-grip was intended in "Le Jeu De La Hache".

25. Lovett, Rob "Le Jeu de la Hache Seminar for AEMMA 2000" http://www.the-exiles.org/

26. The "agent", in English fencing convention, is the aggressor, while the "patient agent" is the defender.

27. *Mandritta*: a blow delivered from your right side to your opponent's left side

 Roverso: a blow delivered from your left side to your opponent's right side

 Squalembrato: a diagonally descending blow
 Tondo: a horizontal blow
 Fendente: a vertically descending blow

28. For example, see Talhoffer, Hans, *Fechtbuch aus dem Jahre 1467*, tafel 1 & 6

29. Lovett, Rob "Le Jeu de la Hache Seminar for AEMMA 2000" http://www.the-exiles.org/

30. Swetnam, Joseph, "The Schoole of the Noble and Worthy Science of Defence", 1617. Pt. 22.

31. Swetnam also provides a second counter to the bind, where the front hand is removed from the shaft, allowing the staff to flip around into a hanging ward. This move, however, suffers even worse when it is "born downward" to the ground.

32 "Le Jeu De La Hache", Point. 32

33. MacBane, Donald "The Expert Swordsman's Companion", 1728, p68

References

Agrippa, Camillo, *Trattato di scienta d'arme*, Rome 1553

Allanson-Winn R. G. and C. Phillipps-Wolley *Broadsword and Singlestick with chapters on Quarterstaff, Bayonet, Shillalah, Walking-Stick, Umbrella and Other Weapons of Self Defence*, London 1890

Anglo, Sydney *"Le Jeu de la Hache: A 15th century Treatise on the Technique of Chivalric Axe Combat"*, Archaeologia, CIX (1991) pp 113-128

Anonymous. *Scout Charts No.12: Quarter-staff play*, London 1909

Di Grassi, Giacomo, *His True Arte of Defence*, London 1594

Fiore Furlan dei Liberi da Premariacco *Flos duellatorum*, ca.1410 Venice or Padua (Pisan-Dossi MS) in Novati, F. *Flos duellatorum: Il Fior di battaglia di maestro Fiore dei Liberi da Premariacco* (Bergamo, 1902)

Galas, S. Matthew, *Kindred Spirits: The Art of the Sword in Germany and Japan*, in Journal of Asian Martial Arts, vol. 6, #3, 1997

Lebkommer, Hans, *Der Allten Fechter grundtliche Kunst*, (Frankfurt, c.1531)

Lovett, Rob *Le Jeu de la Hache Lesson Plan for AEMMA October 2000*, http://www.the-exiles.freeservers.com, 2000

MacBane, Donald *The Expert Swordsman's Companion*, London 1728

McCarthy, Thomas *Quarter-staff: a practical manual*, London 1883

Mair, Paulus Hector, *Opus amplissimum de arte athletica*, 1510-1550

Meyer, Joachim, *Kunst des Fechten*, c.1570

Pistofilo, Bonaventura, "Il Torneo", 1627

Silver, George, *Bref Instructions upo my Pradoxes of Defence*, ed. Matthey, Col. Cyril, 1898, London

Sloane MS. 376, c.1600

Sutor, Jakob *New Kunstlitches Fectbuch* 1849 Stuttgart: J. Scheible. (original 1612)

Swetnam, Joseph *The Schoole of the Noble and Worthy Science of Defence*, London 1617

Talhoffer, Hans, *Fechtbuch aus dem Jahre 1467*, Gerichtliche und andere Zweikampfe darstellend, ed. Gustav Hergsell, Prag, J.G. Calve, 1887

Vadi, Filippo, *De Arte Gladiatoria Dimicandi*, Padua Italy 1482-1487 , codice 1324, fondo Vittorio Emanuele della Biblioteca Nazionale di Roma

Wylde, Zachary *The English Master of Defence*, London 1711

A BRIEF LOOK AT GRAPPLING AND WRESTLING
IN RENAISSANCE FENCING

By John Clements

"If I can close with him, I care not for his thrust."
- *Henry IV*, Act II, Scene I

The Medieval Legacy

The skills of grappling and the art of wrestling have a long legacy in Europe and all historical armed combat involved some degree of unarmed techniques. While their use is integral in popular armed fighting arts of Asia, Western fencing for more than the last two centuries has all but ignored its own similarly rich tradition. As few Renaissance fencing manuals include detailed sections on grappling and wrestling or seizures and hand disarms, the popular assumption has been that they were either not used or were always viewed with disdain. Yet when the evidence is examined, even briefly, a very different impression comes to light. The purpose of this paper then is to take a brief look at how grappling and wrestling was viewed and applied by fencers in the 1500s and 1600s and what it can mean to modern practitioners of the subject.

It should be prefaced that the difference between grappling and wrestling is not precise and in some languages there is no distinction between the two words, which are in a large part synonymous. Generally, it can be said that grappling in fencing can refer to seizing the opponent in some way and using the hands or arms and legs to affect them so that a weapon can then be used more effectively. While wrestling in Renaissance fencing can refer to unarmed techniques for when one or both parties become dis-armed. In the early 1500s, many soldiers, scholars, priests, and nobles wrote that wrestling was important in preparing aristocratic youth for military service. The Medieval legacy of unarmed fighting skills is becoming increasingly well-recognized. There are detailed depictions of unarmed techniques in numerous Medieval fencing manuals and such skills were closely integrated with fencing. The great German master Johannes Liechtenauer, for example, instructed

to *Ringet gutt* or "wrestle well". He also tells us "With ducking under, one comes into wrestling", meaning by closing in underneath the opponent's weapon you can and should seize it. In regard to his knight *Sir Thopas* for instance, Chaucer informs us that, "Of wrastlyng was ther noon his peer".[1]

The master, Fiore De' Liberi da Premariacco in his *Flos Duellatorum* of 1410 based his fighting method logically enough on his wrestling principles and similarly the Hispano-Italian master Pietro Monte in the 1480's recognized wrestling as the foundation of all fighting, armed or unarmed.[2] Accounts of grappling and wrestling also abound in descriptions of judicial contests and tournaments.[3] During a judicial fight in 1367 the knight Sir John Chandos was "grappled by a huge Castillian knight of noted prowess", Martin Fenant.[4] As Fenant was above the prone Chandos, Chandos managed to withdraw his dagger and repeatedly stabbed him in the back and ribs. A 1442 tournament fight in Paris conducted "with weapons as we are accustomed to carrying in battle" included in its fourth article the stipulation "that each of us may help each other with wrestling, using legs, feet, arms or hands."[5] That same year, a judicial duel between Sir John Astley and Philip Boyle of Aragon included the rule: "wrestling with legs and feet, arms and hands, shall be allowed".[6] A 14th century, *Ordinances and Statutes and Rules for Joust*, by the Lord Tiptofte, Earle of Worchester, in contrast stated, "At Tournay…All gripes, shockes, and foule play forbidden."[7] Yet in, *The Booke of Certaine Triumphes*, from c. 1507, one tournament during the reign of King Henry VIII included rules: "To Fight on foot…with Gripe, or otherwise."[8] The reference to "grip or otherwise" is interesting in that it ostensibly allowed a range of grappling. The tournament of "Lady Maies servants" also called for sword combat at the barriers by eight strokes "every man to his best advantage with gripe or otherwise".[9] After a tournament in 1520, Henry VIII even practiced wrestling with King Francis I of France.

From the same period the Emperor Maximilian I was well-known for his enthusiastic practice of the martial arts. George Puttenham in his 1569, *The Arte of English Poesie*, wrote of the Kaiser that he "would take any common souldier to taske at wrestling, or weapon, or in any other activitie and feates of armes".[10] Another challenge of this time mentioned as one of the contest "wrestling, fighting at the barriers".[11] A 1510 challenge to the "Feate called the Barriers" requiring "Bastard-Sword, Poynt and Edge Rebated" was conducted for seven "strokes with the sword point and edge rebated without Close or gripping one another with [hands]" upon pain of punishment.[12] The artist Albrecht Duerer's Fechtbuch of 1512 even contains more material on wrestling than it does on swordplay and the relationship between the two is clearly noticeable. But just how all this heritage relates to the foyning fence of the Renaissance is less well understood.

Martial Exercise and Martial Sport

Approval of grappling and wrestling in the period was inconsistent and was typically curtailed during fencing practice. Understanding its true value can therefore be confusing now for modern students unfamiliar with either the actual evidence or the actual techniques. One view of Renaissance fencing has been that unarmed and pugilistic attacks are mere unskilled thuggery practiced only by the lower classes. After all, surely you should not need to grapple in an encounter if you knew the sword "to perfection"? (…and yet we might ask how many are "perfect" with their sword?). Yet, this perspective makes sense, after all, a slender cut-and-thrust sword or rapier is a weapon whose characteristics are perfectly suited to keeping an opponent away and killing him at range. Intentionally closing-in to resort to hands-on brute strength would seem antithetical to the very nature and advantage of skillfully employing a weapon. In actuality, the matter is that such actions did not rely on primitive brute strength, but were advanced techniques that required considerable practice and skill to execute –and knowing them could make a fighter a

more well-rounded and dangerous opponent in combat.[13] Yet, fencing historians (and practitioners) have typically downplayed or ignored the elements of close-in fighting and grappling in historical swordplay. Part of this prejudice perhaps stems from the surviving 18th and 19th century view of swordplay as essentially being that of personal "duel of honor" or gentlemanly private quarrel. The traditional focus of this time was on fencing as "blade on blade" action rather than on "fighting" with swords in war or in sudden assault. This was not the case in the 1500's and 1600's. Armed fighting consisted of all manner of encounters with all manner of bladed weapons.

About c. 1451 William Worcester wrote in his *Boke of Noblesse* (British Museum, Royal 18 B XXII), that there was a need to school those of noble blood in all forms of armed combat frum jousting to wrestling in order that it make them 'hardie, deliver, and well brethed'"[14] In the early 1500's the Italian solider-priest Celio Calacagnini listed wrestling as an exercise required for preparing upper-class youths for military service, while Girolamo Muzio, commenting in *La Faustina* on the importance of chivalry, noted that a man was no knight if he was merely skilled *only* in wrestling and handling all manners of arms. Wrestling was also part of the academic program for upper class youths in Renaissance Florence. Between 1508 and 1513, the courtier Baldassare Castiglione wrote, "it is of the highest importance to know how to wrestle, since this often accompanies combat on foot."[15] In 1531 the English scholar and diplomat Sir Thomas Elyot wrote, "There be divers maners of wrastlinges" and "undoubtedly it shall be founde profitable in warres, in case that a capitayne shall be constrayned to cope with his aduersary hande to hande, havyng his weapon broken or loste. Also it hath ben sene that the waiker persone, by the sleight of wrastlyng, hath ouerthrowen the strenger…or he coulde fasten on the other any violent stroke."[16]

Writing in 1550 after spending time on the continent, Roger Ascham, tutor to Elizabeth I, advised in *The Scholemaster* that young gentlemen should delight in all exercises for war and pastimes for peace "verie necessarie, for a Courtlie gentleman to use." Ascham counseled "to plaie at all weapones" and "to wrestle."[17] In his 1575, *Essais*, Michel de Montaigne, the French Renaissance thinker and courtier referred to "our very exercises and recreations, running, wrestling …and fencing".[18] In 1523 the educational reformer Ulrich Zwingli favored "the exercise of weapons, and wrestling" as part of the proper education of Christian youth. The English pedagogue Richard Mulcaster in 1581 also advocated wrestling and fencing should be included in school curriculum.[19] The famed Elizabethan, Captain Andrew Hallydean, was himself described as "a fair wrestler and much better fencer".[20] As well, between 1580 and 1585 the French general Francois de la Noue proposed that military academies in Paris and three other French cities would teach youths various skills including the handling of weapons and wrestling.[21] The famed 16th century chronicler of duels, Brantome, also tells us that during this time wrestling was highly regarded at the French court. To instruct aristocratic youths in skills which included wrestling, fencing, riding, dancing, tennis, and firearms, a *Ritterakedemie* or "Knight's School" was reportedly set up in 1589 at the *Collegium Illustre* in Tübingen, Germany.[22] During the early 1600s, Peter Ernest of Mansfeld was sent at the age of 11 to be a page and learn from the *escuyer* horsemanship and management of weapons and to compete in wrestling.[23]

In the 1599, *Basilikon Doron*, King James I of England warned his son the prince not to participate in "rough and tumble" sports such as football, but instead, to engage in "safe sports" such as wrestling. Evidence that nobles and cavaliers for the large part practiced a more honorable or polite court fencing seems lacking. In 1659, the master Johann Georg Pascha declared *Ringen* (wrestling) a useful *exercitium* that history had shown was practiced not only for fun but also in earnest. The German Heinrich Von Gunterrodt in 1579 observed: "Fencing is a worthy, manly, and most noble Gymnastic art, established by principles of nature…which serves both gladiator and soldier, indeed everyone, in …battles, and single-combats, with every hand-to-hand weapon, and also wrestling, for strongly defending, and achieving victory." John Milton in his 1644 essay, *Of Education*, described the ideal public school education as including an hour a day of fencing or wrestling exercise explaining that youths should "be also practiz'd in all the Locks and Gripes of

Wrastling…as need may often be in fight to tugg or grapple, and to close".[24] As has pointed out however, Englishman Henry Peacham in 1622 questioned whether "throwing and wrestling" were more befitting common soldiers rather than nobility, while his contemporary Lord Herbert of Cherbury who studied martial arts in France, found them "qualities of great use".[25] Herbert had put such skills to use as, while riding in London, he was ambushed in broad day light by Sir John Ayres and four lackeys. In the course of the assault he managed with a broken sword to stab Ayres in the chest and knock him down. Herbert then struck Ayres on the head, knocking him to the ground a second time. Injured and still surrounded, Herbert, who for all we know may have very well exaggerated the account, tells how "kneeling on the ground and bestriding him, I struck him as hard as I could with my piece of sword."[26]

In his 1938 work on Renaissance Italian dueling, Frederick Bryson cited Paris de Puteo (c. 1470) as stating that in a formal duel if a sword was broken the fighter might properly continue the combat by twisting his opponent's arm or biting him, etc. But Bryson added that according to the Venetian, Antonio Possevino, by 1553 the notion of purposely discarding a serviceable weapon in favor of fist fighting or engaging in wrestling, kicking, etc. was dishonorable because the contest should test the strength not of the body but of the soul.[27] Such actions were typically deemed appropriate for dueling gentry only if conducted *within* the course of an armed struggle. To consider the awareness of closing among Renaissance fencers we need only make consideration of the entering in to push the opponent's chest or face while simultaneously placing the leg strategically behind the opponent's knee that is depicted in so many manuals from Marozzo's and Agrippa's to Thibault's and L'Ange's.[28] Actions of stepping in against an opponent to pull or push them off balance are arguably a fundamental aspect of sword or rapier combat. The skills of grappling were not only for defeating an opponent but could also be employed in offering him mercy. Giraldi Cinzio for example described a duel from c. 1564 in which an old fencing master named Pirro at Beneveto fought with Sergesto, a young former student. Pirro struck him on the back of the knee with the flat of his blade, pushed the younger fighter to the ground, disarmed him, and seizing his throat made him surrender.[29]

As one modern historian of France in the late Renaissance has noted: "Once a physical fight had begun, the rule often seems to have been a kind of pugilistic opportunism. There was no particular pattern or etiquette to the brawls and beatings that took place…not to lessen the arguments that…combat was the end of, or at least part of, a 'ritual' of sorts."[30] Perhaps the psychology at work in dueling accounts for the disparity between records of actual Renaissance duels and the theoretical teachings of some treatises on fencing from the period. As Practical and necessary as grappling and wrestling skills could be, for dueling among the gentry fighting weapon on weapon or blade on blade was a sign of one's noble status. Its very nature therefore, to a large degree, contrasted with the possibility of unarmed brawling. The French historian Billacois informs us: "Hand-to-hand fighting, the direct contact and the opponent's touch without the distance imposed by a weapon removes respect, both for oneself and for the other, and the sense of justice…to defend oneself with a sword, looking one's opponent in the eye, is to consider him (in both senses of the word), it is to salute and honour him as one strikes."[31] One historian of the Renaissance tells us, "under the influence of the fencing schools wrestling, which was declining in repute as an exercise for the gentleman, was modified into a respectable and useful form of judo, with special emphasis on the unarmed man's defense against an armed assailant".[32] This is partially correct, as martial systems of wrestling had already existed in Europe for several centuries. Just as his Medieval forbears had, the German master Joachim Meyer offered significant elements of grappling and wrestling during swordplay in his Fechtbuch of 1570. In the attractive woodcut of Meyer's manual students are depicted learning actions of twisting swords out of their opponent's hands or forcing them to the ground with various elbow locks and shoulder holds.[33] J. D. Aylward describe that, "One of the things which betray the preoccupation of the earlier masters with cold steel is the fact that all of them…devote almost disproportionate attention to the description of tricks not really dependent upon swordsmanship at all, but rather upon coming to physical grips with the opponent. If these were carried out correctly, it was claimed that the other man could be disarmed, thrown on the ground, or otherwise rendered incapable of continuing the conflict."[34] Anglo points out that "a distinguishing feature of medieval and renaissance personal combat was the combination of two interrelated and legitimate assumptions", one being that the *prese* (or "close quarter trick") which "might often prove decisive, when fighting with swords or staff weapons" and two, that unarmed skills could effectively be used against armed attacks.[35] He adds that it was only slowly, and very unevenly, that these assumptions were later discarded and that some masters even recognized this as an unfortunate development.

Intention and Actuality

Accounts of individual combats in the 1500s and 1600s bear witness to the frequency and effectiveness which grappling and wrestling actions were employed. Even in the notorious 1547 duel between the nobles Jarnac and Chastaignerai, Jarnac was so concerned at Chastaignerai's well known skill as a wrestler (not to mention fencing) that to avoid the chance of a close struggle, he insisted both parties each wear two daggers. Alfred Hutton offered an account from Vulson de la Colombière's description of a 1549 judicial combat with bastard swords between Claude d'Aguerre, Baron of Vienne le Chastel, and Jacques de Fontaine, Lord of Fendailles. Hutton stated, "D'aguerre let fall his sword, and being an expert wrestler (for be it understood that no one in those days was considered a complete man-at-arms unless he was proficient in the wrestling art), threw his enemy, held him down, and, having disarmed him of his morion, dealt him many severe blows on the head and face with it…"[36] After tackling his opponent and beating him with his own helmet, D'aguerre also reportedly stuffed dirt into Fontaine's mouth causing him to gag. During a practice bout with his Milanese instructor Pompée, in 1565 for instance, the young king of France, Charles IX, was allowed to knock his teacher to the ground and pretended to kill him. Charles's younger brother (later Henry III) did the same to his own teacher Sylvie, using a sword and round shield.[37] In their quarrel of c. 1600, the celebrated French rapier duelists Lagarde and Bazanez ended up on the ground violently stabbing and fighting each other.[38] Lagarde's young brother Mirabel at this time fought against Bazanez's cousin, Fermontez. After being stabbed by Mirabel, Fermontez rushed to close on Mirabel and attempted to wrestle, but he expired from his wound.[39] In his history of dueling Millingen described a 1613 rapier duel between Lord Bruce and Sir John Heidon, the Earl of Dorset, that resulted in several non-lethal thrusts. In his personal account of the vicious fight, the Earl of Dorset wrote: "Grabbing each other's blades… yet keeping our holds, …with a kick and a wrench together I freed my long-captive weapon…"[40] Dorset did not in anyway remark as if anything that occurred, including blade grabbing and kicking, was unusual for a duel between two gentleman of such high social status.

Another integral element of grappling or wrestling in Renaissance fencing is that of closing to grab an adversary's sword arm or weapon itself. The Bolognese master, Lelio de Tedeschi, even produced a manual on the art of disarming in 1603. In 1617 English master of defence Joseph Swetnam in his section on a "Close at back-sword" instructed: "then catch hold on they enemies Sword-hilt, or his hand-wrist, with thy left hand…and then you may either trip up his heeles, or cut, or thrust him with your weapon, and in this manner you maie close with a Rapier also".[41] Swetnam commented as well on the value of skill in wrestling for staff fighting. Elizabethan George Silver's views advocating *closes and grips* in swordplay are well known. From section 15, of his 1599, *Paradoxes of Defence*, Silver stated the importance of "closes and gryps, striking with the hilts, daggers, bucklers, wrestlings, striking with the foot or knee in the coddes" and how "all these are safely defended in learning perfectly of the grips".[42] In his praising of the virtues of the short sword over the rapier, George Silver also noted how men coming to blows would, "lay on, having the use of blows and grips…and many times hurling together."[43] Silver's concern was clearly one of a skill of *general* fighting, meaning that which prepared men not for the civilian duel alone but for war, battle, and all occasions of violent combat. Interestingly though, Silver lamented how such things were no longer being taught by teachers of defence, saying "…there are now in these dayes no gripes, closes, wrestlings, striking with the hilts, daggers, or bucklers, used in Fence-schools."[44] We may ponder if perhaps Silver was referring not only to the English fighting guilds but to foreign rapier teachers in England who did not bother to teach such street necessities to their well-born clients?

In section 31 of his *Paradoxes*, Silver actually complained that rather than *discouraging* it the rapier's excessive length *allowed* for close-in fighting without much fear because there was little threat to prevent it once the point was displaced. He wrote: "Of the long single Rapier fight betweene valiant men, having both skill, he that is the best wrestler, or if neither of them can wrastle, the strongest man most commonly killleth the other, or leaveth him at his mercie".[45] He then described what typically happened when rapier fighters both rushed together, explaining:

> "When two valiant men of skill at single Rapier do fight, one or both of them most commonly standing upon their strength or skill in wrestling, will presently seeke to run into the close…but hapning both of one mind, the rather do bring themselves together: that being done, no skil with Rapiers availeth, they presently grapple fast their hilts, wrists, armes, bodies or neckes, as in …wrestling, or striving together, they may best find for their advantages: whereby it most commonly falleth out, that he that is the best wrastler, or strongest man (if neither of them can wrestle) overcometh, wrestling by strength, or fine skill in wrestling, the Rapier from his adversarie, or casting him frō him, either to the ground, or to such distance, that he may by reason therof, use the edge or point of his rapier, to strike or thrust him, leaving him dead or alive at his mercie."[46]

Silver's descriptions above sound quite familiar and reasonable to those who today practice more inclusive rapier fencing with guidelines for intentional close-contact. They coincide closely with some modern day reconstructions. Similarly, Alfred Hutton also related how in the year 1626, the Marquis de Beuvron and Francois de Montmorency, Comte de Boutteville, the notorious rabid duelist and bully, fought a duel together in which both attacked "each other so furiously that they soon come to such close quarters that their long rapiers are useless. They throw them aside, and, grappling with one another, attempt to bring their daggers into play."[47] In section 34, *Of the long single rapier, or rapier and poniard fight between two unskillful men being valiant*, Silver further observed:

"When two unskillful men (being valiant) shall fight with long single Rapiers, there is less danger in that kind of fight, by reason of their distance in convenient length, waight, and unwieldinesse, then is with short Rapiers: whereby it commeth to passe, that what hurt shall happen to be done, if anie with the edge or point of their Rapiers is done in a moment, and presently will grapple and wrastle together, wherin most commonly the strongest or best Wrastler overcommeth, and the like fight falleth out betweene them, at the long Rapier and Poiniard, but much more deadly, because instead of Close and Wrastling, they fall most commonly to stabbing with their Poiniardes."[48]

Of course, it might be argued Silver was not a "rapier master" and so did not understand "proper" rapier fencing. Regardless, he was obviously a highly skilled martial artist and experienced expert swordsman who had actually seen rapier fighting in person. Earlier in 1579, Von Gunterrodt had noted that in fencing, "when one will not cede to the other, but they press one against the other and rush close, there is almost no use for arms, especially long ones, but grappling begins, where each seeks to throw down the other or cast him on the ground, and to harm and overcome him with many other means."[49] This sounds very much like the advise from master Sigmund Ringeck of the early 1400s in his commentary on Liechtenauer's verses: "So be flexible in your defense and aim your sword at one opening after another so that he can not get through with any of his own techniques. But if he moves around your sword and closes in, then start wrestling [*Ringen*]."[50] Ludovico Ariosto in his 1523 poem, *Orlando Furioso* writes of a combat between two knights that includes not only a classic example of *mezza-spada*, but of a not too unfamiliar account of close fighting: "At half-sword's engage the struggling foes; And –such their stubborn mood –with shortened brand; They still approach, and now so fiercely close, They

cannot choose but grapple, hand to hand. Her sword, no longer needful, each foregoes" (Canto 36, XLIX, 1523). Having closed with one another the two fighters resorted to half-sword techniques and from there to wrestling when their blades became a hindrance.[51] It is no surprise then that closing-in to strike, to grab, trip, throw, or push the opponent down is seen in Renaissance fencing manuals from the cut-and-thrust style swords of Achille Marozzo in 1536 and Camillo Agrippa in 1553, to the slender rapier of Giovanni Lovino in 1580 and L'Lange in 1664.[52] Jacob Wallhausen's 1616 depictions of military combat (armored and unarmored) show much the same techniques. Dr. Anglo has called this desperate armed or unarmed combat of the Renaissance "all-in fighting" –as opposed to formal duels with rules –and describes it as: "one other area of personal combat which was taught by masters throughout Europe…practiced at every level of the social hierarchy whether the antagonists were clad in defensive armor or not".[53] He adds that, "Even in Spain, where it might be thought that mathematical and philosophical speculation had eliminated such sordid realities, wrestling tricks were still taught by the masters –as is well illustrated in an early seventeenth-century manuscript treatise by Pedro de Heredia, cavalry captain and member of the war council of the King of Spain."[54]

The use of the legs to trip or sweep an opponent is another integral element in any close-in fighting or grappling. Through out his *Bref Instructions* Silver for example made repeated admonitions to "strike up his heels."[55] Scooping an opponent off his feet by hooking his leg with your arm was not unknown in rapier fencing either. Earlier, 15th century masters such as Fiore dei Liberi had included such actions as well as direct kicks in their fighting. Even staid master Girard Thibault in 1630 in his highly systematic rapier style illustrated a frontal kick.[56] Silver noted Rocco Bonetti's sword and rapier encounter with Austen Bagger in the 1590's describing how Bagger: "stroke up his heeles, and cut him over the breech, and trode upon him, and most grievously hurt him under his feet."[57] Though Bagger had spared the Italian, Bonetti later died of the injuries.[58] In 1625, Englishman Richard Peeke fought similarly during a rapier duel at Sherries, in Spain, defeating the Spaniard Tiago by sweeping his legs out from under him. As Peeke tells it: "A *Spanish* Champion presents himselfe, Named *Signior Tiage*; When after wee had played some reasonable good time, I disarmed, as thus, I caught his Rapier betwixt the Barres of my Poniard, and there held it, till I closed in with him, and tripping up his Heeles, I took his Weapons out of his hands".[59] Peeke described himself as being but a common sailor and soldier saying his "breeding had been rough, scorning delicacy" and calling himself "blunt, plaine, and unpolished". Whether Tiago was familiar with such moves of Peeke or not is unclear from the account, but his defeat certainly surprised Peeke's courtly hosts.

The Italian master Salvatore Fabris in 1606 depicted a range of close-in and second-hand actions like those in Medieval texts in a section on coming to grips and seizing the sword, even teaching to take the opponent down by grabbing him around the waist. Yet Fabris only included material on grips and seizing reluctantly, because his text was focused on *perfect* defense with the sword in a way that gentlemen would not need to come to grips on the seizing of swords except by accidents of scuffling that might occur. He stated for example, "Thus we proposed to treat only of the thrust and the cut, believing that, whoever can defend and attack in time with these, would never need to come to grips on the seizing of swords."[60] Fabris had even advocated leaving your blade separated from the opponent's rather than touching it noting that the attempt to continually keep it in contact "often degenerates into a wrestle and a hand-to-hand."[61] As with other masters, his method was essentially aimed at encounters of honor within the *code duello*. Apparently though, whatever his opinion of them as appropriate for his readers he did understand and teach these other skills in some way to prepare his students for them. Fabris' close-in moves were influential enough to be copied by several later rapier masters, including Heussler in 1615, L'Lange in 1664, and Porath as late as 1693.[62] In fact, a variety of closing actions and grapples similar to Fabris' were included by Siegmund Weischner in his smallsword treatise, *Die Ritterliche Geschicklichkeit im Fechten*, of 1765.

A 1625 edition of the short text, *Gioielo di sapienza*, or "Jewel of Wisdom", features an assortment of fencing tips, apparently written by a

commoner, that included disarming actions and armed ground-fighting.[63] Among its material on single sword, sword and cape, dagger, halberd and unarmed skills, Section 4 offered advice "For one who, finding himself without arms, might be assaulted by an enemy." Section 6 offered advice what do when on the ground while armed. This section advises when on the ground and with no time to get to one's feet, one must cut the enemy's legs. It then recounts a case where a French boy killed his standing adversary in this way. Other sections cover how to fight while unarmed against an attacker including disarming a halberd.[64] In his work Johann Georg Pascha also revealed an extraordinary range of unarmed techniques. It would not be difficult to believe that Pascha, who was also a rapier master, would have widely utilized the techniques in his fencing method. A fighter always uses what he knows. In the words of Captain Sir Richard Burton, "The complete swordsman studies his own physical prowess and discovers the utmost use that can be made of them."[65]

The close-in techniques employed with Renaissance swords were not ignored by later fencers using smallswords either. In 1671 an affray took place in Montreal, Canada, between two soldiers. The two men drew swords and exchanged blows and after several wounds both wrestled briefly before one struck the other repeatedly on the head with his pommel. They were then separated by some five passing onlookers and both combatants survived.[66] In his 1693, *Some Thoughts Concerning Education*, the philosopher John Locke wrote, "a man of courage, who cannot fence at all, and therefore will put all upon one thrust and not stand parrying, has the odds against a moderate fencer, especially if he has skill in wrestling".[67] Locke believed for a man to prepare his son for duels, "I had much rather mine should be a good wrestler than an ordinary fencer; which the most any gentleman can attain to in it, unless he will be constantly in the fencing school, and every day exercising."[68] In a 1712 small-sword duel between Duke Hamilton and Lord Mohun, the Duke got on top of the fallen Mohun and killed him but not before Mohun was able to first shorten his sword and stab the Duke through to the heart.[69] In this same duel, Colonel Hamilton fought Colonel Maccartney (themselves each acting as seconds). As Maccartney made a full pass at Hamilton, he parried downward wounding himself in his instep in the process, yet he still took the opportunity to immediately close with and disarm Maccartney.[70]

Scot fencing master Sir William Hope in his 1707, "New Method" fencing book also spoke highly of grips and tripping (although not as something to be casually practiced in class). Hope tellingly declared: "Because, however allowable such active and nimble defences may be upon a pich at sharps, yet in a school-assault, all such kind of struggling between scholars is rude and undecent."[71] Hope also commented on the value of using entering techniques by a student when "commanding of his adversary's sword, if he be strong enof to grapple with and master him; or only in forcing of himself close upon his adversary for his own security."[72] Hope had his "Scholar" conversationally ask: "but I see that a man in making use of this kind of en-closing, may be in a great deal of hazard, if he be not all the experter in this art." To which Hope's "Master" replies: "Sir, I tell you again that a man should never attempt to play any of the difficult lessons, when he is assaulting, until by practice upon a master's breast, he hath become master of them."[73] Hope's writings reveal the fencing in his school was open to public viewing and this itself may be the very reason for many of his classroom restrictions on grappling and wrestling, since those watching might have been shocked by it. His statement banning wrestling was qualified by another comment about "however allowable it may be in a pinch at sharps", suggesting that wrestling was considered quite acceptable when one's life was at stake.[74]

Sir Thomas Parkyns in his 1720, *Cornish-Hugg Wrestler*, called wrestling "of great use to such who understand the small-sword in fencing".[75] Parkyns explained, "I illustrate how useful Wrestling is to a Gentleman in Fencing, in…parrying, and leave it to the ingenious, to make a farther Application as oft as an Opportunity shall offer itself."[76] In his 1771 fencer's guide for broadsword, the Eng-lish fencer A. Lonnergan at one point instructed, "When I begin to advance the left hand to disarm you, spring back, making a blow at it; or, if you think yourself as powerful as your adversary, op-pose force to force, then the weaker must go to the ground, if some knowledge of wrestling does not prevent it."[77] Similarly, the 1772 smallsword duel

between Sheridan and Mathews ended in their wrestling together on the ground bashing at one another. Their seconds did not intervene.

The In-Complete Fencer?

That some Renaissance fencing masters and courtiers however may have frowned on close-fighting actions seems understandable. It has been said of personal combat in the period, "There were always upper class fools willing to observe the niceties."[78] Perhaps some teachers felt no cause to address certain possibilities that would more or less be unlikely to be employed by par-ties in a formal aristocratic duel. The view that a lengthy agile sword should alone be sufficient for defense is a reasonable one (and is highly reminis-cent today of the recent grappling/ground-fight-ing deficiency so effectively argued against the more traditional "stand-up kick/punch" martial artists). As has been concluded, "Whatever the theoretical status of wrestling among the learned and knightly classes, it is obvious from surviving treatises that, up to the early seventeenth century and even beyond, many master of arms recognized the advantage bestowed upon their pupils by the physical exercise of wrestling – in order to develop agility, strength, and dexterity – and by practicing unarmed combat to use against the assaults of an armed assailant or in any other mortal affray".[79] Thus, when reconstructing Renaissance fencing today, it can be narrow and self-defeating for us to canonize the masters who failed to address or disapproved of close-fighting over those who recommended it.

Where then does this brief look at grappling and wrestling in Renaissance fencing lead us? What can be surmised? For modern practitioners one obvious conclusion is: do not overlook the area of close-in fighting. It may be that it was only after grappling and wrestling was limited, first within certain tournaments and judicial duels and then later within the Code Duello, that private armed combat came to be characterized as something other than "close-combat" (i.e., fighting at a range *other* than the weapon's own reach). It would ap-parently seem it was not until close-in actions were later disavowed or discarded from fencing that a view developed that considered them "improper". As historians Barber and Barker acknowledged in their work on tournaments "Fencing became an aristocratic pastime only when the element of wrestling disappeared, and pure swordplay was the accepted form of combat."[80] Grappling, throws, and take-downs in swordplay may be considered *unseemly brawling* only when there is no technique or method involved, when they are haphazard, accidental and impromptu, otherwise such actions reflect skill and an art. They require extensive practice and their execution takes expert timing and balance. For example, in a 1750 small-sword duel between two German noblemen, Swiegel and Freychappel, the combat lasted nearly an hour during which both were many times wounded. Eventually, Freychappel in trying to rush and close with his opponent, tripped and fell and was instantly run through and killed by Swiegel.[81]

In his instructions on footwork from his 1536, *Opera Nova*, Achille Marozzo states it is those who understand timing, who know how to get in and out in close-measure, that must be recognized as excellent and perfect fencers. This tacit acknowledgment of the skill necessary to effectively close to advantage against an armed opponent is demonstrable still today. After all, one cannot expect to be a highly skilled swordsman if one cannot prevent an opponent simply closing-in to punch you in the mouth or easily trip you on to the floor.[82] But, it is understandable that as such actions were used less and less in formal duels, they were no longer taught, and not being taught they fell out of use. Intentionally or not, one fights the way one trains after all. Wisely, a fighter would not attempt actions against an opponent unless he had practiced them considerably in the first place; otherwise they would certainly be foolish except in desperation (which did occur). As Nicholaes Petter said in his 1674 text on wrestling, "Practice perfects knowledge! It is not enough to understand matters with a quick mind, only one who has practiced will be able to apply his knowledge. There must also be instruction to make an art known to others, without which it would disappear with him that invented it."[83] In fact, Silver himself in General rule 26 of Chapter 4 in his, *Bref Instructions*, declared, "never attempt to close or come to grip at these weapons unless it be upon the slow motion or disorder of your enemy." He then cautioned, "But if he will close with you, then you may take the grip of him safely at his coming in." Seizures, disarms, close-

in grabs, and left-hand parries have always been tricky, always been risky, and always required practice in all types of fencing. Perhaps there have always been fencers too conservative to approve of them or to risk coming corps-a-corps ("body to body") at all. But this does not mean that they did not work and cannot again be reconstructed now. These things were (and are) advanced techniques and even for advanced students may not always work perfectly. But then, we might ask what fighting technique does?

The abandonment by later generations of duelists (fighting under very different conditions) of those techniques, which were a part of the repertoire of a many Renaissance swordsmen, surely does not negate either the evidence here or the significance and effectiveness of these skills.[84] Even Egerton Castle in 1891 cited the importance of knowing, not only the proper manner of "coming to point" in "matters of honourable difficulty", but also of the "less decorous methods of dealing scientifically with a rough antagonist, by enclosing and disarming in case of a sudden rencounter".[85] Historians of dueling have pointed out that frequently in the 1500s and 1600s little distinction was made between brawls, sudden affrays, rencounters, private assaults, and "duels". This distinction even appears to have been the exception rather than the rule. Dr. Sydney Anglo, surely the foremost scholar of historical fencing texts, astutely comments on the styles of fighting in the Renaissance stating: "The techniques involved – dealing with unequal odds, left hand parrying, wrestling throws, ruthless battering about the head, stabbings, wards, and a total commitment to death and destruction – are all much the same as those described and illustrated by masters of arms from the late fourteenth century onwards. And, however much such behavior may later have been frowned upon by academic fencers, similar practices were still being taught long after they are conventionally supposed to have vanished from the sophisticated swordsman's repertory."[86] Accordingly, Anglo has declared, "I would argue that the onus of proof is on those who believe that men fighting for their lives scrupulously followed the rules codified in theoretical treatises."[87]

The persuasiveness of the evidence undermines the view there was no effective grappling or wrestling in Renaissance fencing or rapier combat and that these were clumsy tricks used in placed of "proper" fencing. The belief that they could not have been effectively used because an opponent would be hit before closing to range seems not to be borne out by period accounts. The view that Renaissance swords and rapiers were too quick to allow successful closing or grappling is also mistaken given modern experiment and practice. There is still more that can be said about this subject and this has been only a brief look. What becomes remarkable though as we begin to study historical fencing as a martial art again, is not that there is so much evidence for grappling and wrestling in Renaissance fencing, but that grappling and wrestling in swordplay seemingly has been overlooked for so long.[88] The skills of entering in close to grab an opponent's arm, hand or blade, disarm them or trap them were used and are something that today's student of historical fencing should explore in detail by students. The techniques of closing to take down or trip up an opponent can make all the difference in a real sword fight and today are elements worthy of long-term investigation. As Burton wrote, "You are never thoroughly safe until you have learned to defend yourself against any attempt which might have a fatal result."[89]

In the words of the Bolognese Master of Arms, Philippo Vadi, in c. 1480 taught, you can also use in this art strokes and close techniques that you find simpler; leave the more complex, take those favoring your side and often you will have honour in the art.[90] Thus, with so many soldiers, swordsmen, and gentlemen courtiers, throughout the Renaissance acknowledging and practicing grappling and wrestling skills, can we seriously consider that such skills were ignored when swords were drawn? After all, in fighting the objective is not a prolonged session of fencing, free-playing, bouting, or exchange of tourney blows, but rather to immediately control the encounter as swiftly and effectively as possible. Perhaps Shakespeare expresses the whole matter best when in part two of *King Henry IV* (Act II, Scene I), written around 1598, two characters set out on the street to arrest Sir John Falstaff: Mistress Quickly declares of Falstaff, "If his weapon be out, he will foin like any devil; he will spare neither man, woman, nor child." To which, undaunted, the sheriff's officer

Master Fang tellingly responds, "If I can close with him, I care not for his thrust."[91]

Bibliography:
Anglin, Jay P. "The Schools of Defense in Elizabethan London", in *Renaissance Quarterly* (Vol. XXXVII No. 3, AUTUMN, 1984. Renaissance Society Of America, NY).
Anglo, Sydney. *Chivalry in the Renaissance*. (Woodbridge; Boydell Press, 1990).
Anglo, Sydney. *The Martial Arts of Renaissance Europe*. (Yale University Press, UK 2000).
Ascham, Roger. *The Scholemater*. (Da Capo Press, NY, 1968).
Aylward, J.D. *The Small-Sword in England its History, its Forms, its Makers, and its Masters*. (Hutchinson of London, London, 1945).
Baldick, Robert. **The Duel - A History of Dueling.** (Spring Books, 1965).
Barber, Richard and Juliet Barker. *Tournaments - Jousts, Chivalry, and Pageants in the Middle Ages*. (The Boydell Press, UK 1989).
Berry, Herbert. *The Noble Science, a Study and Transcription of Sloane MS. 2530, Papers of the Masters of Defence of London, Temp. Henry VIII to 1590*. (Associated University Presses, London, 1991).
Billacois, Francois. *The Duel Its Rise and Fall in Early Modern France*. (Yale University Press, New Haven and London 1990).
Bosquett, Abraham. *A Treatise on Dueling together with the Annals of Chivalry- the Ordeal and judicial Combat from Earliest Times*. (London, H. Scofield, 1818).
Bryson, Frederick R. *The Sixteenth-Century Italian Duel – A study in Renaissance Social History*. (University of Chicago Press. 1938).
Burton, Richard F. *The Sentiment of the Sword: A Country-House Dialogue, Part I*, Edited, with Notes, by A. Forbes Seiveking. (London, Horace Cox, 1911).
Castiglione, Baldesar. *The Book of the Courtier*. Translated by George Bull. (Penguin Classics, 1967).
Clephan, R. Coltman. *The Mediaeval Tournament*. (Dover Edition, New York, 1995).
Craig, W. J. ed. *The Complete Works of William Shakespeare*. (London, Oxford University Press, 1914).
Cripps-Day, Francis Henry. Harleian MS. 69 fo. I, as cited in Appendix IV, p. xxiv. *The History of the Tournament in England and in France*. (Bernard Quartrich Ltd. London 1918).
Davies, William Shears. *Life in Elizabethan Days*. Harper & Brothers. (UK, London, 1930).
Davis, Robert C. *The War of the Fists – Popular Culture and Public Violence in Late Renaissance Venice*. (Oxford University Press. 1994).
Dillon Viscount. "On a MS Collection of ordinances of Chivalry of the Fifteenth Century", in "Archaeology" (#57. I, 190029-70).
Educational Writings of John Locke. Edited by John William Adamson. (Cambridge University Press, 1922).
Elyot, Thomas. *The Boke named The Governour*. (J. M. Dent & Co, London, 1531).
Fabris, Salvator. *De lo Schermo Overo Scienza D'Arme*. (Copenhagen 1606, Translation by A. F. Johnson).
Greenshields, Malcolm. *An Economy of Violence in Early Modern France Crime and Justice in the Haute Auvergne, 1587-1664*. (The Pennsylvania State University Prewss, University Park,

Pennsylvania. 1994).

Hale, J. R. *The Military Education of the Officer Class in Renaissance War Studies.* (Hambledon Press, London, 1983).

Halliday, Hugh A. *Murder Among Gentlemen – A History of a Dueling in Canada.* (Robin Brass Studio, Toronto, 1999).

Hope, William. *A New Short, and Easy Method of Fencing.* (Edinburgh, 1707).

Hutton, Alfred. *Sword and the Centuries*, London, 1901. (Barnes & Noble reprint, 1995).

Lonnergan, A. *The Fencer's Guide; Being a Series of every Branch required to compose A Complete System of Defence.* (London, W. Griffin, 1771).

Lucas-Dubreton, J. *Daily Life in Florence.* (Translated from the French by A. Lytton Sells. MacMillian, NY, 1961).

Luxon, Thomas H., Ed. *The Milton Reading Room.* (http://www.dartmouth.edu/~milton, March, 1997).

Matthey, Cyril G. R. *The Works of George Silver.* (George Bell and Sons. London, 1898).

Medieval Knighthood V, Papers from the Fifth Strawberry Hill Conference 1990. (Edt. By Christopher Harper-Bill and Ruth Harvey. Boydell Press, UK, 1992).

Millingen, J. G.. *The History of Dueling.* (Vol. II, 1841, R. Bentley, London).

Newark, Timothy. *Medieval Warfare.* (Jupiter Books Ltd., London, 1979).

Parkyns, Thomas. *The Inn-Play: Or Cornish-Hugg Wrestler.* (London, 1727).

Petter, Nicolaes. *Clear Instructions to the Excellent Art of Wrestling.* (Reprinted in Amsterdam by Johannes Janssonius Van Waesberge. Anno 1674).

Puttenham, George. *The Arte of English Poesie.* (Scholar Press, Menston, 1968. Scholar Press facsimile of the 1569 edition).

Quintino, Antonio. *Gioielo di sapienza.* (Milan, 1613).

Riverside Chaucer. (Ed. L. D. Benson, Oxford, 1988).

Rowe, F. Brooking. *Manyly Peeke of Tavistock.* (William Brendon and Son, Plymouth, England, 1879).

Silver, George. *Paradoxes of Defence.* (Unpublished, 1598. Shakespeare Association Facsimile No. 6, Oxford University Press, 1933).

Swetnam, Joseph. *Schoole of the Noble and Worthy Science of Defence*, Nicholas Oaks, London, 1617.

"Story of Swordsmanship, The". in *The Illustrated London News.* (March 7, 1891).

Thimm, Carl. *A Complete Bibliography of Fencing and Dueling.* (London, 1896, Pelican Press edition, 1998).

Truman, Ben C. *The Field of Honor: Being A Complete and Comprehensive History of Dueling in All Countries; Including the Judicial Duel of Europe, the Private Duel of the Civilised World, and Specific Descriptions of All the Noted Hostile Meetings in Europe and America.* (Fords, Howard, & Hulbert, NY, 1883).

Vadi, Filippo. *De arte gladiatoria dimicandi.* (Urbino (?) c. 1482-87)

Notes

[1] *Riverside Chaucer.* (ed. L. D. Benson, Oxford, 1988). Line 740.

[2] Sydney Anglo. *The Martial Arts of Renaissance Europe.* (Yale University Press, UK 2000) p. 173.

[3] In the late 15th century *Freydal de Kaisers Maximilian I* (*Turnier und Mummereien*, ed. Quirin von Leiter, Vienna, 1880), the Emperor Maximilian I himself is shown using his feet to expertly kick, stomp, and trip his opponents in friendly bouts.

[4] Timothy Newark. *Medieval Warfare.* (Jupiter Books Ltd., London, 1979) p. 63.

[5] R. Coltman Clephan. *The Mediaeval Tournament.* (Dover Edition, New York, 1995) p. 82.

[6] Viscount Dillon. "On a MS Collection of ordinances of Chivalry of the Fifteenth Century". (Archaeology 57. I, 190029-70).

[7] Francis Henry Cripps-Day. Harleian MS. 69 fo. I, as cited in Appendix IV, p. xxiv. *The History of the Tournament in England and in France.* (Bernard Quartrich Ltd. London 1918), p. 123. "Tournay" it should be noted however, usually referred to mounted combat.

[8] Harleian MS. 69 fo. I, as cited in Appendix VI, p. xlv. *The History of the Tournament in England and in France.* (Francis Henry Cripps-Day. Bernard Quartrich Ltd. London 1918).

[9] Sydney Anglo. *The Great Tournament Roll of Westminster. Acollotype Reproduction of the Manuscript.* (Clarendon Press, Oxford, 1968) p. 43.

[10] George Puttenham. *The Arte of English Poesie.* (Scholar Press facsimile of the 1569 edition, 1968) p. 206.

[11] Francis Henry Cripps-Day. *The History of the Tournament in England and in France.* (Bernard Quartrich Ltd. London 1918) p. 123

[12] Cripps-Day, Ibid. Bryson cites a formal duel from the early 1500's sanctioned by the Grand Duke Alphonso I in Ferrara, Italy, where (in an obvious effort to prevent such actions) the challenged party attempted to wear armor with sharp projections at places where one would typically try to grab and take hold. In response, the Duke summoned a smith to file down the sharp points on grounds it was not the proper manner of armor worn by knights in war and thus should not be allowed. Frederick R. Bryson. *The Sixteenth-Century Italian Duel – A study in Renaissance Social History.* (University of Chicago Press. 1938) p. 49.

[13] It is perhaps worth noting that in the *mostre* boxing duels of the Venetian *guerre di pugni* during the early 1600s, "Grappling and wrestling were condemned less as unfair fighting than as a coward's way of avoiding his rival's punches; when

a duelist would not allow himself to be turned into a beast." Robert C. Davis. *The War of the Fists – Popular Culture and Public Violence in Late Renaissance Venice.* (Oxford University Press. 1994) p. 70.

[14] *Medieval Knighthood V, Papers from the Fifth Strawberry Hill Conference 1990.* (Edt. By Christopher Harper-Bill and Ruth Harvey. Boydell Press, UK, 1992) p. 135.

[15] Baldesar Castiglione. *The Book of the Courtier.* (Translated by George Bull, Penguin Classics, 1967) p. 62. Castiglione's *Il Cortagio* was originally published in 1528.

[16] *Sir Thomas Elyot, The Boke named The Governour.* (J. M. Dent & Co, London, 1531, Chapter XVII) p. I3r.

[17] Roger Ascham. *The Scholemater.* (Da Capo Press, NY, 1968) p. 19-20.

[18] From Chapter I, *Of Custom, And That We Should Not Easily Change A Law Received.*

[19] Sydney Anglo. *The Martial Arts of Renaissance Europe.* (Yale University Press, UK 2000) p. 29.

[20] William Shears Davies. *Life in Elizabethan Days.* (Harper & Brothers, London, 1930) p. 245.

[21] J. R. Hale, *The Military Education of the Officer Class in Renaissance War Studies.* (Hambledon Press, London, 1983) p. 238.

[22] J. Lucas-Dubreton. *Daily Life in Florence,* Translated from the French by A. Lytton Sells. (MacMillian, NY, 1961) p. 111.

[23] J. R. Hale, *The Military Education of the Officer Class in Renaissance War Studies.* (Hambledon Press, London, 1983) p. 231.

[24] Luxon, Thomas H., ed. *The Milton Reading Room,* http://www.dartmouth.edu/~milton, March, 1997.

[25] Sydney Anglo. *The Martial Arts of Renaissance Europe.* (Yale University Press, UK 2000) p. 175-176.

[26] Sydney Anglo. *The Martial Arts of Renaissance Europe.* (Yale University Press, UK 2000) p. 273-274.

[27] Frederick R. Bryson. *The Sixteenth-Century Italian Duel – A study in Renaissance Social History.* (University of Chicago Press. 1938) p. 50.

[28] For at least nine convenient examples of this see Sydney Anglo. *The Martial Arts of Renaissance Europe.* (Yale University Press, UK 2000) p. 25, 38, 80, 275, 277, 302, and 303.

[29] Frederick R. Bryson. *The Sixteenth-Century Italian Duel – A study in Renaissance Social History.* (University of Chicago Press. 1938) p. 183.

[30] Malcolm Greenshields, *An Economy of Violence in Early Modern France Crime and Justice in the Haute Auvergne, 1587-1664.* (The Pennsylvania State University Prewss, University Park, Pennsylvania. 1994) p. 95.

[31] Billacois, Francois, *The Duel Its Rise and Fall in Early Modern France.* (Yale University Press, New Haven and London 1990) p. 195.

[32] J. R. Hale, *The Military Education of the Officer Class in Renaissance War Studies.* (Hambledon Press, London, 1983) p. 236.

[33] Anglo points out that by 1612, Jacob Sutor's version of Meyer's teachings included only a vestigial presence of unarmed techniques in swordplay. See Sydney Anglo. *The Martial Arts of Renaissance Europe.* (Yale University Press, UK 2000) p. 190.

[34] Aylward, J.D. *The Small-Sword in England its History, its Forms, its Makers, and its Masters.* (Hutchinson of London, London, 1945) p. 127. One humane consequence of using such actions would also be perhaps to disable an opponent without killing him.

[35] Sydney Anglo. *The Martial Arts of Renaissance Europe.* (Yale University Press, UK 2000) p. 172.

[36] Alfred Hutton, *The Sword and the Centuries.* (London, 1901. Barnes & Noble reprint, 1995) p. 33.

[37] Sydney Anglo. *Chivalry in the Renaissance.* (Woodbridge; Boydell Press, 1990) p. 10, citing Brantôme.

[38] Robert Baldick. **The Duel - A History of Dueling.** (Spring Books, 1965,) p. 53.

[39] Alfred Hutton, *The Sword and the Centuries.* (London, 1901. Barnes & Noble reprint, 1995) p. 148.

[40] J. G. Millingen. *The History of Dueling,* Vol. II. (R. Bentley, London, 1841, p. 27-28).

[41] Joseph Swetnam. *Schoole of the Noble and Worthy Science of Defence.* (Nicholas Oaks, London, 1617) p. 127-128.

[42] George Silver. *Paradoxes of Defence.* Unpublished 1599 (Shakespeare Association Facsimile No. 6, Oxford University Press, edition 1933) p. 25.

[43] George Silver, *Paradoxes of Defence,* Unpublished 1599 (Shakespeare Association Facsimile No. 6, Oxford University Press, edition 1933) Section 3, p. 33.

[44] George Silver, *Paradoxes of Defence,* Unpublished 1599 (Shakespeare Association Facsimile No. 6, Oxford University Press, edition 1933) p.24.

[45] George Silver, *Paradoxes of Defence,* Unpublished 1599 (Shakespeare Association Facsimile No. 6, Oxford University Press, edition 1933) p.47.

[46] George Silver, *Paradoxes of Defence,* Unpublished 1599 (Shakespeare Association Facsimile No. 6, Oxford University Press, edition 1933) p.47-48.

[47] Alfred Hutton, *The Sword and the Centuries.* (London, 1901.

Barnes & Noble reprint, 1995) p. 169.

[48]George Silver, *Paradoxes of Defence*, Unpublished 1599 (Shakespeare Association Facsimile No. 6, Oxford University Press, edition 1933) p. 50.

[49] Translation by Dr. Jeffrey Singman, November 2000. Work forthcoming.

[50] *So arbayt in der versatzung behentlich fur dich mitt dem schwert von ainer blöss zu der anderen; so mag er vor deiner arbayt zu seinen stucken nicht kommen.Aber laufft er dir eynn, so komme vor mitt dem ringen.*(Wierschin Munchen 1965 p.99). English translation by David Lindholm & Peter Svärd, 2001, work forthcoming.

[51] Gathered from World Wide Web, E-book edition. http://www.bookrags.com/books/orfur/PART37.htm.

[52] The application of the empty second hand to seize the opponent's blade, hilt, arm, or body to trip or hold (not to mention strike a blow) is itself so frequently depicted in Renaissance fencing manuals as to require a separate article.

[53] Sydney Anglo. *The Martial Arts of Renaissance Europe*. (Yale University Press, UK 2000) p. 171.

[54] Sydney Anglo. *The Martial Arts of Renaissance Europe*. (Yale University Press, UK 2000) p. 181. Heredia's illustrations of rapier fights in his *Tratado de la armas* include several effective close-in actions that hark back to similar techniques that can be seen illustrated in the work of Marozzo in 1536 and even to Fiore Dei Liberi in 1410. See Anglo, pages 302 and 303 for plates of Heredia.

[55] See Matthey, G. R. *The Works of George Silver*, 1598, edited with an Introduction by Cyril G. R. Matthey, George Bell and Sons, London, 1898.

[56] Sydney Anglo. *The Martial Arts of Renaissance Europe*. (Yale University Press, UK 2000) p. 80.

[57] George Silver, *Paradoxes of Defence*, Unpublished 1599 (Shakespeare Association Facsimile No. 6, Oxford University Press, edition 1933) p. 65-66.

[58] Jay P. Anglin. "The Schools of Defense in Elizabethan London". in *Renaissance Quarterly* (Vol. XXXVII No. 3, AUTUMN, 1984. Renaissance Society Of America, NY) p. 410.

[59] F. Brooking Rowe, *Manyly Peeke of Tavistock*. (William Brendon and Son, Plymouth, England, 1879) p. 7 & 15.

[60] "*Cosi parimenti haueuamo in animo di non trattare d'altro, che della punta, & del taglio, parendoci, che chi sapra con quelle diffendersi, & offendere in tempo non douesse hauere di bisogno, ne di lotte ne di prese.*" Salvator Fabris, *De lo Schermo Overo Scienza D'Arme*. (Copenhagen 1606, Translation by A.F. Johnson) p. 244,

[61] Ibid, page 12.

[62] To be balanced, there is evidence close-in techniques were excluded from the German Fechtschulen events of the 1500s where, in order to perform safe displays, rules were in place to prevent such techniques. Similarly, the 1573 Sloane Manuscript 2530 of the London Masters of Defence states that in Prize Playing events "who soever dothe play agaynst ye prizor, and doth strike his blowe and close withall so that the prizor cannot strike his blowe after agayne, shall Wynn no game for anny Veneye". (Herbert Berry. The Noble Science, a Study and Transcription of Sloane MS. 2530, Papers of the Masters of Defence of London, Temp. Henry VIII to 1590. Associated University Presses, London, 1991), p 73. Yet, the obvious implication is that while close-in techniques of closing and seizing were effective and understood, they were inappropriate for public display intended to safely showcase a student's skill at defending and delivering blows.

[63] Its true authorship is obscure. Titled in English: "Advertisements necessary for defending oneself against an enemy in many ways, according to various accidents which might occur. Added thereunto also the way to keep yourself safe from many harmful animals...Collected by Giovanni Briccio, Roman. And brought to light by Lorenzo Leandro, Venetian." Viterbo, 1613. It was first printed in Genoa. Carl Thimm also under a "Boiccio" lists the work as edited by one Antonio Quintino and entitled, *Gioielo di sapienza* or "Jewel of Wisdom in which are contained wonderful secrets and necessary advertisements for defending oneself against men and many animals...." (Milan, 1613). Carl Thimm. *A Complete Bibliography of Fencing and Dueling*. (London, 1896, pelican Press edition, 1998) p, 33.

[64] Sydney Anglo. Personal correspondence with the author, September 23, 2001.

[65] Burton, *The Sentiment of the Sword: A Country-House Dialogue, Part I*. Edited, with Notes, by A. Forbes Seiveking. (London, Horace Cox, 1911) p. 104.

[66] Hugh A. Halliday. *Murder Among Gentlemen – A History of a Dueling in Canada*. (Robin Brass Studio, Toronto, 1999) p. 10.

[67] *Educational Writings of John Locke*. (edited by John William Adamson, Cambridge University Press, 1922) p. 199.

[68] Sydney Anglo. *The Martial Arts of Renaissance Europe*. (Yale University Press, UK 2000) p. 176.

[69] *A Treatise on Dueling together with the Annals of Chivalry- the Ordeal and judicial Combat from Earliest Times*. Abraham Bosquett, Esq. (London, H. Scofield, 1818) p. 45.

[70] Alfred Hutton, *The Sword and the Centuries*. (London, 1901. Barnes & Noble reprint, 1995) p. 224.

[71] Sir William Hope, *A New Short, and Easy Method of Fencing*. (Edinburgh, 1707). This is Hope's rule XIII from the fold out sheet included in the book, no page number.

[72] Ibid, p. 141.

[73] Ibid, p. 84.

[74] Ibid. This quote from Hope's rules for the salle was part of an unnumbered fold-out plate in his *New Method*. The entire quote reads as: "XIII. Upon commanding no struggling is to be allowed to the person commanded, after his fleuret is once cacht hold of, nor tripping to the person commanding, after he is master of it; Because, however allowable such active and nimble defences may be upon a pinch at sharps, yet in a school assault, all such kind of struling betwixt scholars is rude and undecent."

[75] Sir Thomas Parkyns, *The Inn-Play: Or Cornish-Hugg Wrestler.* (London, 1727) p. 33.

[76] Parkyns, Ibid, p. 33.

[77] A. Lonnergan, *The Fencer's Guide; Being a Series of every Branch required to compose A Complete System of Defence.* (London, W. Griffin, 1771) p. 217.

[78] Sydney Anglo. *The Martial Arts of Renaissance Europe.* (Yale University Press, UK 2000) p. 37.

[79] Sydney Anglo. *The Martial Arts of Renaissance Europe.* (Yale University Press, UK 2000) p. 176.

[80] Richard Barber and Juliet Barker, *Tournaments - Jousts, Chivalry, and Pageants in the Middle Ages.* (The Boydell Press, UK 1989) p. 211.

[81] Major Ben C. Truman. *The Field of Honor: Being A Complete and Comprehensive History of Dueling in All Countries; Including the Judicial Duel of Europe, the Private Duel of the Civilised World, and Specific Descriptions of All the Noted Hostile Meetings in Europe and America.* (Fords, Howard, & Hulbert, NY, 1883) p. 226.

[82] When exploring the use of grappling and wrestling grappling actions in our modern Renaissance fencing practice, we can reasonably surmise that of three or four actions a Master may have included in his work, each can have multiple applications and variations. Since in the process of practicing them several obvious alternatives easily make themselves evident, it would be reasonable to surmise these few fundamental techniques were not meant to be the only ones he knew or the only one he considered viable. The theoretical instructions of masters must after all be somewhat balanced with the historical accounts of actual combats.

[83] *Clear Instructions to the Excellent Art of Wrestling, Teaching how one can defend oneself in all occurrences of violence, and how to counter all grips, pushes, punches &c. Most useful against troublemakers and those seeking to offend others, or that threaten one with a knife. Developed by the very famous and well-known wrestler Nicolaes Petter.* Reprinted in Amsterdam by Johannes Janssonius Van Waesberge. Anno 1674.

[84] Interestingly, some schools and masters were still teaching grips and seizures up to the 19th century. Against a lighter, shorter blade, these actions are indeed harder to effect, but that only meant a swordsman would have to be careful in the attempt -which was true with earlier weapons, as well.

[85] "The Story of Swordsmanship", in *The Illustrated London News.* (March 7, 1891) p. 299.

[86] Sydney Anglo. *The Martial Arts of Renaissance Europe.* (Yale University Press, UK 2000) p. 274.

[87] Personal correspondence with the author, August 2001.

[88] For example, since its beginnings ARMA (The Association for Renaissance Martial Arts) has in its study emphasized seizures, disarms, grappling, and close entering actions as crucial, vital, and integral elements in all historical armed combat, including rapier. Our approach has been that these actions were real, they were historical, and they worked and were used by all manners of fighters from all classes of society. In our modern practice now we believe we must not suppress them, ignore them, or make excuses for our ignorance of them because they do not somehow fit a preconceived notion of how "proper" fencing (whether Medieval or Renaissance) should have been conducted. Instead, we must expose them, explore them, and try to master them. Our perspective is that of training and instructing. Hence, our purpose is to interpret and reconstruct this subject as a martial art and to train in these skills as if they were really intended to be used.

[89] Burton, *The Sentiment of the Sword: A Country-House Dialogue, Part I.* Edited, with Notes, by A. Forbes Seiveking. (London, Horace Cox, 1911) p. 70.

[90] *Filippo Vadi "De arte gladiatoria dimicandi ("About the Gladiatorial Art of Fighting").* Urbino (?) 1482-87, Codice della Biblioteca Nazionale di Roma, Fondo Vittorio Emanuele, Codice 1324. Parzialmente ripubblicato in Bascetta, Carlo ; Sport e giuochi : trattati e scritti dal XV al XVIII secolo a cura di Carlo Bascetta; Milano : Il Polifilo, 1978, a cui rimandiamo per un buon apparato di note terminologiche e lessicali sul testo. Translation by Luca Porzio. Personal Correspondence. Cap. XV. "Ti poi adoprar ancor in questa arte, ferrire e strette che te sien più destre, lassa la più sinestre, tiente a quel che la man te dà favore, che spesso te farà ne l'arte onore."

[91] Craig, W.J., ed. *The Complete Works of William Shakespeare.* (London: Oxford University Press: 1914; Bartleby.com, 2000. www.bartleby.com/70/).

FOUNDATIONS OF ITALIAN RAPIER

ByWilliam E. Wilson

The main focus of this paper is to introduce the reader to the early 16th C rapier combat of Achille Marozzo. As a full discussion of Marozzo's techniques can fill a book, this paper will touch upon the guards of Marozzo and a few other supporting topics.

According to Maestro Andrea Lupo-Sinclair, one of the weapons used during Marozzo's time period was called the *Spada da Lato* in Italian (sidesword), rapier in English, and was primarily a cutting weapon.[1] In the early 16th C in Italy, Achille Marozzo wrote his *Opera Nova*, a fencing manual that covered a number of different types of weapons, only one being the sidesword. This is the earliest surviving manuscript of its type and is very important as it is the first known treatise covering civilian use of weapons. A number of editions of his book were published under two different titles, *Opera Nova*[2] and *Arte dell' Armi*.[3] The book is divided into five sections: section one and two deal with the sword (*spada sola*) alone or used in conjunction with the dagger (*pugnale*), round shield (*rotella*), square buckler (*targa*), round buckler (*brochiero*), or cloak (*cappa*). Section three deals with the spadone, a two handed sword. Section four is devoted to pole type weapons that include the pike, partisan, voulge and poleaxe. Section five covers the philosophy of fighting and the duel.[4]

Castle considers Marozzo "the greatest teacher of the old school."[5] This old school was founded by Master Filippo (or Lippo) di Bartolomeo Bardi (Neppo Bardi) at Bologna. Bardi was not only a fencing master but also an astrologer and mathematician. He wrote a book on the relations between fencing and geometry, which has subsequently been lost. He died in 1464, and one of his best scholars was Guido Antonio di Luca, Marozzo's Master. Other students of di Luca included

Manciolino, Altoni and possibly dall'Agocchie (who later went on to write a fencing manual that is helpful in understanding Marozzo).[6]

The sidesword (*spada da lato*) was primarily a cutting weapon although the use of the point was also taught. Maestro William Gaugler describes this sword as having a short grip, a large, spherical pommel, crossbar (*quillon*), and a long slender blade that tapered to a point.[7] Arthur Wise on the other hand described the sword as heavy and ill-balanced.[8] Maestro Andrea Lupo Sinclair of Italy describes the sword as being a light and agile weapon. The sword was long, approximately half the height of the fencer (the quillons at the hip with the tip of the sword on the ground). The width of the blade at the ricasso was approximately 3 cm.[9] In my own studies of sideswords from the Howard de Walden Collection at Dean Castle in Scotland and the Royal Museum of Scotland in Edinburgh, I agree with Maestro Sinclair that the sidesword is a very agile weapon that is easily wielded. The sideswords that I examined weighed approximately one kilogram (2.2 pounds) and had blade lengths from 85 to 96.5 centimeters (33.5-38 inches).[10]

To begin I will quote from Marozzo, Capitula 137, Castle translation:

"I wish thee to make thy scholar practice these things – the cuts and parries in the form of counter attacks – during four or five days with thee. As soon as he knows them well, I wish thee to begin and examine him in every guard, but especially in those of Porta di ferro larga, stretta, o alta, also in Coda lunga e stretta. This thou shalt do as in a combat with sword and target or shield or buckler, or with the sword alone. Let this indicate to thee that in teaching a scholar to play with any of the above weapons, thou must make him understand all these guards, one by one, step by step, with their attacks and parries and everything pro and contra. Thou shalt see in these writings, and in the figures therein to be found – and therefore do not fail to succeed in teaching the same – that I make no difference in the guards on account of the weapons. But, in order not to cover too much space and to avoid repitition, I explain them merely in connection with the sword alone, or with the sword and buckler.[11]"

Marozzo instructed in technique on the primary cuts and thrusts used during the period. He also taught a number of guard positions. I will cover the cuts and the guards.

The cuts were described in far more detail than the thrusts. Marozzo categorized the cuts as *mandritti* and *roversi*. The *mandritti* were cuts delivered from the right and the *roversi* from the left. Both were issued with the right (also known as true) edge (dritto filo). Some of the cuts were delivered with the false or back edge of the blade. The cuts with the right edge were subdivided by the general angle of attack:

> **Tondo**: A circular cut delivered horizontally
> **Sgualembrato**: An oblique downwards cut
> **Fendente**: A vertical downwards cut
> **Montante**: A vertical upwards cut
> **Redoppio**: An oblique upwards cut

As noted previously cuts could also be delivered with the false or back edge of the blade. Marozzo called cuts with the false edge from the right falso dritto and from the left *falso manco*.[12] As far as attacks go, Marozzo said "And I tell you again that you must never attack without defending, nor defend without attacking, and if you do this you shall not fail.[13]" (Author's translation). The cut diagram from *Arte dell' Armi* is given from the perspective of the one issuing the cut. Other manuals that have similar cut diagrams show it from the perspective of the target.[14]

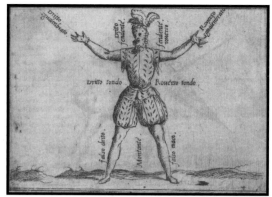

Fig. 1: Marozzo's cutting diagram

Although the term parry was used, no actual parries are defined. According to Castle all attacks were to be countered with a counter-attack or a displacement of the body or else they were to be warded with a buckler, cloak or dagger.[15] This being the case, Marozzo's guard positions are not parries but more invitations or positions to launch an attack from. The parries consisted of blocks with the false edge (weapon in same line of attack), beats and expulsions.[16]

Foot movement was used to maintain a proper fighting distance from an opponent. A number of specific steps were noted and others can be inferred from Marozzo's text. The following is a list of the steps with brief descriptions:[17]

> **Passo**: A simple step. The feet do not pass by each other with this step. Similar to a classical advance and retreat.
> **Passata**: A passing step where one foot passes by the other.
> **Inquartata**: A circular step where the back foot makes a quarter circle behind the forward foot.
> **Intagliata**: An angular step to the left when starting with the right foot foremost.
> **Mezzo passo**: A sideways step to the right or left.
> **Gran passo**: A large step used when making an attack. It may almost be considered a demi-lunge.

Sidesword combat should flow smoothly with the combatants moving from guard to guard, blades engaged at times and moving with absence of blade at others. The different guards must be learned and internalized so that they are used subconsciously to close lines and to provide invitations.

Marozzo showed through illustrations and text some fifteen guards. These guards were described with the single sword or with the sword and buckler. I group his guards into six series: *coda lunga*, *porta di ferro*, *cinghiara*, *guardia alta*, *guardia di faccia*, and *becca*.[18] Each member of a series may be more advantageous for defense or for preparing to launch an attack. The low guards are invitations from middle distance. These guards are useful for determining your opponent's skill. The high guards are invitations to attack in time, counterattack or attack with disengagements. It is my opinion that the sidesword is a weapon to be used with binding actions and actions with the blade. Certain guards like the *coda lunga e stretta*, *porta di ferro e stretta* and the *becca cesa* may be made with engagement of the blade (blades touching) and narrower distance between the fencers than say the *guardia alta* or the *coda lunga e distesa* where there will be absence of blade (blades not touching) and wider distance.

The illustrations used in this paper are from the 1568 edition of Marozzo's *Arte dell' Armi*.

The Coda Lunga Series

Four guards comprise this series: *coda lunga e stretta*, *coda lunga e alta*, *coda lunga e larga*, and *coda lunga e distesa*.

In Chapter 138 of *Opera Nova* Marozzo said "You will set your student with the right leg forward and his sword and buckler straight towards his enemy and place the right hand just outside the right knee, with the wrist towards the ground as in the illustration[19]." This is the general position of the hand for the coda lunga series, just outside the right knee.[20]

At times Marozzo is difficult to understand. Luckily for scholars of historical fencing another master of the time, *Dall'Agocchie*, helped to describe and define what Marozzo was teaching. Giovanni Rapisardi in his paper *Teachings of Marozzo* gives a number of translations of Agocchie's text which you may refer to for further information.[21]

Coda Lunga e Stretta

"Let thy scholar stand with the right leg foremost, with the sword and the target well out, and see that his right hand be well outside his right knee with the thumb turned downwards as may be seen in the figure. This is called the coda lunga e stretta, and is meant for striking and parrying. The scholar being in this guard, thou wilt show him how many attacks he can therefrom being agent, and how many parries with the shield he can perform as patient, from above and from below, and likewise their variations one from the other. Thou wilt also show him the parries against his own attacks."[22]

The hand is basically in pronation, the Italian second hand position, and the right leg is forward. This is a defensive posture that also allows for the launching of a number of cuts or thrusts.

Fig. 2: *Marozzo's* Coda Lunga e Stretta

Coda Lunga e Alta

"I wish thee to know that, when remaining patiente, this is a good guard, and most useful, and accordingly advise thee to tell thy pupil that he had better assume this guard on the defensive, and make him understand all that can be done on it, pro and contra...."[23]

This guard is the same as the *coda lunga e stretta* except that the left leg is forward. This is a defensive guard, especially when using a defensive device such as a buckler as it places the buckler extended out in front of your body.

Fig. 3:
Marozzo's Guardia di Coda Longa e Alta

Fig. 4:
Marozzo's Guardia di Coda Lunga e Larga

Coda Lunga e larga

"Take notice that on this guard thou canst both assault and defend, for it is possible to use the false edge from the left, and to cut tramazone with both right or false edge, or tramazone roverso, or false filo tondo, or roverso sgualembrato, by turning the sword to its proper place. Likewise thou canst deliver thrusts from the right or left, with or without feints, and all the roversi that belong to them, &c..."[24]

This guard is made with the right leg forward and the sword low with the hand held outside and behind the right knee. The point of the sword is lower than the guard and is trained in the general direction of your opponent. It is a good position to defend as well as attack.

Coda Lunga e Distesa

"Being on this guard you will cause him to be agente, especially with dritti falsi, or with the point, with roversi, and such other attacks, as can be derived from the said guard. Thou must also teach him the parries thereto, since the art of striking is

but little in comparison with a knowledge of the parries, which a fine and more useful thing."[25]

This guard was taught as early as by Fiore de' Liberi in his treatise on two-handed sword.[26] The guard is an offensive guard in that you are set like a spring ready to strike. The stance is made with the left leg forward and the weapon trailing behind as in the illustration.

Fig. 5:
Marozzo's Guardia di Coda Lunga Distesa

The Porta di Ferro Series

Dall'Agocchie describes this guard as an iron door that is very hard to smash down[27]. This is one of the base guards that Marozzo indicates to use as a starting guard[28]. The standard porta di ferro is made with the right foot forward and the right hand held with the hand over the right knee.

The palm of the hand faces left. There are three variants to the *porta di ferro* series: *porta di ferro e stretta*, *porta di ferro larga*, and *porta di ferro alta*.

Porta di Ferro e Stretta

This guard is made by leading with the right foot and positioning the right hand above the right knee. I use this guard as a base ward for novice fencers as it it possible to launch a number of different cuts and thrust from this guard.

Fig. 6:
Marozzo's Guardia di Porta Ferro e Stretta

Fig. 7:
Marozzo's Guardia di Porta Ferro e Alta

Porta di Ferro Alta

Alta variant is made by raising the hand slightly as may be seen in the illustration. This guard may be more aptly used as an ending position resulting from a thrust delivered from the right.

The *Cinghiara Porta di Ferro* Series

The cinghiara (wild boar) porta di ferro is made with the left foot forward and the right hand inside, over the left knee. This guard is called the wild boar since the wild boar does not attack in a straight line with its fangs[29].

Cuts and thrusts from the left side may most easily be delivered from this guard.

Fig. 8:
Marozzo's Cinghiara Porta di Ferro

Guardia Alta Series

I group two guards into this series as they both are made with the point high and the hand at head level or above. These are the guardia alta proper and the guardia di testa.

Guardia Alta

I consider this guard a very offensive guard in that you stand ready to strike if your opponent approaches. From this guard you may make strong cuts in a downward direction. You may also easily counter attack your opponent's arm in conjunction with a backwards step if they thrust at your body. Marozzo said the following:

> "Thy scholar being placed on that guard, thou wilt show him how many cuts are derived therefrom, carefully remarking that this guard is meant chiefly for the attack."[30]

This guard may be made with either the right or left foot forward. The sword is held high above the head ready to strike.

Fig. 9:
Marozzo's
Guardia Alta

Guardia di testa

"In this head guard one can be both agente and patiente, but I shall first speak of defense. If any one should cut at him with a mandrtitto fendente or sgualembrato, or a tramazone, thou wilt make him parry in head guard, and then from this guard to pass to the attack; he can do so with a thrust from the right over the hand, or a mandritto fendente, or tondo, or sgualembrato, or falso dritto. From this head guard, thou wilt make him proceed with a thrust from the left in his adversary's face, and advance his left leg. . ."[31]

This guard is similar to an invitation in fifth in modern Italian fencing.[32] This guard is good for protecting the upper body. The guard may also be used for inviting an attack. In the event that your opponent makes a cut at your head you can parry in this position and follow it up with a point thrust over your opponent's hand ending up in the *guardia di intrare*.

Fig. 10:
Marozzo's Guardia di Testa

Guardia di Faccia Series

Guardia di Faccia

"Having made him assume this guardia di faccia, inform him that in this he can both assault and defend at the same time. On his adversary's cutting mandritto tondo, or fendente dritto, he should thrust at the same time at his face."[33]

This guard is made with the palm up and the arm extended out towards your opponent. This is a very imposing and offensive guard. With the point directed at the opponent's face and the arm extended you heavily threaten your adversary.

Fig. 11:
Marozzo's
Guardia Faccia

Guardia d'intrare

"On this guard one must be patiente, as few attacks can be made from it. . ."[34]

Even though Marozzo indicates that there are few attacks that may be made form this guard it can be used as an end position resulting from a counterattack resulting in a point thrust to the face with an oblique step to the left.

Fig. 12: *Marozzo's* Guardia Intrare

This guard is similar to the later broadsword hanging guard[37] that is used to protect the fencer from downward strokes but is made with the left leg forward.

Fig. 13: *Marozzo's* Becca Possa

Beca Cesa

"And the swordarm is held high and extended, turning the wrist outside and placing the point of the sword towards his face and the fist well extended; this is the becca cesa.[38]"

The becca cesa is similar to Fabris' guard[39] of 1st although with Fabris' style the arm is much more extended and with Marozzo the point of the sword is pointed more at the lower extremities of the opponent or the ground. Marozzo shows this guard in use when describing his circular combat in chapter 144. To quote:

"This is the sign, where you'll make your students walking on it, stepping back and forward, handling their weapons, turning around, putting their feet on the lines that cut the circle...[40]"

Becca Series
The etymology of these two guards is not clear. The term *becca* was used to describe a kind of baldic worn by medeival knights. The word *cessa* may have been derived from *caesa* meaning killed or defeated. *Possa* may be a derivation of possum, to be able or powerful. So, this guard may cross the body like a baldric on the strong and weak side.[35] *Becco* in modern Italian means beak. Another interpretation of the name may be a beaked position as in the upper part of a bird's beak.

Becca Possa

"Having thus examined thy scholar in every guard, I am of the opinion that on his assuming the becca possa, thou shouldst advise him to oppose it to his adversary whenever the latter assumes that of porta di ferro larga, or stretta, or alta, and to follow him step by step, and from guard to guard. That is, if the adversary goes in coda lunga e distesa he must go into becca cesa; . ."[36]

Conclusion

Marozzo's guards were meant to be used in combinations and in his treatise he moves a student from one guard to the next in progression.[41] Castle provides a translation of this section of Marozzo's book. The various cuts and thrusts should be practiced from the guard positions to gain expertise. Oppose your opponent's guard with one that will cover you best from attacks that

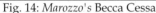

Fig. 14: *Marozzo's* Becca Cessa

Fig. 15: *Marozzo's Circle*

can be launched from his guard. When defending with the buckler, parry at an oblique angle so the cutting blade will slide outwards away from your body. When using the buckler against a thrust beat the blade forcefully aside with the buckler while at the same time delivering a counter thrust or cut. Always use footwork with your counter attack to gain a better angle and to not be where your opponent aimed their attack.

Marozzo's work is quite extensive. A comprehensive discussion of Marozzo's sidesword technique would be the subject of a whole book. Start your study by learning the guards and use them in your practice.

BIBLIOGRAPHY

Agocchie, Giovanni Dall'. *Dell' Arte Discrimia Libri Tre* (Venetia, 1622)

Brown, Terry. *English Martial Arts.* (Norfolk, 1997)

Castle, Egerton. *Schools and Masters of Fence from the Middle Ages to the 18th Century.* (London,1892)

Fabris, Salvatore. *Sienz e Practica d'Arme.* (Copenhagen, 1606)

Gaugler, William M. *The History of Fencing: Foundations of Modern European Swordplay.* (1998)

Gaugler, William. *The Science of Fencing.* (1997)

Hutton, Alfred. *The Sword and the Centuries.* (USA, 1995)

Hutton, Alfred. *Old Sword Play.* (London, 1892)

Liberi, Fiore di. *Flos Duellatorum.* (Getty, 1410)

Manciolino, Di Antonio. *Bolognese, opera nova dove sono tutti li documti e vantaggi che si ponno havere ne mestier de l'armi d'agni sorte, novemente correcta et stampata.* (Vinegia, 1531)

Marozzo, Achille. *Opera nova di achille Marozzo, Bolognese, Maestro Generale de l'arte de l'armi.* (Venetia, 1517)
Marozzo, Achille. *Arte dell' Armi.* (Venetia, 1568.)

Morton, E.D. *A-Z of Fencing.* (London)

Norman, V.B. *The Rapier and the small-sword,* 1460-1820. (London, 1980)

Novati, Francesco. *Flos duellatorum in armis, sine armis, equester, pedester; il fior di battaglia di maestro Fiore dei Liberi da Premariacco. Testo inedito del MCCCX publicato ed illustrato a cura di Francesco Novati; Bergamo Istituto Italiano d'Arti Grafiche.* (Italia, 1902)

Pendragon, Joshua. *Fencing: On the Science of Arms. A translation of De Lo Schermo, overo scienza d'arme. (Copenhagen: 1606) by A. F. Johnson.* (UK, In progress)

Rapisardi, Giovanni. *The Teachings of Marozzo.* (http://jan.ucc.nau.edu/~wew/other/gr/, 1999).

Thimm, Carl A. *A Complete Bibliography of Fencing & Dueling.* (New York, 1968).

Wise, Arthur. *The History and Art of Personal Combat.* (London, 1971)

(Footnotes)

[1] Andrea Lupo-Sincliar, Italian Sidesword Seminar, Lansing Swordfighting Convention, July 2001.

[2] Published in 1536, 1540, 1550, and 1568. Although Manciolino's manual was published earlier. It was Marozzo's manual that took off and was looked to as the basis of this style of combat.

[3] Published in 1568, 1615, and 1892.

[4] Although Marozzo's book is one of the only known surviving copy of its type, earlier manuscripts have been located from Italy as well as other countries that do cover swordplay and combat with other weapons. One of these is Flos Duellatorum by Fiore di Liberi. This manual covers unarmed, dagger, arming sword, longsword and armored combat. For more information on this fighting form you may go to http://www.aemma.org and look in the Knowledge Base.

[5] Egerton Castle. *Schools and Masters of Fence from the Middle Ages to the 18ᵗʰ Century.* (London, 1892) P. 48

[6] Francesco Novati. *Flos Duellatorum in armis, equester, pedester;* p. 108

[7] William Gaugler. *History of Fencing.* P. 2

[8] Arthur Wise. *History and Art of Personal Combat.* P. 36

[9] This information comes from personal communications with Maestro Andrea Lupo-Sinclair during 2001.

[10] I viewed the swords with Master Paul Macdonald of Edinburgh Scotland in June, 2001. As a representative sample here are the measurements of a sword from the Howard de Walden Collection: early 16ᵗʰ C. sidesword - overall length 40 1/8 inches (102cm) with a blade length of 33 ½ inches (85.1cm). The ricasso is 1 inch wide (2.5cm) and the shoulder of the sword is 1 3/8 inches (3.5cm). The balance point is 3 ½ inches (8.9cm) from the cross.

[11] Egerton Castle. *Schools and Masters of Fence from the Middle Ages to the 18ᵗʰ Century.* (London, 1892). P. 52. Achille Marozzo. *Arte dell' Armi.* Cap 137.

[12] Egerton Castle. *Schools and Masters of Fence from the Middle Ages to the 18ᵗʰ Century.* (London, 1892). P. 49

[13] Achille Marozzo. *Arte dell' Armi.* Cap 2. "Et anchora te dico, che tu non gli dia mai ferire senza il suo parato, et cosi parato senza il suo ferire, et se cosi farai non portrai fallire."

[14] For example Salvator Fabris. *Sienz e Practica d'Arme.* (Copenhagen, 1606). p. 30.

[15] Egerton Castle. *Schools and Masters of Fence from the Middle Ages to the 18ᵗʰ Century.* (London, 1892) P.50

[16] Andrea Lupo-Sinclair. *Italian Sidesword Seminar.* Lansing Swordfighting Convention. July 2001; Egerton Castle. *Schools and Masters of Fence from the Middle Ages to the 18ᵗʰ Century. (London, 1892)* p. 50

[17] Andrea Lupo-Sinclair. *Italian Sidesword Seminar.* Lansing Swordfighting Convention. July 2001.

[18] I follow Giovanni Rapisardi's example in collapsing the guards into groupings although I group them in a slightly different fashion. See the bibliographic entry for Rapisardi to view his work on the world wide web. In this paper I will touch upon the most well described of Marozzo's guards.

[19] Marozzo. *Arte dell' Armi, 1568, Cap. 138.* Giovanni Rapisardi. *The Teachings of Marozzo.* Webpage. Original text reads "Farai assettare il ditto scholare con la gamba dritta innanzi, con la spada, et il brochiero over targa a bene distesa over lo dritto del nemico, et sua spada accompagnata insieme, et fa che la sua mano dritta sia di fuori dal suo ginocchio dritto con il polso della mano dalla spada volto all'ingiuso verso terra, . . ."

[20] For a left handed fencer the hand would be positioned outside the left knee.

[21] See bibliographic entry for webpage url.

[22] Egerton Castle. *Schools and Masters of Fence from the Middle Ages to the 18th Century.* (London, 1892). p. 52. Original text reads "Farai assettare il detto scholare con la gamba dritta innanzi con la spada, et il brocchiero, overo targa bene distesa per lo dritto del nemico, et la sua spada accompagnata insieme, et fa che la sua mano dritta. si di fuori dal suo ginnocchio dritto con il polso della mano dalla spada volto all'ingiuso verso terra, come puoi vedere nell'antecedente figura, et questa si dimamda coda lunga et stretta, et sta cosi per ferire, come per parare, et pero essendo il ditto scholare nella ditta guardia li mostrerai quanti ferire si puo fare volendo esser lui agente, e dapoi essendo paziente li mostrerai quanti parati si posson fare da alto, et da basso variati l'uno dall'altro, et gli darai li parati con li suoi ferire di quella natura…"

[23] Achille Marozzo. Arte dell' Armi, 1568. Cap 141. Translated by Egerton Castle. *Schools and Masters of Fence from the Middle Ages to the 18th Century.* (London, 1892). p. 54. Original text reads "Voglio che tu sappi, ch'e essendo tu paziente, questa è una buona, & utile guardia, et per questo io ti dico, che tu debbi dire alli tuoi scholari, che loro si debbano mettere per sua diffensione contra il suo nimico in questa guardia, . . ."

[24] Achille Marozzo. Arte dell' Armi, 1568. Cap 143. Translated by Egerton Castle. *Schools and Masters of Fence from the Middle Ages to the 18th Century.* (London, 1892). p. 57. Original text reads "Nota che in ditta guardia si può essere agente, & paziente, perche di qui si può tirere falso, & roverso, & tramazzone dritto, & falso, & tramazzone roverso, & falso fil rtondo, co'l roverso sgualembrato

tornando la spada al luoco suo, . . ."

[25] Achille Marozzo. Arte dell' Armi, 1568. Cap 143. Translated by Egerton Castle. *Schools and Masters of Fence from the Middle Ages to the 18th Century.* (London, 1892). p. 55. Original text reads "Essendo il tuo scholare nella ditta guardia, tu lo farai essere agente, massime con falsi dritti, o varrai conponte, o roversi, et altre botte, che li può nascere della ditta guardia, . . ."

[26] Fiore di Liberi. Flos Duellatorum. (Italy, 1410) p. 24v.

[27] Giovanni Rapisardi. *The Teachings of Marozzo.* Webpage.

[28] See footnote 11.

[29] Giovanni Rapisardi. *The Teachings of Marozzo.* Webpage.

[30] Achille Marozzo. Arte dell' Armi, 1568. Cap. 140. Translated by Egerton Castle. *Schools and Masters of Fence from the Middle Ages to the 18th Century.* (London, 1892). p. 54. Original text reads "Essendo il tuo scholare nella ditta guardia alta, gli mostrerai quanti feriri si puòcavare di essa facendoti intendere, . . ."

[31] Achille Marozzo. Arte dell' Armi, 1568. Cap 143. Translated by Egerton Castle. *Schools and Masters of Fence from the Middle Ages to the 18th Century.* (London, 1892). P. 56. Original text reads "In ditta guardia di testa si puòessere agente, & paziente, ma prima diremo del paziente; . . ."

[32] William Gaugler. Science of Fencing. (Bangor, 1997). p. 195.

[33] Achille Marozzo. Arte dell' Armi, 1568. Cap 143. Translated by Egerton Castle. *Schools and Masters of Fence from the Middle Ages to the 18th Century.* (London, 1892). P. 58. Original text reads "Havendo fatto andare il predetto in guardia di faccia, tu gli dirai che in questa guardia glie' paziente, & agente in uno istesso tempo; . . ."

[34] Achille Marozzo. Arte dell' Armi, 1568. Cap 143. Translated by Egerton Castle. *Schools and Masters of Fence from the Middle Ages to the 18th Century.* (London, 1892). P. 57. Original text reads "Es-

sendo nella ditta guardia ti conviene esser per forza patiente, . . ."

[35] Giovanni Rapisardi. *The Teachings of Marozzo.* Webpage.

[36] Achille Marozzo. Arte dell' Armi, 1568. Cap. 143. Translated by Egerton Castle. *Schools and Masters of Fence from the Middle Ages to the 18th Century.* (London, 1892). p. 58. Original text reads "Havendo io esaminato il ditto scholare di guardia in guardia, ho considerato ch'e essendo in ditta guardia di becca possa, che consorti il tuo scholare, che'l debba andare in questa guardia quando il suo nemico andasse à porta di ferro larga, o stretta, o alta, seguendolo di passo in passo, & di guardia in guardia: . . ."

[37] Terry Brown. *English Martial Arts.* (Norfolk, 1997). p. 99.

[38] Achille Marozzo. Arte dell' Armi, 1568. Cap 142. Translated by the Author. Original text reads "& braccio della spada all'insuso, alto, e disteso, voltando il polso della mano di fuori, facendo tenere la ponta della spada sua nella faccia, o al pugno del predetto, ben distesa; & questa e becca cesa."

[39] Salvator Fabris. Sienz e Practica d'Arme. (Copenhagen, 1606). p 31.

[40] Achille Marozzo. *Arte dell' Armi*, 1568. Cap. 144. Translation by Andrea Lupo-Sinclair given in personal communication with the author. Original text reads "Questo é il segno, dove to farai sopra passegiare li detti tuoi scholari di passo in passo, cosi innanzi come indrieto, con le armi in mano, attorno attorno, mettendo li piedi in su questi fili, che attraversano li segni tondi."

[41] Achille Marozzo. *Arte dell' Armi.* 1568. Starting at Cap. 138 Marozzo gives the following progression of guards for the student to use in sequence: coda lunga e stretta, cinghiara porta di ferro, guardia alta, coda lunga e alta, porta di ferro stretta overo larga, coda lunga e distesa, guardia di testa, guargia di intrare, coda lunga e larga, becca possa, guardia di faccia, becca cesa.

SPANISH INFLUENCE IN THE RAPIER PLAY
OF VINCENTIO SAVIOLO

By Stephen Hand & Ramon Martinez

Introduction

Prior to May 2000 neither author had entertained the thesis that there were major Spanish influences in the work of the 16th century Italian rapier master Vincentio Saviolo. The train of thought that lead to this paper can be traced to a single incident. During a demonstration of the techniques of Saviolo by Stephen Hand in Lansing Michigan in May 2000 Jared Kirby, a student of Maestro Martinez watched a technique being executed and said "that's Spanish". This came as a surprise to the first author who had not studied Spanish rapier fencing, or prior to that date even met anyone who had studied it. Later in the same month Jared's suspicions were confirmed when the two authors met for the first time. In Maestro Martinez's opinion, although Saviolo's style was predominantly Italian, some of his techniques were typical of *La Verdadera Destreza*, the style of Spanish rapier fencing developed by Hieronymo Carrança in the mid 16th century. It is the aim of this paper to identify those elements of Saviolo's style which, in the authors' opinions are of Spanish origin.

How does one prove that a technique came from a particular fencing system? Of course, without an explicit admission that "I learned this technique from Master X" one cannot. However, it will be demonstrated that many of the actions and techniques described by Saviolo were used by Spanish fencing masters, but not by Italian fencing masters other than Saviolo himself[1]. A similarity between techniques does not prove that Saviolo learned these techniques from a Spanish master. However, there is circumstantial evidence that Saviolo studied in Spain. While the thesis can not be proved "beyond reasonable doubt" the authors feel that the available evidence (preserved in Saviolo's treatise) strongly favours the conclusion that Saviolo studied under a Spanish master and in-

corporated elements of Spanish rapier play into his dominantly Italian style. The only alternative, that he developed these techniques in isolation, is possible, but fails the test of Occam's Razor.[2]

Vincentio Saviolo: His Practise

Vincentio Saviolo was born in Padua[3] and according to Aylward, arrived in England in 1590.[4] It is known that Saviolo was in England by 1591 because in that year his friend, the author John Florio writes about the former's school in his book *Second Frutes*.[5]. In the words of George Silver; Saviolo and Jeronimo ("that was Signior Rocko his boy,")[6] "taught Rapier-fight at the Court, at London, and in the countrey, by the space of seaven or eight yeares or thereabouts.."[7] By the time Silver published in 1599, Saviolo was dead.[8]

In 1595 Saviolo published *Vincentio Saviolo his Practise. In two Bookes. The first intreating of the use of the Rapier and Dagger. The second, of Honor and honorable Quarrels.* There is some uncertainty as to whether *his Practise* was ghost written. Both Aylward[9] and Rossi[10] suggest that the fencing manual was actually written by Saviolo's friend John Florio. Certainly, some literary similarities exist between *his Practise* and Florio's previous work, *Second Frutes.*[11] Whoever wrote the English text of *his Practise*, the content is Saviolo's, so while speculation about the authorship may be of historical interest it has no bearing on Saviolo's system of rapier fencing.

That Saviolo had trained in Spanish swordsmanship is not a new idea. Aylward states that "Saviolo was a professional teacher of the sword who had gone through a long and arduous training. Not content with what he could learn in Italy, he had studied in Spain, formulating from his experience of the methods of the two countries a system of fence, which he believed, combined the best features of both."[12] Aylward offers no evidence for this statement. He is, perhaps, following Castle, who stated of Saviolo that "This popular teacher was a master of his art, to judge from the report of fame and from the inherent qualities of his treatise. His progression, as moderns would call the systematic arrangements of his passes, is very cleverly devised, and as far as can be seen he was acquainted with both Spanish and Italian fashions."[13]. Once again, the reader is offered nothing more than the one tantalizing statement.

Francisco Moreno wrote his 1904 monograph *Esgrima Española (Apuntes para su Historia)* as a strong rebuttal against the erroneous conclusions about the history of fencing in Spain made by Castle. However, Moreno concurs with Castle when he says; ".... Henri Sainct Didier in France, Meyer in Germany and Saviolo of England, each founders in their respective countries, of the modern school of fence and the much celebrated teacher Girard Thibaust as well as Salvator Fabris, came to Spain to learn from the disciples of Carranza and Pacheco de Narvaez, not only thrusting play, but also that science of attack and parrying blows with settled measure,…"[14]. Like Aylward and Castle, Moreno offers no evidence for his assertions.

Saviolo's knowledge of both systems of rapier fence seems to have been assumed by these authors. Nowhere in his own work does Saviolo say who his masters were, nor do the aforesaid writers provide sufficient documentation to establish a link through ordinary scholarly means. One suspects that it is a statement written by one author and accepted by successive generations. However, Castle was an experienced fencer. Did he notice Spanish elements within Saviolo's *Practise*? Ultimately it is impossible to determine. Because the authors of secondary works failed to supply any evidence for their assertions, their statements lack weight. We must go back to primary sources, including Saviolo's own treatise and work from first principles.

So what, if any evidence did Saviolo present in *his Practise* that he studied in Spain?

Saviolo writes that "Since my childhoode I haue seene verie many masters the which haue taken great paines in teaching, and I haue marked their diuerse manners of playe and indangering: wherefore (both for the particular contentment & pleasure of the Gentlemen my friends, and for the general help & benefit of many) I haue changed fiue or six sundry maner of plaies, taught me by diuerse masters, and reduced them vnto one by my no little labour and paine,"[15] This passage suggests that Saviolo went out of his way to observe the different styles of rapier fencing, but it still doesn't prove that he studied Spanish rapier fencing. In order to demonstrate where Saviolo's techniques derive from, we must examine them, comparing each technique with those described in contemporary Spanish and Italian sources.

A close technical examination of some of the sequences found in Saviolo's treatise, shows a clear Hispanic influence in his system. Historically speaking, such an influence is more than plausible. In fact Saviolo may not even have had to travel to Spain to be exposed to Spanish rapier fencing. Spain was a dominant power in the late 16th century, holding possessions across most of Europe, including an important one, close to Saviolo's birthplace. As stated above, Vincentio Saviolo was from Padua. The dominions of Spain during the 16th century included many parts of Europe, among which was the duchy of Milan in northern Italy. In fact, one of King Phillip II's titles was Duke of Milan. Padua is also in northern Italy, 150 miles southeast of Milan. Therefore it is reasonable to surmise that Saviolo may have studied not only in his native city, but also in Milan, which was a city that was heavily influenced by Spain, and where there was much contact and interchange through commerce and politics between the two cultures.

Don Hieronymo Sanchez De Carrança, the father of the Spanish school of rapier fence worked on his system for many years before publishing it. He finished the first manuscript of his work, *De la filosofia de las armas,* in San Lucar in 1569 at the age of thirty-five, but few copies were printed. It did not reach general circulation until 1582. Don Luis Pacheco De Narvaez, Carrança's disciple, did not publish his work *Libro de las grandezas de la espada…* in Madrid until between 1599 and 1600. However, it should be noted that Carranza had other followers besides Narvaez, although Don Luis was the

Fig. 1: *Saviolo's stance. The figures are illustrated closer together than described in the text.*

The wards (or, as the fencing position is known in Spanish, *affirmarse*, literally "to steady oneself"[17]) of Saviolo are not as upright as the ones of Carranza or Narvaez, and the unarmed hand position is held up in front of the upper chest in a relaxed manner typical of Italian rapier.[18]

Nevertheless, the center of gravity is much higher than in the typical Italian *guardia*,[19] but lower than the Spanish one[20]. The knees are also not held as

best politically connected, and thus became the most celebrated Spanish master after the "Father of the Science" (which also generated some resentment and opposition from his colleagues when Narvaez was appointed Grand Examiner by Phillip IV). We can therefore reasonably surmise that *La Verdadera Destreza* had been established by the time Saviolo began his career[16].

Saviolo, being a contemporary of both Carrança and Narvaez, and coming from a part of Italy that was heavily influenced by Spain, may very likely have been at least exposed to Spanish swordsmanship during his training. We can speculate that this may have prompted him to go to Spain to receive training from its source. There is no record of Saviolo ever leaving England after his arrival in 1590, so it can be said with some degree of certainty that his system was already established and tested long before his arrival in England.

Fig. 2:
Spanish stance as illustrated by Narvaez

Fig. 3: *Capo Ferro's stance*

Comparison of Techniques

In the latter part of the year 2000 a number of Saviolo's sequences were demonstrated by the first author to the second author who compared them to the large body of Spanish and Italian rapier techniques with which he is familiar. Out of these sequences , the authors chose a few, which contain elements typical of Spanish rapier fencing, but are not found in any other Italian fencing manual which the authors are familiar with. It should be noted that these sequences were interpreted by the first author prior to his meeting with the second author. No element of these sequences has been reinterpreted as a result of contact between the authors. Therefore there is no possibility that the interpretation of Saviolo may have been affected by prior knowledge of *La Destreza*.

straight as in the Spanish school, and the space between the feet is ever so slightly wider. This stance seems to be midway between a Spanish and an Italian stance and would therefore give Saviolo's methods a facility to go from Spanish to Italian. Whether this was deliberate policy on the part of Saviolo is not known. Early Masters of Italian rapier (the early rapier or Spada da lato[21] was arguably a different weapon than the one used by Saviolo, but nonetheless, the early treatises and the Masters who wrote them influenced later practice) such as Di Grassi and Viggiani used stances much like Saviolo.[22]

The first technique to be discussed is, in fact, the very first one described by Saviolo. The protagonists in the sequences are "the maister" (Vincentio, or simply V.) and his "scholler" (Luke or simply L).[23]

> "then shall the maister begin to teach him, moving his right foot somewhat on the right side in circle wise, putting the point of his Rapier under his schollers Rapier, and so giving him a thrust in the belly.

> "L. And what then must the scholler doo?

> "V. At the selfesame time the scholler must remove with like measure or counter-time with his right foote a little aside, and let the left foote follow the right, turning a little his bodye on the right side, thrusting with the point of his Rapier at the belly of his teacher, turning readily his hand that the fingers be inward toward the body, and the joint of the wrist shall be outward. In this sorte the saide scholler shall learne to strike and not be stricken, as I alwaies advise the noble-men and gentlemen whit whome I have to deale, that if they cannot hit or hurt their enemy, that they learn to defend them selves that they be not hurt."[24]

From an engagement in Saviolo's first ward (an extended ward in terza[25] (fig.4)) the Master commences with a cavatione[26], simultaneously making a slope pace[27] forward and right and thrusting a stoccata at the belly of his Scholar (fig. 5). The thrust should be made close to the Scholar's rapier with the hand in quarta, closing the inside line. The turning of the hand into quarta and the closure of the line are not described by Saviolo, but are typical of Italian rapier fencing. The passage below (from Pallas Armata, 1639) describes how a thrust is to be made.

> "11. Thy thrust thou must make close to thine adversaries Rapier, as if thou wouldest strike fire out of his weapon, which if thou dost not doe, you will both be hurt if neither of you have skill; if one of you have but skill, and knoweth to observe this then

hee onely will bee endangered that doth not thrust close to his adversaries Rapier.

> "12. Yet this is not all, but thou must like wise thust close to the *Secunde* or weakest part of his Rapier, with thy *Prime* or strongest part of thy Rapier, for if thou canst doe that, he cannot put thee by.

> "13. When thou dost thrust at thine adversary without, over his right arme, thou must do it with a *Secunde*. When thou makest a thrust at thine adversary within, thou art to doe it with a *Quarte*."[28]

Fig. 4 *Stephen, on the right, playing the part of the Master, faces Volker, on the left, playing the part of the Scholar in Saviolo's first ward, the extended ward in Terza*

Fig. 5 *Stephen disengages and thrusts at Volker, closing the line as he does so.*

In response to the Master's thrust the Scholar takes a circular half pace to the right with his right foot so that it is pointing directly at the Master. This is immediately followed by a larger circular half pace to the right with his left foot (the feet move through the same angle but the rear foot, being further from the Master must move a greater distance). As the Scholar traverses away from the Master's attack he should thrust at his Master's belly. The hand should be turned into quarta and the thrust should be along the Master's rapier, to close the line of his attack.

Fig. 6 *Volker traverses right and counterthrusts with opposition at Stephen*

Fig. 7 *The same action viewed from above.*

Saviolo does not continue the phrase past this point, but in the opinion of the first author it may (at least in theory) be continued ad infinitum. The Master has taken only one step during his attack. It is natural for him to recover forwards with his rear foot. If he steps forward and right with his left foot he may easily close the line of the Scholar's counterattack, successfully thrusting in opposition.

Similarly, the Scholar may continue to traverse circularly to the right, changing his line and retaking opposition against the Master's blade. In theory the phrase could go on, but in practice by the first author and his students it has never progressed past this point.

La Verdadera Destreza differs from Italian rapier fencing in that although some sequences such as those described by Saviolo are described, techniques are not.

Techniques (*treta*) are built up from a number of *movimientos*, specific isolated actions of the arm and/or weapon[29] Therefore it is difficult to find a

Fig. 8 *Stephen traverses right and counterthrusts with opposition at Volker.*

Fig. 9 *The same action observed from above.*

Spanish sequence equivalent to Saviolo's. In one instance a matching sequence has been found. In the absence of others it is necessary to look at the movements which comprise Saviolo's sequence and to compare these to the *movimientos* of La Verdadera Destreza.

In the sequence described and illustrated above, the two fencers begin on opposite ends to the diameter of the imaginary circle[30]

The Master launches an angular attack by stepping off the diameter to the right, whereupon the Scholar defends himself by slightly sidestepping to the right and closing the line of attack. The Master continues his movement to the right, displacing his body while maintaining opposition (Spanish: *atajo*, Italian: *stringer della spada*) and thrusting (Spanish: *estocada*, Italian: *stoccata*)[31]. While the elements of this sequence are present in both Italian and Spanish rapier fencing, no sequence like this exists in other Italian rapier fencing treatises. In contrast, the concept of moving circularly around the opponent and thrusting in opposition are at the core of La Destreza.

The second sequence is "an imbroccata in manner of a stoccata"[32], or a thrust from over the hand in the manner of a thrust from under the hand[33].

> "V. With all my heart, and therefore I must tell you of an imbroccata in manner of a stoccata, which is verie good and excellent, as well for practise of plaie, as for fight, but they must be most readie both with hand and foot that use it: therefore when the scholler shall find his masters Rapier in this ward, that it bee helde upright or toward his face, then the scholler shall winne ground a little with his right foote, beeing mooved somewhat aside, and withall let him remove with his left foot, that it be toward the right foot of the teacher, and that your right foot be against the middest of his left, as I have said before, and in removing let him turne his Rapier hand, that the pointe bee conveighed under his masters weapon, which being done, promptly and readily his point will be towards the belly of his master, which must bee followed with the left hand, & let the scholler lift up his hand to the ward that his fist be somewhat high, and let him take heed that he loose not his point, because the teacher may give him a stoccata or thrust in the belly or face, for that he hath lost his time.

> "L. But I pray you, cannot the teacher then defende himselfe?

> "V. He may do the self same, which I told you before, when I spake of the imbroccata delivered above the Rapier, and certainly this is a verie good play when it is performed with good measure, and great agilitie and readines."[34]

This is a difficult passage to interpret. The phrase "upright or toward his face" seems to be contradictory, how can something at once be vertical and towards the opponent's face? An alternative definition of upright, one used in the 16th century is 'at full length' and 'with the face upwards; supine'[35]. Using this definition the remainder of the passage becomes far easier to interpret. The Master's rapier is extended directly at the Scholar's face with the hand supine. This is the basic guard or *affirmarse* (which literally means; "to steady oneself"[36]) of La Destreza. The diestro assumes an upright semi-profiled posture, legs straight and heels slightly apart. The sword-arm is held straight out at shoulder level, the sword blade parallel to the ground. The sword is positioned in such a way as to have the point constantly menacing the adversary. A similar guard (although intended to be used quite differently) is shown by Marozzo, the Guardia di Facia[37]. Frankly it is irrelevant whether Saviolo intends the technique described to be used against the Spanish or Italian variant of this guard. The guard with the rapier extended at the face is not recommended by Saviolo, he merely includes it in order to describe his response to someone adopting it.

It is unclear whether the Scholar is intended to win ground on the Master's right or on the left. If he moves to the Master's left then his attack will be a stoccata delivered with opposition in quarta. This does not adequately explain the *remove*[38] with the left foot or the reference to the left hand and in any case can hardly be described as an imbroccata. If the ground is won on the Master's right then there are two ways that the Scholar can "lift up his hand to the ward that his fist be somewhat high". Firstly he can turn his hand into quarta. I consider this unlikely because it does not close the line and because a thrust in quarta would be described as a stoccata or a punta riversa, not as an imbroccata. The other alternative, and the one which seems to best fit the text is that the Scholar raises his hand into seconda. This gives opposition and explains the phrase "loose not his point". From there the hand may stay in seconda or be rotated into prima, whichever delivers the most satisfactory opposition. If the Scholar's "fist be somewhat high" then his point will be "conveighed under his masters weapon" and "his point will be towards the belly of his master". The point will be below the Master's rapier hand – an imbroccata "in manner of a stoccata".

Fig. 10 *Stephen, playing the part of the Master is in a ward resembling that used in La Verdadera Destreza. Volker is in Saviolo's second ward, a close ward in terza.*

Saviolo uses the term "remove" in reference to the movement of the left foot. He only uses the word remove to refer to passes[39]. Therefore the Scholar's footwork is a step to the left with his right foot followed by a pass forward and left with his left foot. The reference to the left hand could be referring to a technique in which the hand braces the sword about 3/4 of the way down the blade. This is identical to a technique which Saviolo uses later[40] and is perfectly suited to a forward pass to a left-leg forward stance. Alternatively it could refer to the Scholar simply raising his hand and guarding his face.

Fig. 11 *Volker has stepped to the left with his right foot.*

Fig. 12 *Pivoting on his right foot, Volker passes circularly forward and left, thrusting with opposition.*

Fig. 13 The same action observed from above.

In response to this action Saviolo recommends doing "The self same, which I told you before". In other words the Master must use a technique previously described by Saviolo. The last mention of the imbroccata is on page 19V (also labeled 13V). "the scholler must bee readie and nimble to remoove with his left foote, that the point or ende thereof bee against the middest of his masters right foot, turning his Rapier hand, and that his point be in imbrocata-wise above his teachers Rapier,". This is almost identical to the technique used by the Scholar in this sequence. Therefore Saviolo is telling Luke that the Master should use the same response against the Scholar's "imbrocata in manner of a stoccata" as he used against the last imbroccata he described. Therefore we need to look to Saviolo's response to the technique on pages 19V (also labeled 13V) which is found on page 20R (also labeled 14R). "When the schollar remoueth with his left foot, the master must steppe backe, but yet in such sorte, that the left foote be behinde the right, and that he remoue[41] to the right side, and shall strike a mandritta at the head of the scholler," So the Master steps back and to the right with his left foot, followed by his right, striking a mandritta fendente or squalambrato at the head of the Scholar.

Fig. 14. *Stephen steps back and to the right with his left foot, raising his arm.*

Fig. 15. *Stephen steps back and to the right with his right foot, cutting at Volker's face.*

Fig. 16. *The cut viewed from above.*

So to recap, the entire second sequence is as follows. The Master's rapier is horizontal or near horizontal, held out at length towards the scholar's face. The Scholar steps forward and to the left with his right foot, taking opposition against his opponent's blade and then passes forward, thrusting an *imbroccata* in *seconda*, possibly at the half-sword. The Master steps back and to the right with his left foot followed by his right, striking a *mandritta fendente* or *squalambrato* at the head of the Scholar.

The first step made by the Scholar is called a *transversal* by Don Francisco Lorenz de Rada[42] The second step is a *passada*. This is a term common to Spanish and Italian systems. However, the meaning differs. In Italian rapier fencing the term passada, passata or passade refers to a step in which one leg moves past the other as in a normal walking motion[43]. In La Destreza a *passada* uses the same walking motion but is executed when both feet have completed the pace. It is a pace that is not hurried and as when walking involves moving both feet[44]. The pass made in the sequence above is more Italian in nature than Spanish. Therefore this

sequence commences with a Spanish *transversal* step and follows with an Italian style *passada*.

During the execution of the pass the Scholar maintains opposition (*atajo*) and thrusts (*estocada* – a Spanish word obviously coming from the same root as Stoccata)[45]. The cut (*tajo*) is from the wrist and is hence a *mandoble* in the terminology of La Verdadera Destreza[46].

The third of Saviolo's sequences to be discussed is a response to an attempted parry-riposte that finishes with a hilt grab and thrust in opposition.

> "Also if you should deliver a stoccata to your enemie, and that he should breake it with his Rapier, immediatly you might remove with your lefte foot, your left hand, waiting on the weapon of your enemie, and give him an imbroccata or foine under or above his Rapier, and may bee master of his weapon."[47]

Fig. 17. *Stephen and Volker are on guard in Saviolo's second ward, a close ward in terza.*

Fig. 18. *Stephen thrusts a stoccata at his "enemie" Volker, who attempts to parry the thrust in quarta.*

Fig. 19. *The parry viewed from above.*

So, as you "deliver a stoccata to your enemie", in Spanish parlance a committed action or *acometimiento*[48] he attempts to parry it across his body (a parry in quarta).

Saviolo then recommends that you should remove or pass with your left foot and grip your enemy's weapon. He has previously told his student that he must grip the hilt and not his enemy's arm[49] and that passes in which the left hand is brought forward to grasp the hilt must be circular (*compass curvo*[50]) , not straight forward. The latter is described in an almost identical sequence earlier in Saviolo's *Practise*.

> "when the master and scoller stand upon this ward, and that the point of the schollers weapon is towarde the face of the teacher, and the point of the masters without the bodie of the scholler toward the right side, both of them being upon this ward, the scholler must bee readie and nimble to remoove with his left foote, that the point or ende thereof bee against the middest of his masters right foot, turning his Rapier hand, and that his point be in imbrocata-wise above his teachers Rapier, and that his left hand bee toward the ward of his teacher: and let all this be done at once, by which meanes the scholler shall come to have his masters weapon at commandment, and if it were in fight, his enemies.

> "L. This plaie which now you tell me of, me thinkes is contrarie to many other, and I my selfe have seen many plaie and

teache cleane after another fashion, for I have seene them all remove in a right line, and therfore you shall doe mee a pleasure to tell mee which in your opinion, is best to use, either the right or circular line.

> "V. I will tell you, when you stand upon this ward, if you remove in a right line, your teacher or your adversarie may give you a stoccata either in the bellie or in the face. Besides, if your master or your adversarie have a Dagger he may doo the like, hitting you with his dagger either in the belly or on the face, besides other harms which I list not to write. And therefore to proceede, I saie, that in my opinion and judgement, it is not good to use the right line, whereas in remooving in circular-wise, you are more safe from your enemie, who cannot in such sort hurt you, and you have his weapon at commandement: yea although he had a dagger hee coulde not doo you anie harme."[51]

Saviolo does not mention what must be done with the blade as the pass and grip are made, but if nothing is done, your pass takes you onto your opponent's riposte (Saviolo does not mention a riposte either, but to assume that an opponent will parry and not riposte is unrealistic). Hence, for the action to succeed some sort of defence must be offered against the riposte.

In both the third sequence and the technique described above, the Scholar's rapier must maintain opposition (*atajo*) throughout the action in order to cover the Scholar as he passes circularly forward. In the above technique, the rapier is engaged as the action commences. In the third sequence your rapier has been parried away to your right. Therefore you must make a cavatione and take opposition against your "enemie's" rapier in seconda. At this point a critical difference emerges between the two techniques. In the third sequence if the arm continues forward with the body as the pass is made, not only will a parry in seconda be impractical, but so will the final action described by Saviolo, the imbroccata. Therefore, in order for your rapier to be in the correct position to parry and to deliver an imbroccata with opposition, it must not go forward with the body. To achieve this the sword arm must bend as the body goes forward in the pass. This is a peculiarly Spanish position, that of *estraño*, literally "strange"[52].

The *movimiento estraño* is used in a parrying technique (*desvio*[53]) as the adversary attacks, by yielding to the blade pressure and pivoting on the lead foot thus derailing the attack. The *diestro* will find himself next to his adversary and in a position to take control of the adversary's rapier hilt or arm. An *estraño* can also be applied as an *atajo* technique as in a counter opposition. As the adversary executes a parry the *diestro* can pivot on the lead foot and apply a counter pressure on the blade with his own blade. This is done by bending the arm at the elbow (*estraño*) and placing the strong part of the blade against the weak part of the adversary's. In the same instant the *diestro* pivots around to the side of the adversary again finding himself next to him in a position where he can thrust while maintaining his blade contact (*atajo*). The use of the movimiento, *estraño* in this manner is not found in any Italian fencing manual other than Saviolo's.

Fig. 20. *Stephen makes cavatione and takes opposition against the inside of Volker's rapier with his hand in seconda.*

Fig. 21. *The action viewed from above.*

Fig. 22. *Stephen passes forward and grips Volker's hilt, maintaining opposition (atajo) through use of the movimiento estraño.*

Fig. 23. *The same action viewed from above.*

Finally opposition (*atajo*) is maintained as an *imbroccata* thrust (*estocada*) is delivered. This thrust can easily be imagined from the position shown in figures 22 and 23.

The actions in this sequence can be opposed in the same fashion as illustrated in figures 14-16, except that either a cut or a thrust may be used.

This last sequence is of special interest because an almost identical sequence has been found in Narvaez.

"If you are parried , enter with the left foot and hold the [adversary's] sword with your hand.

"In this instance enter with the left foot.

"He who fights within his own work takes counsel conforming to the variety of the causes which are offered, and they [the causes] themselves proceed to dictate and advise what needs to be done to come out of danger. Even though the movement or defense that the adversary may make or which is commonly done, is easy, of little artifice and of less consideration; and which you will recognize in the beginning of your [technique].

"(and please excuse me for placing it here so that nothing remains in confusion, nor will there be a need to labor in studying it.) you will become aware of the remedy to the strike by thrust, which is indicated in the previous demonstration. It is a common recourse to wish to catch the point of the sword that strikes on the guard (hilt) of your own lifting it upward solely with the determination to parry the strike, but not to offend with one that they may anticipate; nor should this be attempted because this is the function of the art and skill: to wound and defend [oneself] from the adversary. For this reason, it gives more place and more security to offend [the adversary] because they do not attempt to offend but to defend themselves, they give place so that you may execute many strikes until one of them arrives to effect and harm [the adversary] all at once. Therefore, if your adversary executes such a parry, knowing the principle of the movement, and knowing that it is primary to bring your sword to the obtuse angle, and that he will parry the point of your sword from in front of your body; with great quickness you will make a curved step from point C to point E., entering with the left foot profiling your body, holding the guard (hilt) with your left hand, which you will be able to do because of your being close. And forming a *reves* (a reverse cut with the back edge)[54] which should be done as we have stated in other parts, stamping with the right leg like those who cut flax, executing it [the cut] on the right side of the head. You can also strike by thrust, as one or the other will be in your hand and the adversary will not be able to retreat with such quickness that before he comes out with his intent you have obtained yours."[55]

Fig. 24: *Maestri Ramon Martinez and Jeannette Acosta-Martinez stand (Affirmarse) on opposite ends of an imaginary circle.*

Fig. 25: *Maestro Acosta-Martinez has stepped to her left and has made a threat to Maestro Martinez's outside line.*

Fig. 26: *Maestro Martinez has opposed/parried while stepping to his left.*

Saviolo describes other sequences which contain Spanish movimientos, but none which contain movimientos in addition to those described in the sequences above. The purpose of this paper is to present the hypothesis that Saviolo studied La Verdadera Destreza and incorporated some elements of it into his system of rapier fencing. It is not the authors' intention to present a comprehensive listing of from where Saviolo derived each of his techniques. Hence additional techniques which the authors believe to contain Spanish elements have been omitted.

Fig. 27:
On Maestro Martinez's parry Maestro Acosta-Martinez has pivoted on her right foot bringing her left foot forward (compass curvo) while executing an estrano and at the same time seizing Maestro Martinez's hilt.

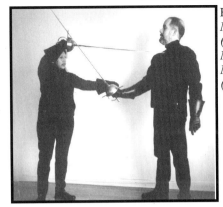

Fig. 28:
Maintaining opposition (atajo) Maestro Acosta-Martinez thrusts to Maestro Martinez's chest (estocada).

Conclusions

Vincentio Saviolo was an Italian fencing master. His system of rapier fencing is dominantly Italian. His wards and attacks are typical of those described in other Italian fencing treatises. Saviolo's terminology, stoccata, imbroccata etc. is Italian. There can be no argument that the main influence on Saviolo's fencing system were the existing Italian schools of swordsmanship. However, there are a number of elements in Vincentio Saviolo's rapier play that are found in the Spanish fencing system La Verdadera Destreza but are not found in the works of other Italian masters.

At the heart of Saviolo's system is the principle of moving circularly around an opponent while creating opposition in the exposed line. For example, in the first sequence discussed, movement is circularly to the outside line (assuming right handed fencers; to the right), while opposition is created in the inside line, i.e. to the left with the blade in *quarta*. In the third sequence, movement is circularly to the inside line while opposition is created in the outside line, with the blade in *seconda*. This principle is at the heart of La Destreza but not of Italian rapier fencing. Opposition is important in Italian rapier play, but the overall movement style is far more linear. Linear attacks, like the lunge are unknown in La Verdadera Destreza[56] until Thibault[57] in whose work appears what is really a type of "demi-lunge" or "half-lunge" and not the lunge as shown in the Italian treatises.

The lunge first appears in the mainstream of the Spanish School in Rada's treatise of 1705[58]. The Spanish ward used by Saviolo in the second sequence and the cut of *mandoble* are unlike any ward or cut seen in Italian rapier play. The movimiento estraño is also typical of Spanish play, but unknown in Italian.

Saviolo had the opportunity to study under Spanish masters. He admits to having created his style by having taken "fiue or six sundry maner of plaies, taught me by diuerse masters, and reduced them vnto one by my no little labour and paine,"[59]. Neither Saviolo nor any of his contemporaries stated that his system was an amalgam of Italian and Spanish elements. It is conceivable that Saviolo invented the "Spanish" elements of his style by himself. However we have Saviolo's own word that the style was an amalgam, and we see distinct and recognizable elements of contemporary Spanish rapier play within it. The most logical conclusion is that Saviolo studied under a teacher of La Verdadera Destreza and that he incorporated elements of that style into a predominantly Italian framework. It is the opinion of the authors that any other conclusion would be perverse.

Acknowledgements

The authors would like to thank Maestro Jeannette Acosta Martinez for her assistance with Spanish sources and the reconstruction of la Verdadera Destreza. Volker Stephens is thanked for assisting Stephen Hand in the reconstruction of Saviolo's rapier play. Thanks are also due to Paul Wagner and Kim Moser for assistance with photography. Paul also assisted with cleaning up the artwork. Finally, the authors would like to thank Jared Kirby for having a sharp eye and recognising the Spanish in Saviolo.

William Wilson, Mark Rector and Roger Siggs read this paper and offered constructive criticism which resulted in several improvements being made.

Bibliography

Agrippa, Camillo, *Trattato di Scientia d'Arme*, Roma 1553

Aylward, J.D., *The English Master of Arms*, London 1956

Bondi Di Mazzo, *La Spada Maestra*, Venetia 1696

Capo Ferro, Ridolfo, *Gran Simvlacro Dell'Arte Edell'Vso Della Scherma*, Siena 1610

Carrança, Hieronymo, *De la filosofia de las armas*, Lisbon 1582

Castle, Egerton, *Schools and Masters of the fence from the middle ages to the 18ᵗʰ century*, London 1884

Dall'Agocchie, Giovanni, *Dell'Arte Discrimia Libri Tre*, Venetia 1572

Fabris, Salvator, *De Lo Schermo Overo Scienza D'Arme*, Copenhagen 1606

Florio, Blasco *La Scienza Della Scherma*, Catania 1844

Florio, John, *Second Frutes*, London 1591

Giganti, Nicoletto, *Scola Ouero Teatro*, Venetia 1606

Grassi, Giacomo Di, *Ragione Di Adoprar Sicvramente L'Arme si da Offesa, Come da Difesa*, Venetia 1570

Grassi, Giacomo Di, *his True Arte of Defence*, London 1594

Marcelli, Francesco Antonio, *Regole della Scherma*, Roma 1686

Marozzo, Achille, *Opera Nova*, Bologna 1536

Moreno, Francisco, *Esgrima Espanola (Apuntes para su Historia)*, Third Edition, Madrid 1904

Narvaez, Don Luis Pacheco De, *Libro de las Grandezas de la Espada*, Madrid 1600

Narvaez, Don Luis Pacheco De, *Llave y gobierno de la destreza. De una filosofia de las armas."* Unpublished MS. 1608, ed. Fernando Fernandez Lanza University of Alcala de Henares, Spain, 1991

Pallavacini, Giuseppe Morsicarto *La Scherma Ilustrata*, Palermo 1673

Rada, Francisco Lorenz de, *La Nobleza de la Espada*, Madrid 1705

Rossi, Sergio, *Vincentio Saviolo his Practise 1595: A Problem of Authorship. in England and the Continental Renaissance. Essays in Honour of J.B. Trapp*, ed. E Chaney and P. Mack, Woodbridge 1990, pp. 165-75

Saviolo, Vincentio, *his Practise*, London 1595

Scorza, Rasaroll & Grisetti, Pietro. *La Scienza Della Scherma*, Milano 1803

Silver, George, *Paradoxes of Defence*, London 1599, in Mathey, Cyril (ed). *Works of George Silver*, London 1898

Thibault, Gerard, *Académie de l'espée*, Leyden 1630

Viggiani, Angelo, *Lo Schermo*, Vinetia 1575

(Footnotes)

[1] By which the authors mean that they have not come across these techniques in their extensive reading of Italian rapier fencing treatises. Of course it is impossible to compare Saviolo's techniques with every technique of every Italian rapier fencing master.

[2] The principle espoused by William of Occam in the 14ᵗʰ century that if there are two possible solutions to a problem, the simpler solution is more likely to be the correct one.

[3] *Vincentio Saviolo his Practise.* London 1595 p.152R Saviolo writes, "At Padua where I was borne,"

[4] J.D. Aylward. *The English Master of Arms.* London 1956 p.51

[5] John Florio. Second Frutes. London 1591 pp. 111-125

[6] George Silver. *Paradoxes of Defence.* London 1599, in Cyril Mathey (ed). *Works of George Silver*, London 1898, p. 64 Jeronimo was perhaps the son or servant of Rocco Bonetti, the first Italian rapier fencing teacher in London.

[7] Ibid. p. 66

[8] Ibid. "This Vincentio proued himselfe a stout man not long before he died," p. 68

[9] J.D. Aylward. *The English Master of Arms.* London 1956 pp. 59-60

[10] Sergio Rossi. *Vincentio Saviolo his Practise (1595): A Problem of Authorship.* in England and the Continental Renaissance. Essays in Honour of J.B. Trapp, ed. E. Chaney and P. Mack (Woodbridge 1990) pp.165-175

[11] John Florio. Second Frutes. London 1591

[12] J.D. Aylward. *The English Master of Arms.* London 1956 p. 51

[13] Egerton Castle. *Schools and Masters of the fence from the middle ages to the 18ᵗʰ century.* London 1884 p. 79

[14] Francisco Moreno, *Esgrima Espanola (Apuntes para su Historia)*, Third Edition Madrid 1904 pp. 80-81 The original text reads ""...Henri Sainct en Francia, Meyer en Alemania y Saviolo en Inglaterra, fundadores cada uno en su respectivo pais, de la moderna escuela de esgrima y que tanto el celebre profesor Girard Thibaust como Salvator Fabris, vinieron a Espana a aprender de los discupulos de Carranza y Pacheco de Narvaez ,

no solamente el juego de punta, sino tambien esa ciencia de atacar y parar los golpes con reposada mesura,…" Translation by Ramon Martinez.

[15] *Vincentio Saviolo his Practise.* London 1595 p. 1V

[16] Though we do not know when this was. From what has been written about Saviolo it would seem unlikely that he was elderly when he was teaching in England. He was challenged to combat by George Silver and others which suggests that he was not so old as to make a combat farcical (see George Silver, *Paradoxes of Defence*, London 1599 in Cyril Mathey (ed). *Works of George Silver*, London 1898, pp. 66-70).

[17] Hieronymo Carrança, *De la filosofia de las armas,* Lisbon 1582, The term affirmarse is explained in the section *Declaracion de lo que Significa Cada Vocabulo de los que tocan á la Theorica de la Arte*. The pages in this section are unnumbered. See also note 35.

[18] Similar hand positions can be observed in many Italian rapier treatises, such as Viggiani (1575), Di Grassi (1594), Fabris (1606), Giganti (1606), Capo Ferro (1610), Alfieri, (1640), *La Scherma Illustrata* Palermo, (1673) by Giuseppe Morsicato Pallavicini, *Regole della Scherma* Roma, (1686) by Francesco Antonio Marcelli, and in *La Spada Maestra* Venetia, (1696) by Bondi Di Mazo. In Italian rapier fencing the left hand and/or arm was always held in a position of readiness in front of the chest or along the left side of the head (eg: Fabris) for defensive actions such as deflecting the attacking blade (parry) or for seizing the adversary's blade, hilt or arm. In fact the practice of using the unarmed hand or arm for defence persisted in the Italian Schools into the 19th century and can be seen in two of the most important treatises of the classical period which are in *La Scienza Della Scherma* Milano, (1803) by Rassaroll Scorza & Pietro Grisetti and in *La La Scienza Della Scherma* Catania, (1844) by Blasco Florio. This practice gradually began to disappear in the so-called Northern Italian Schools only after contact was made with the French School during and after the Napoleonic wars, thus clearly evidencing that some influence was made by French theory and practice in the Italian Schools; which is something that the Italian masters do not readily admit. By contrast although Spanish swordsmen did use the unarmed hand in auxiliary techniques it was always commonly held straight down along side the body. The authors

have found no reference or illustration in an Italian treatise that corresponds exactly to the manner in which a Spanish swordsman held his left arm. In *La Verdadera Destreza* the emphasis (in the use of the rapier when used without the dagger.) was to rely on the blade for both defence and offence. The unarmed hand was used only when the opportunity or need presented itself.

[19] See for example Salvator Fabris, *De Lo Schermo Overo Scienza D'Arme,* Copenhagen 1606, plates 1-16, Nicoletto Giganti, *Scola Ouero Teatro*, Venetia 1606, plate 2 and Ridolfo Capo Ferro, *Gran Simulacro Dell'Arte Edell'vso Della Scherma*, Siena 1610, 2-4 and 6

[20] The proper stance of La Verdadera Destreza, is one in which the swordsman assumes an upright semi-profiled posture, legs straight and heels slightly apart. The sword arm is held straight out at shoulder level and the left arm is held straight downward usually with the index finger pointing at the ground. The stance or guard position is described by Hieronymo Carrança, *De la filosofia de las armas*, Lisbon 1582 on pages 28 & 163 and by Don Luys Pacheco De Narvaez , *Libro de las Grandezas de la Espada*, Madrid 1600 pages 36-40.

[21] See Camillo Agrippa, *Trattato di Scientia d'Arme*, Roma 1553, p. 1V, Angelo Viggiani, *Lo Schermo*, Vinetia 1575, p.54R

[22] Giacomo Di Grassi, *Ragione Di Adoprar Sicvramente L'Arme si da Offesa, Come da Difesa*, Venetia 1570, See any of the stances illustrated on pages 18-21. Angelo Viggiani, *Lo Schermo*, Vinetia 1575, See for example plate 2, "Seconda Guardia Alta, Offensiva, Perfetta" (High Second Guard, Offensive and Perfect) Author's Translation.

[23] *Vincentio Saviolo his Practise*, London 1595, the hypothetical "maister" and "scholler" are introduced by Saviolo on page 14R (also labelled page 8). Interestingly Saviolo uses the words *maister* and *teacher* interchangeably.

[24] Ibid. pp. 14V-15R (also labelled pages 8 and 9)

[25] The four hand positions of Italian rapier fencing are best described in the anonymous *Pallas Armata The Gentlemans Armorie*. London 1639 on pages 7-9 (Note that *Pallas Armata* uses the French terms *Prime, Secunde, Tertz,* and *Quarte* rather than the Italian *Prima, Seconda, Terza* and *Quarta* used in this paper) "1. There are but foure guards according to the foure wayes thou canst turne thy hand, *viz. Prime, Secunde, Tertz*, and *Quarte*.

2. The *Prime* is when thou houldest thy Rapier in

such a manner that the outside side of thy hand doth looke towards thy left side out, and the inside of thy hand looke towards thy right side out...

...3. The *Secunde* is, when thou holdest thy Rapier in such a sort that the outside of thy hand looketh upwards, and the inside of thy hand towards the ground...

...3. The *Tertz* is when thou dost holde thy Rapier in such fashion that the outside of thy hand looks towards thy right side out, and the inside of thy hand towards thy left side out...

...4. The *Quarte* is when thou holdest thy Rapier in such a manner with a bended arme, that the outside of thy hand looke downe towards the ground, but the inside upwards.

[26] A circular disengage under the opponent's weapon. See Salvator Fabris *De Lo Schermo Overo Scienza D'Arme* Copenhagen 1606. Cap.11 p.15 "Che Cosa Sia Cavatione, Contracavatione, Ricavatione, meggia cavatione, & commettere di spada & come, & quando si debbano usare." (What is the disengagement, counter-disengagement, re-disengagement (or double disengagement), half-disengagement, committment of the sword and how and when they are to be used.) Translation by Stephen Hand.

[27] *Di Grassi his true Arte of Defence*, London 1594. The terminology used for Saviolo's footwork is borrowed from the English translation of Di Grassi. With the exception of the word remove, which Saviolo uses to describe the pass (see note 33), Saviolo did not use any technical terms to describe his footwork. See pages 14V-17R for Di Grassi's full description of the type of footwork used in his fencing style.

[28] Anonymous. *Pallas Armata The Gentlemans Armorie.* London 1639 pp. 4-5

[29] The *movimientos* are all described in detail in the first volume of Francisco Rada's *La Nobleza de la Espada* (1705), pages 78-79. More contemporary to Saviolo, definitions of some of the various primary *movimientos* may also be found in Narvaez' treatise of 1600 on page 85 (Cardinal Movements)

"Cardinal movements, what are they?"

"Cardinal movements whose names are, violent movement, natural movement, *remisso* movement, and mixed movement which are born and produce different effects, according to the how they accompany one another and at the instant that all of these the wound is formed."

The original text reads,

"Movimientos cardinales , quales son?"

"...Movimientos cardinales, cuyos nombres son, Movimiento violento, Movimiento natural, Movimiento remisso, y Movimiento mixto los quales nace y se produzen diferentes efectos, segun la compania que haze el un con el otro, y asi mismo, la vez que con todos ellos se forma la herida..."

on page 107 (concerning the arrebatar, or cut from the shoulder)

"The most famous technique of the common Destreza., whose name is snatch (literally, to violently seize away) and cut"

"...to snatch (violently seize away) and cut, is with the entire arm with all of its length and that of the sword."

The original text reads,

"La mas famosa treta de la comun Destreza, cuuyo nombre es: Arrebatar y tajo"

"...para arrebatar, es con todo el braco, y tan largo, quanto su largura, y la de la espada."

on page 269 (the remisso, or withdrawal of the arm on either side of the adversary's blade)

"The *remisso* movement as we have stated is that which the sword makes to either of the sides (of the <adversary's> sword)..."

The original text reads,

"El movimiento remisso ya hemos dicho que es aquel que haze la espada a qualquiera de los lados,.."

on page 270 (the mixto, or mixed movement intended to maintain control of the adversary's sword)

"Mixed movement what it is and why it is called thus."

"The mixed movement is that which is made to either of the sides (of the sword) and is called mixed because it is done together by taking the contrary sword as when we parry (literally, to re-route or derail)."

The original text reads,

"Movimiento mixto qual es porque se llama asi"

"El movimiento mixto es aquel que se haze a qualquiera de los lados y llamasse mixto, porque se haze llevando juntamente la espada contraria como quando la desviamos,..."

on page 268 (concerning the movimientos violento, or sudden upward movement of the arm, and natural, or deliberate downward movement of the arm).

"...on lifting the arm upward (which is the violent movement)."

The original text reads,

"...*que al levanter el braco en alto (que es el moviento violento)*"
and
"...that the corruption of the violent movement is the cause from which the natural movement is engendered."
The original text reads,
"...*que la corrupcion del movimiento violento es causa que se engendre el natural,...*" Translation by Ramon Martinez.
Finally, Carrança, the father of the school, lists all the movimientos in the back of his book in the sections titled, "Declaracion de lo que Significa Cada Vocabulo de los que tocan á la Theorica de la Arte" and the following Tabula. However, to list all of these would take a treatise in and of itself.

[30] La Verdadera Destreza is based on geometrical principles. At any stage of an encounter the position of the fencers can be described on an imaginary circle. This circle exists in the minds of the fencers, and would only ever have been drawn on the ground as a training tool. Spanish swordsmen stand facing each other at opposite ends of the diameter of an imaginary circle and assume their stance. They will then commence to step around each other along the circumference of this imaginary circle. The *Diestros* will endeavor to maintain their position on the diameter of the circle as they walk around the circle because it is the most safe position for them to be. If the swordsmen attack along the diameter of the circle they would impale each other. The attack is always executed at an angle to the adversary's blade. In order for an attack to be successful one *Diestro* has to lead the other off the diameter by carefully executed footwork. At that moment the swordsman who has not maintained his position on the diameter and has permitted himself to be led to a less strategic position, is vulnerable to attack.

[31] The Spanish terms may be found in Hieronymo Carrança, *De la filosofia de las armas,* Lisbon 1582, The terms *atajo* and *estocada* are explained in the section *Declaracion de lo que Significa Cada Vocabulo de los que tocan á la Theorica de la Arte. Stringer della Spada* is discussed by Ridolfo Capo Ferro, Gran Simvlacro Dell'Arte Edell'Vso Della Scherma. Siena 1610 p. 38. *Stoccata* is used freely by Saviolo in *Vincentio Saviolo his Practise.* London 1595, initially on page 9V

[32] *Vincentio Saviolo his Practise,* London 1595 p. 20V (also labeled page 14)

[33] From Saviolo's usage it is clear that he uses Dall'Agocchie's definitions of the terms imbroccata, stoccata and punta riversa. Dall'Agocchie writes "But the thrust that is delivered from over the hand is named imbroccata: & that is from under the hand, stoccata: & that starts from the left side is named punta riversa" Translation by Stephen Hand. The original text reads "Ma venendo alle punte, quella che si fa sopra mano, fu detta imbroccata: & quella che si fa sotto mano, stoccata: & quella che dal le parti manche si diparte, punta riversa:" Giovanni Dall'Agocchie, *Dell'Arte Discrimia Libri Tre*, Venetia 1572 p. 8V

[34] *Vincentio Saviolo his Practise*, London 1595 p. 20V (also labelled page 14)

[35] "2. Lying or so as to lie at full length, flat or recumbent, on the back and with the face upward; supine. Usu. with lie" *Oxford English Dictionary*, 2nd Edition Vol. XIX, p.130

[36] Don Luys Pacheco De Narvaez , *Libro de las Grandezas de la Espada*, Madrid 1600 The correct stance is described on pages 37-41. Translation by Ramon Martinez. See also note 17.

[37] Achille Marozzo, *Opera Nova*, Bologna 1536 p.46R

[38] *Remove* is the word which Saviolo uses instead of the word pass or the Italian equivalents passo, passare or passade. In *Giacomo Di Grassi his True Arte of Defence* London 1594 p. 15V the pass (translated into the English as pace) is described thus, "It is to be knowen that the feete moue either streightly, either circulerly: If streitly, then either forwardes or backwards: but when they move directly forwards, they frame either a halfe or a whol pace. By whole pace is vnderstood when the foot is carried from behind forwards, kepinge stedfast the forefoot."

[39] *Vincentio Saviolo his Practise.* London 1595 For example, "the teacher...shall remoue his right foot behinde his left striking a crosse blow at the head. L. And the scholler what shall he doo: V. When I remoue with my foote and lift vp my hand, let the scholler passe with his left foote where his right was," p. 15R (also labelled page 9)

[40] Ibid. p. 24V (also labeled page 19)

[41] Note the use of the word remove in this instance to denote a traverse rather than a pass. There is clearly not a 1:1 correlation between the words remove and pass.

[42] Don Francisco Lorenz de Rada, *La Nobleza de la Espada ...Madrid* 1705, Vol. 2 Book 3 p. 399. In Vol.

1 Book 2 p.45 Rada claims that Narvaez uses the term, but the authors have been unable to find the term *transversal* in Narvaez's treatiseof 1600.

[43] As for example in Salvator Fabris, *De Lo Schermo Overo Scienza D'Arme* Copenhagen 1606, the text accompanying plate 40 in which the fencer being struck has stepped forward past his right foot with his left leg. "This hit in seconda against one in quarta who has passed with the left foot may easily arise in the following way," p.67 Translation by Stephen Hand. The original text reads "Qvesta ferita di seconda contra vna qvarta passata di pié sinistro inanzi facilmente è deriuata dall' essere andato collui,". In the anonymous *Pallas Armata The Gentlemans Armorie*. London 1639 the word *passade* is used on page 10 with an accompanying illustration on page 11 showing a step forward, past the right foot with the left leg.

[44] Don Luys Pacheco De Narvaez , *Libro de las Grandezas de la Espada*, Madrid 1600, pp. 62-64

[45] Hieronymo Carrança, *De la filosofia de las armas*, Lisbon 1582, The terms *atajo* and *estocada*, are explained in the section *Declaracion de lo que Significa Cada Vocabulo de los que tocan á la Theorica de la Arte*.

[46] Ibid, The term *tajo*, is explained in the section *Declaracion de lo que Significa Cada Vocabulo de los que tocan á la Theorica de la Arte*. *Mandoble* is explained on page 155.

[47] Vincentio Saviolo his Practise. London 1595 pp. 26R&V (also labelled pages 20)

[48] Hieronymo Carrança, *De la filosofia de las armas*, Lisbon 1582, The term *acometimiento*, is explained in the section *Declaracion de lo que Significa Cada Vocabulo de los que tocan á la Theorica de la Arte*.

[49] Vincentio Saviolo his Practise. London 1595 "L. But tell mee I praie you, is it not all one if I take hold of the arme of my teacher or adversarie, in sted of laying my hande uppon his warde?
V. No in deede, for if your enemie were skilfull in this art, whilest you catch him by the hand or arme, hee might with his lefte hand seize upon his weapon & put you in danger of your life. So that you must take heed to have all advantage of your enemie, that hee may not in anie sort do you anie harme: in dooing of which, you shall alwaies be to good for him." pp. 21R&V (also labelled pages 15)

[50] Hieronymo Carrança, *De la filosofia de las armas*, Lisbon 1582, The term *compass curvo*, is explained in the section *Declaracion de lo que Significa Cada*

Vocabulo de los que tocan á la Theorica de la Arte.

[51] Vincentio Saviolo his Practise. London 1595, pp. 19V-20R (also labelled pages 13 and 14)

[52] Hieronymo Carrança, *De la filosofia de las armas*, Lisbon 1582, The term *estraño*, is explained in the section *Declaracion de lo que Significa Cada Vocabulo de los que tocan á la Theorica de la Arte*. Note that while positions with a bent arm can be seen in Italian texts, notably in plates 45 and 119 of Salvator Fabris' *De Lo Schermo Overo Scienza D'Arme*, Copenhagen 1606, these are not *estraño* because the bent arm is used in a very different way. In the first example from Fabris, the bent arm is used to attack in an open line and reduce the distance. In the second example the bent arm is used as a means of a direct attack in opposition. Neither of these examples are defensive as the *estraño* is used in La Destreza. In the second example the posture of the body is very low and is moving forwards below the adversary's blade, quite different to la Destreza. Finally the bent arm is held above the head which is not common to La Destreza. In contrast, Saviolo's uses of the bent arm is to close the distance while keeping a line of attack closed, as practiced in La Destreza.

[53] Ibid. The term *desvio*, is explained in the section *Declaracion de lo que Significa Cada Vocabulo de los que tocan á la Theorica de la Arte*.

[54] Hieronymo Carrança, *De la filosofia de las armas*, Lisbon 1582, The term *reves*, is explained in the section *Declaracion de lo que Significa Cada Vocabulo de los que tocan á la Theorica de la Arte*.

[55] Luis Pacheco De Narvaez, *Llave y gobierno de la destreza. De una filosofia de las armas."* Unpublished MS. 1608, ed. Fernando Fernandez Lanza, University of Alcala de Henares, Spain , 1991, p. 429. The original text reads,

"Si desviare, meter pie izquiredo y sujetar su espada con la mano
Aqui se mete pie izquierdo.
Aquel que pelea en la propia obra, toma el consejo conforme la variedad de los casos que se le ofrecen, y ellos propios le van dictando y aconsejando lo que ha de hacer para salir sin peligo. Y aunque el movimiento o defensa, que podra hacer el contrario, o la comunmente se hace, es facil y de poco artificio y menos consideracion; y que al principio suyo lo conocierades (y pudiera excusarme de ponerla aqui, porque no quede nada en confuso, ni que sea menester poner trabajo en

estudiarlo) advertireis su remedio a la herida de estocada, que senala al demostracion antes de esta. Es usado y comun remedio, querer coger la punta de la espada que le va a herir, en la guarnacion de la suya, levantando hacia arriba, solo con determinacion de quitar la herida, pero no de ofender con otra que ellos llevan prevenida; ni hay que tartar de tal porque este es oficio de la destreza verdader: dar herida y defender la contraria. Por lo cual, da mas lugar y mas seguridad para ofenderles, porque como ellos no procuran ofender sino defenderse, dan lugar a que se les vaya ejecutando muchas heridas hasta que de alguna llegue el efecto y su dano todo junto. Pues si vuestro contrario hiciere el tal desvio, conociendo el principio del movimiento, y conociendo que es primera llevar vuestra espada al angulo obtuso, y quitara la punta de la suya de delante de vuestro cuerpo; con grandisima presteza daries compas curvo de punto C. a punto E., metiendo pie izquierdo perfilando el cuerpo, sujetando la guarnacion con la mano izquierda, que lo podreis hacer por estar cerca. Y formareis un reves que ha de ir, como ya en otras partes hemos dicho, pegando con el muslo derecho como los que espadan lino, ejecutandolo en la cabeza en el lado derecho. Y tambien podries herir de estocada, pues lo uno y lo otro estara en vuestra mano y el contrario no pueda retirarse con tanta presteza, que antes que salga con su intento hayais conseguido el vuestro." Translation by Ramon Martinez.

[56] Don Luys Pacheco De Narvaez, *Libro de las Grandezas de la Espada*, Madrid 1600 p.60 *"Por la linea del diametro no se puede caminar sin peligro."* (Along the line of the diameter one can not walk without peril.) Translation by Ramon Martinez. The diameter is the straight line between the two fencers.

[57] Gerard Thibault, *Académie de l'espée*, Leyden 1630

[58] Francisco Lorenz de Rada, *La Nobleza de la Espada*, Madrid 1705

[59] *Vincentio Saviolo his Practise*. London 1595 p. 1V

HIGHLAND SWORDSMANSHIP

By Paul Wagner

Introduction

The Scottish Highlanders were the last of Europe's tribal societies, and inherited many customs and institutions virtually unchanged from the ancient Celtic tribes. The sword in particular held a special place in Highland culture, and they were one of history's very few primarily sword-armed armies, amassing a remarkable series of victories over conventional troops throughout the 16th, 17th and 18th centuries. The fighting methods of the Highlanders are thus of considerable interest to both historical fencers and military historians. Most analysis, however, has been at the tactical level, for example on the origin and effectiveness of the "Highland charge"[1]. In contrast, Gaelic swordsmanship itself has received little attention, and is often dismissed as being "simple" or "crude" (in keeping with the historically prejudiced view of Gaelic civilisation) - for example, a recent book on the use of Highland broadsword and targe was reviewed with dismissive comments such as "the Scot weapons themselves are fairly simple and without any sophisticated method of their own"[2] and "the Art of the Scottish Broadsword and Targe as featured 42 small-format pages probably corresponds very closely to what a knock-kneed Highlander must have known about the use of his sidearm as he felt a draft of cold air up his kilt at Culloden"[3]. However, it could be argued that the secret of the Highlander's military success must have lain primarily at the level of the individual swordsman.

The only way the famously "undisciplined" Highlanders, whose primary tactic was to "run towards the enemy in a disorderly manner,"[4] could have prevailed so regularly over conventional soldiery was through a clear superiority at close-quarter combat. Accounts of the Highland Charge emphasise the mob-like nature of the clan warriors, whose only real ambition was to close with the enemy as soon as possible and engage in single-combat - for example, after the charge of the Jacobite right wing had triumphed at Sheriffmuir in 1715, an eyewitness described how they "arrived in such confusion that it was impossible to form them according to the line of battle projected...every one posted himself as he found ground"[5]. Although less famous than the great battles, Highlanders preferred small-scale "guerilla warfare" actions where the their martial ability could be used to the best effect, such as the incident in 1655 when Sir Ewen Cameron of Lochiel and 32 of his elite luchd-tagh (household troops) attacked and destroyed 138 English soldiers who had been sent to chop down some of the Cameron's woods, for the loss of only 5 of their own[6]. The eagerness with which Highlanders would attempt to prove their skill at single combat, regardless of wider military considerations, showed (in the words of one British general) "how little they knew of war, except the mere fighting part of it". It is, however, the very part that most interests historical fencers and re-enactors, and thus deserves more serious consideration that it has received to date.

The main reason for the lack of work on Highland swordsmanship would seem to be simply that there is little in the way of concrete evidence about the subject. Celtic culture was, by and large, a non literary one - the Druids had a prohibition on committing their knowledge to written word, and even the clan bards of the 18th century retained this emphasis on oral transition and eidetic memory[7]. The practical upshot is that none of the Welsh, Irish or Highland masters are known to have recorded their knowledge as the English, Germans or Italians did. There are, however, several lines of inquiry that can provide a great deal of information about the native fencing style of the Highlanders.

Highland Warrior Society

As with all Celtic societies, the Scottish Highland warriors were a highly trained and educated social elite. Combat was their primary right and responsibility, and even though the clan armies were bulked out with lower-class clansmen, most of the actual fighting was done by the front ranks of sword-armed clan elite, the "gentlemen" or daoine uaisle ("people of pride"), and the professional warriors or ceathernach[8]. From the age of 10 they spent the summer in "martial academies" where they were taught how to use bows and muskets, dirks, swords and targes. Strength and agility was built in sword dances, wrestling, throwing the stone, tossing the caber and playing camanachd (shinty)[9]. The emphasis was on physical toughness, fieldcraft and individual weapon skill, rather than drill or mass manoeuvres, and the warriors so trained were proud and independent, and primarily concerned with their own individual prowess, honour and glory.

That Highlanders were skilled swordsmen seems undeniable, and was remarked upon regularly - for example, William Sacheverell, Governor of the Isle of Man, made an excursion through the Western Isles in 1688, where he recorded:

"A round target on their backs, a blue bonnet on their heads, in one hand a broad-sword, and a musquet in the other. Perhaps no other nation goes better armed; and I assure you they will handle them with bravery and dexterity, especially the sword and target"[10]

Sacheverell's impression of Highland prowess was confirmed the following year at the battle at Killiekrankie, where the clansmen;

"...fell in pell-mell among the thickest of them with their broadswords ... the noise seemed hushed; and the fire ceasing on both sides, nothing was heard...but the sullen and hollow clashes of broadswords, with the dismall groans and crys of dyeing and wounded men"[11]

The Jacobite era has left dozens of similar descriptions of the carnage inflicted by Highland swordmen on their enemies, and even as late as the battle of Quebec in 1758 Highlanders armed with broadswords proved quite unstoppable;

"When these took to their broadswords, my God! What a havock they made! They drove everything before them, and walls could not resist their fury. Those breechless fellows are an honour to their country. I cannot do justice in my description of them."[12]

Highland Weaponry

Before the disarming act of 1747, the Highland warrior was one of the most completely armed in Europe. A Highlander's weapons were an essential part of his character. They were worn as a normal part of his attire, and rarely did he venture forth without a range of arms upon his person, and in the 18th century it was recorded that;

"it is well known that highlanders go about almost constantly armed, partly with a view of being always ready to defend themselves or to attack their enemies, and partly that being accustomed to the instruments of death they may be less apprehensive of them."[13]

The ownership of and proficiency with weapons were part of the duty of every clansman to his chief, and the Highlands could produce a formidably armoury - a roll taken by the Earl of Atholl in 1638 records that 523 men between them owned 448 broadswords, 3 claymores, 112 guns, 11 pistols, 149 bows, 125 targes, 9 lochaber axes, 2 halberds, 11 breastplates, 8 "headpieces", 2 "steel bonnets", 1 pair of plate sleeves, and 1 coat of mail.[14]

The type and variety of Highland weaponry is well recorded in 16th and 17th century sources, including longbows, spears, darts, halberds, lochaber axes, two-handed "claymores" and dirks (see Figure 1). Of these nothing can really be said of their use, except that it would have presumably been equivalent to that found in other Western European nations.[15] One of the most distinctive armaments, however, was the combination of "a very broad sword" and "a strong handsome target,"[16] which became the standard Highland weaponry dur-

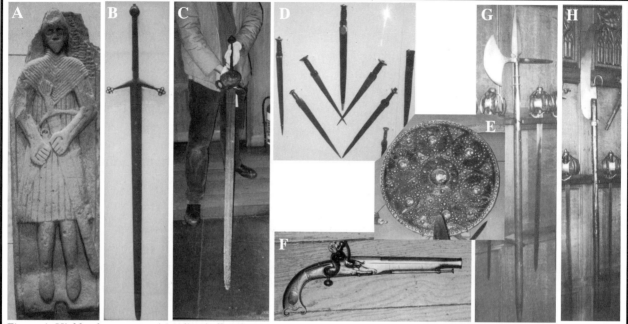

Figure 1. *Highland weaponry. a) Medieval effigy from the Western Highlands, showing a warrior dressed in a quilted leather aketon or cotun, and wearing a long, broad-bladed single-handed sword of the type typical of the 14th-16th century Highlands. b) A 15th century Highland longsword or "claymore." These broad-bladed two-handed sword were optimised for cutting. c) A 17th century "clam-guard" two-handed sword. d) A selection of dirks. e) A studded leather targe. f) An all-steel Highland pistol, which could be used as a club after being discharged. g) A Lochaber axe. There were a huge variety of polearms used by the Gaels, of this was only one general categpry. h) A battle-axe.*

ing the Jacobite era. The distinctive basket-hilted broadsword, also called a "claymore" (see Figure 2), is closely associated with the Highlanders, and of this weapon, at least, some useful information can be extracted.

Descriptions of Highland Swordsmanship

There are many first-hand accounts of Highlanders in battle, all of which emphasise the ferocity of the Highland Charge and the damage done at close quarters by the broadswords. Donald MacBane was on the receiving end at Killiekrankie, which he survived by running away;

> "The sun going down caused the Highland-men to advance upon us like mad men, without shoe of stocking, covering themselves from our fire with their targes. At last they cast away their muskets, drew their broad swords, and advanced furiously on us, and were in the middle of us before we could fire three shots, and obliged us to retreat, some back to the water, and some another way..."[17]

The success of sword-and-shield armed men against pikes or bayonets, although perhaps eas-

ily understood, was not a mere matter of madly charging in and relying on the shield. There are many references to clansmen cutting off pikeheads with their swords before closing,[18] and at Mulroy Hill MacBane reports;

> "...a highlandman attacked me with sword and targe, and cut my wooden handled bayonet out of the muzel of my gun; I then clubed my gun and gave him a stroke with it, which made the butt-end to fly off; Seeing the Highland-men to come fast upon me, I took to my heels and run thirty miles before I looked behind me."[18]

It is clear from the descriptions that the primary attack delivered by Highland swordsmen was a vertically descending cut onto the head. Accounts of Killiekrankie in 1689 talk of "heads lying cloven,"[19] and how "many...were cut down through the scull and neck, to the very breasts,"[20] while at Culloden Lord Robert Kerr died with "his head being cleft from crown to collar-bone."[21] At Clifton the English (dismounted) dragoons sent out to harass the retreating Jacobites were issued with iron helmets to wear beneath their hats, and when charged by the Macphearson rearguard "the poor

HIGHLAND BASKET-HILTED CLAYMORES

Figure 2. *Highland broadswords [Author's collection] The top left example is a Highland manufactured hilt of the type that was fully developed by 1560. The top right example is a simple buff-leather lined hilt of unusual design from around 1640. The lower left sword dates from the last half of the 17th century, and the lower right broadsword is a magnificent example of the fully developed Scottish baskethilt of the kind carried by clan warriors in 1745.*

swords suffered much, as there were no less than fourteen broke on the dragoons skull caps...before it seems the better way was found of doing their business."[22] The "better way" meant the thrust, and despite the surprise of the English armour, the Highland swordsmen still inflicted 40 casualties for the loss of only 5 men in this action.

Although it is clear from the above statistics that the Highlanders were, on the whole, better swordsmen than their military adversaries, the accounts give only a few hints of their technique. There are, however, detailed descriptions of how Highlanders dealt with bayonet lines. By the time of the 1745 Rebellion the British Army had fully developed the concept of "defence in depth". This utilised firing by ranks in order to keep up continuous fire against the charging clansmen, and if the Highlanders even reached their target they would (in theory) have great difficulty penetrating the hedge of bayonets presented by three close ranks.[23] Although often accused of being slow to adapt to new military technology, in fact the Gaels quickly invented a counter to the ranked defence-in-depth;

> "When within reach of the enemies' bayonets, bending their left knee, they, by their attitude, cover their bodies with their targets, that receive the thrusts of the bayonets, which they contrive to parry, while, at the same time, they raise their sword arm and strike their adversary. Having once got within the bayonets, the fate of the battle is decided in an instant, and the carnage follows; the Highlanders bringing down two men at a time, one with their dirk in the left hand, and another with the sword."[24]

or

> "(They) stooped low below the charged bayonets, they tossed them upward by the target, dirking the front rank man with the left hand, while stabbing or hewing down the rear rank man with the right; thus, as usual in all Highland onsets, the whole body of soldiers was broken, trod underfoot, and dispersed in a moment."[25]

The technique described above is extremely sophisticated and difficult to execute - approaching the bayonet line at a run, the swordsman must drop low with the left leg, deflect the front-ranked bayonet upwards with the targe, then pass forward with the right foot, striking the second-rank soldier to the right with the broadsword while simultaneously dirking the front-ranked man in the chest. This is certainly an extremely impressive feat, but it is simply one technique against one particular formation, and says little about the depth of Highland swordsmanship.

Manuals on Highland Broadsword

Although there are no native Gaelic manuals on the use of the basket-hilted broadsword, several fencing manuals were written by Scots who might be expected to be familiar with Highland methods, such as Sir William Hope and Donald MacBane.[26] Hope was a Lowland small-sword master who devoted a surprising proportion of his books instructing his students how to deal with broadsword-armed opponents, and warned them not to lunge, thrust or even "Stand not to an Ordinary Guard, for then he would Disable your Sword Arm."[27] MacBane was an expert with smallsword and spadroon, and his "The Expert Sword-Man's Companion" also offers advice on how to deal with Highlanders armed with broadsword and targe, something he had experienced first hand in a clan fight with the MacDonalds at Mulroy in 1688;

> "The MacDonalds came down the hill upon us without either shoe, stocking or bonnet on their head. They gave a shout...then

Figure 3. *MacBane's stance with the Highland broadsword* [Author's collection]

broke in upon us with their Sword and Target, and Lochaber Axes...Seeing my Captain sore wounded, and a great many more with heads lying cloven....I was sadly affrighted, never having seen the like before."[28]

As Highlanders joined the British Army in increasing numbers during the late 18th and 19th centuries, the "Highland broadsword" became a popular weapon among the troops, and several fencing works were devoted to it. These included Henry Angelo's "Hungarian and Highland broadsword" (1799), Roworth's "The Art of Defence on foot with the broad sword and sabre uniting the Scotch and Austrian methods into one regular system" (1798), John Taylor's "The Art of Defence on Foot with the Broad Sword and Sabre: adapted also to the Spadroon, or Cut-and-Thrust Sword" (1804), Thomas Mathewson's, "A New Treatise on the Art of the Scotch Broadsword" (1805), and the wonderfully entitled "Anti-Pugilism, or the science of defence exemplified in short and easy lessons, for the practice of the Broad Sword and Single Stick. Whereby gentlemen may become proficients in the use of these weapons, without the help of a Master, and be enabled to chastise the insolence and temerity, so frequently met with, from those fashionable gentlemen, the Johnsonians, Big Bennians, and Mendozians of the present Day; a work perhaps better calculated to extirpate this reigning and brutal folly than a whole volume of sermons" of 1790, credited simply to "a Highland officer."

The authors of these works were justifiably proud of the feats the Highland Regiments had performed broadsword-in-hand, and keen to claim their place in the martial tradition of the Gaels; for example, the aforementioned Highland Officer wrote;

> "My countrymen, the Highlanders, have, from time immemorial, evinced the utility of the Broad Sword; and, by their skillful management of it in the day of battle, have gained immortal honour. Such has been the effect of their dexterity and knowledge of this weapon, that undisciplined crowds have made a stand against, nay, and have defeated a regular army." [29]

However, the weakness with using these works

to recreate Highland fighting styles is that they are all relatively late, and influenced by contemporary military techniques which do not necessarily reflect traditional clan methods - in fact, the methods for "Highland broadsword" differ little from those described by earlier English texts such as Lonnergan's "The Fencer's Guide" (1771), Zachary Wylde's "The English Master of Defence" (1711), or Swetnam's "The Schoole of the Noble and Worthy Science of Defence" (1617). Contemporary descriptions of Highland battles, however, would suggest that, rather than the right-foot-forward slashing approach favoured by 18th and 19th century military swordsmen, the Highlanders retained a more medieval style of swordplay from which powerful cuts are delivered "on the pass". Lowland Scottish and English troops were always horrified by the damage done by the Highland broadswords, such as at Killiekrankie in 1689;

> "Many officers and soldiers were cut down through the scull and neck, to the very breasts; others had sculls cut off above the ears. Some had both their bodies and crossbelts cut through at one blow; pikes and small swords were cut like willows."[30]

...or the local newspaper account of the Battle of Prestonpans in 1745;

> "the field of battle presented an appalling spectacle rarely exhibited even in the most bloody conflicts. As almost all the slain were cut down by the broadsword and the scythe, the ground was strewn with heads, legs, arms, hands and mutilated bodies"[31]

In comparison, the style of "Highland Broadsword" taught by Angelo, Taylor, etc, is not designed for cutting off limbs and cleaving heads[32]. For example, the anonymous Highland Officer said clearly that;

> "the motion of the sword is to proceed from the wrist only."[33]

and

"In this movement your wrist exactly performs this figure 8 (turned sideways), which I strongly recommend to beginners the frequent practice of, as not only the success of these two cuts entirely depend on its being neatly executed, but all the cuts and disengagements are a part of it; and it will render the wrist pliant and flexible, which is an indispensible requisite in order to become a master of your weapon."[34]

Even MacBane, who might be most expected to be influenced by the clans, was true to his conventional training in smallsword and spadroon, and his attacks with the broadsword were done by "throwing quick at the Inside and Outside of the Face"[35] (see Figure 3), making slashing cuts from the wrist and forearm rather that the limb-severing, head cleaving style of the Highlanders, whose swords were wielded "circling in the air."[36]

There are, however, occasional echoes of the older style, particularly in Thomas Mathewson's, "A New Treatise on the Art of the Scotch Broadsword" from 1805. Mathewson was the only author to specifically train with the last of the Scottish swordmasters, as he "made it my study to find out and frequent the company of the most able swordsmen and masters,"[37] and in addition to a number of British Army swordsmen he acknowledges five civilians; one Irishman, a Campbell and MacLane of Galloway, MacGregor of Paisley, and Mr Rogerson of Edinburgh. There are two instances where Mathewson is in sharp contrast to all other 17th, 18th and 19th British military swordmasters, and uses techniques which he can only have picked up off the Highlanders.

Firstly, although engaging in a conventional right-foot-forward stance, Mathewson is alone among his contemporaries in recommending attacks be done "on the pass" from a left-foot-forward stance, and that passing back out-of-distance was a better defence than warding with the sword;

"The scholar at the inside guard will move his right leg back, behind the left, and form his hanging guard, step forward with his right foot a full three feet, and throw at his adversary's head; he will immediately recover with his right leg back, forming his hanging guard, and receive his adversary's cut for his head…This is the most useful lesson in learning the Broad Sword, as it gives action to the body to move forward and backward as circumstances may require, and the leg being moved back in place of guarding with the sword, is allowed by the best fencers to be preferable."[38]

What Mathewson is saying here is to pass back to launch the attack (out-of-distance, avoiding the danger of receiving a cut or stop-thrust when raising the sword to attack), pass in to deliver the cut, and then pass back out-of-distance afterwards to avoid any counterattack. These instructions are exactly the same as the George Silver's,[39] except that Silver would, if attacking from "Open Ward", already be starting left-foot-forward and thus skip the first step (see Figure 4).

The second unique aspect of Mathewson's work is advertised in the full title of the manual;

"A New Treatise on the Art of the Scotch Broad Sword: shewing the superiority of that weapon, when opposed to an enemy armed with a spear, pike, or gun and bayonet"

The entire second section "shewing the superiority" of the broadsword over the bayonet consists of a single trick he also presumabiy picked up in the Highlands, but of which he seems extremely

Figure 4. *Thomas Mathewson demonstrates how to pass backwards in order to avoid a counterattack. In the best tradition of English fencing manuals, the pictures rarely match the text. [Author's collection]*

proud. The technique described is, in fact, a variation on Vincent Saviolo's instructions on how to deal with an opponent in the "Spanish Ward,"[40] and if nothing else it indicates that Highland fencing was as sophisticated as the Renaissance rapier schools.

By comparing the published manuals with actual accounts of Highland swordsmanship, it would seem that the British military system of "Highland broadsword" did not evolve directly out of native Gaelic swordsmanship, but was, at it's core, a foreign style foisted upon Regimental recruits by the British military. This view is confirmed by Samuel Johnson and James Boswell, who toured the Hebrides in 1773 and reported that swordsmanship had completely disappeared from the Highlands following the post-Culloden disarming. Johnson wrote;

> "After all that has been said of the force and terrour of the Highland sword, I could not find that the art of defence was any part of common education."[41]

and Boswell recorded the chief of MacLeod lamenting the loss of the martial arts;

> "I am sorry that prize-fighting is gone out; every at should be preserved, and the art of defence is surely important. It is absurd that our soldiers should have swords, and not be taught the use of them."[42]

The complete loss of martial understanding is clearly evident in MacLeod's comment's on his ancestor Rory More's "Glaymore [sic.], which was wielded with both hands, and is of prodigious size,"[43] where the Highlander absurdly claimed;

> "I think the heavy glaymore was an ill-contrived weapon. A man could strike only once with it. It employed both his hands, and he must of course be soon fatigued with wielding it; so that if his antagonist could only keep playing a while, he was sure of him. I would fight with a dirk against Rory More's sword. I could ward off a blow with a dirk, and then run in upon my enemy…"[44]

Illustrations of Highland Swordsmen

In the absence of native Gaelic fencing manuals it is necessary to turn to iconographic evidence to determine what style of fencing the native Highlanders actually practiced prior to the Disarming. There are a number of contemporary illustrations and portraits of sword-armed clansmen, all of which confirm that they retained a style of fencing that had passed out of use elsewhere in Europe by around 1600.

The single most common stance depicted in contemporary artwork is a high ward, held left-foot-forward, with the shield in front of the chest and the sword elevated above the head. In some cases the sword is held either vertically or sloping slightly backwards (Silver's "Open Ward"[45]), or alternatively sloping slightly forwards and diagonally across the head, with the true edge upwards - Richard Watt's "Alastair Grant the Champion" and the Austrian artist Martin Engelbrecht's depiction of a Highlander are some of the better known, but many other contemporary pictures show the same general ward. It is essentially a diagonally-oriented version of the English "St George Ward", and is so typical of Highland swordsmanship I am tempted to label it the "St Andrews Ward"[46] (see Figure 5 and 6).

The two central figures in David Morier's famous painting of Culloden are in a low "Passata" ward[47] (with the hilt low by the right hip and the blade roughly horizontally. pointing forward) and a high "Zornhut" or "Ward of Wrath"[48] (an "Open Ward" variation with the hilt held above the head and blade sloping down behind the back). Laurie and Whittle's 1747 engraving "The Battle of Culloden" has a particularly interesting group of figures representing the charge of the Jacobite right wing, depicting a variety of wards that seem to represent the shift in stance as the clansmen approached the bayonet line. The 4th and 3rd men in the row are in a "Passata" and "Open Ward" respectively, with their shields flat on. The 2nd row figure has brought his shield forward and edge-on beside his sword-hand, in what can only be likened to I.33's "Half-Shield."[49] The figure in the front row has raised his sword into Open Ward, and is being skewered by a British bayonet, but the Highlander next to him is slipping his targe

Figure 5. *Variations on the Gaelic high ward as depicted in period artwork. a) From Blaeu's map of "Scotia Antiqua", 1643; b) Richard Watt's "Alastair Grant the Champion", early 18th century; c) Martin Engelbrecht's Highlander, mid-18th century; d) A propaganda print of Jenny Cameron, 1745; e) Charging Highlander from military print of Culloden, Aberdeen University Library, c.1746. While a) is in a classic Silver "Open Ward", all the others have their swords sloping upwards and forwards over the head in the "St Andrew's Ward"*

Figure 6. *Rob Roy MacGregor [Author's collection]
Two contemporary images of Rob Roy, from Sir Walter Scott's collection at Abbotsford. The first shows Rob in Open Ward with single sword, standing menacingly over a fallen foe. The second is obviously inspired by "Alastair Grant the Champion"*

Figure 7. *Wards of the Highland Charge [Author's collection]. a) The two central figures from David Morier's "Culloden" (1746), painted using captives from the battle as models, in a high Zornhut and low Passata ward. b) Charging Highlanders from Laurie and Whittle's "The Battle of Culloden" (1747). From left to right they are in an Open Ward, Passata, Half-Shield, Open Ward again, and another Half-Shield. The central-right figure is slipping his targe to deflect the bayonet aimed under his sword-arm, a sophisticated movement that is used with both I.33's small buckler and Talhoffer's great duelling shields. This would seem to have been the Highlander's answer to Cumberland's much-vaunted orders to thrust bayonets at the underarm of the clansman to the right rather than the one directly ahead.*

over to his right side to deflect a bayonet aimed at his right armpit, while bringing his sword down on the Redcoat's head[50] (see Figure 7).

The Penicuick Sketches

By far the best record of native Highland sword styles are the "Penicuick Sketches", which clearly demonstrate the commonality between the 18th century Highland style and the pre-Renaissance form of European swordplay (see Figure 8). These are a series of sketches drawn by an unknown artist in the Penicuick area of Scotland during the 1745 Jacobite Rebellion,[51] and consist of around 50 figures, of which around a dozen are armed with sword and/or targe. Of these, most might be said to be in an en guarde stance. Although they have a certain air of caricature about them, the sketches show ample evidence of close

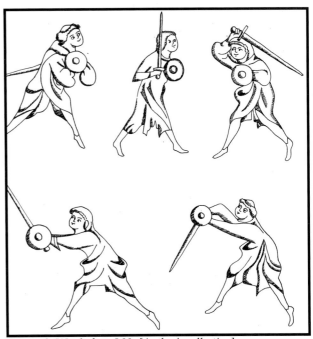

Figure 8. *The wards of the Penicuick Sketches [Author's collection].*
a) A Clan officer with single sword. Is he en guarde or just cranky?;
b) "The Crook". Note how the hilt is held below eye level, a detail
which distinguishes the I.33 ward from other "Hanging Wards",
and is used in the delivery of "stab-knocks". For a functional expla-
nation see "Footwork in Fechtbuch I.33" by the author elsewhere in
this volume; c) The "St Andrews Ward". Note how the shield is held
facing inwards; d) and e) "Walpurgis' Ward", another high ward
variation; f) The same ward held sword-foot-forward; g) Highlander
in an "Iron Door"-like ward; h) A dramatic "Underarm"

L-shape with the front foot pointing at target, and the rear foot roughly at right angles to it. Interestingly, four of the fourteen figures are left-handed, which might be considered artistic licence intended to make the exotic Gaels appear more "sinister" except that they are known individuals, identified by name. Only one figure has a sword alone, and while the rest are all wielding targes none have a dirk drawn. Assuming the drawings are accurate to scale, the shields would range in size from around 18" to perhaps 28" diameter, while surviving targes are generally in the 18-21" range.[52]

The ward positions depicted in the Sketches are varied and particularly revealing, and their relationship to medieval swordplay is immediately obvious (see Figures 9 & 10). Most common is a high ward, with the blade vertical and the sword hilt pulled back roughly level with the right shoulder (like the famous Japanese hasso no kamae ward). The only analogue of this the author is aware of appears in I.33 as one of the Priest's "special wards", held by the enigmatic Walpurgis.[53]

observation of actual Highlanders, with their garb, arms and accoutrements all accurately drawn, including the belted plaid, hose with "castellated" tops, garters and brogues. This attention to detail makes it a fair assumption that the fighting postures illustrated are also an accurate representation of the actual use of Highland weapons.

Some general observations can be made about the figures. Firstly, like other contemporary illustrations, nearly all the combatants are standing sword-foot-back, in the "medieval" style stance from which powerful cuts are delivered on-the-pass. The figures are generally in a low crouch, their feet are widely spaced, forming the typical

Figure 9. *Wards from I.33 [Author's collection]*
Five wards for sword-and-buckler similar to those of the Penicuick
Sketches. a) Walpurgis' Ward; b) The Crook; c) Underarm; d) Half-
Shield; e) The 4th Ward ("zornhut"); The differences in shield
positions between these and the Highlanders is largely explained
by the differences in size and grip between a 12-15" I.33 buckler
and a 20" or larger target.

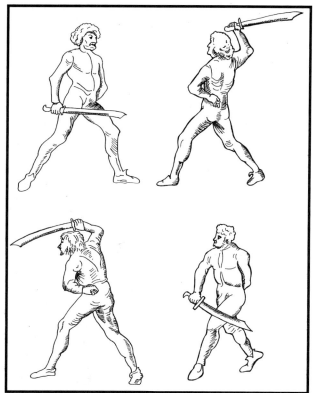

Figure 10. *Wards from Durer [Author's collection] Four wards for single sword similar to those of the Penicuick Sketches.*

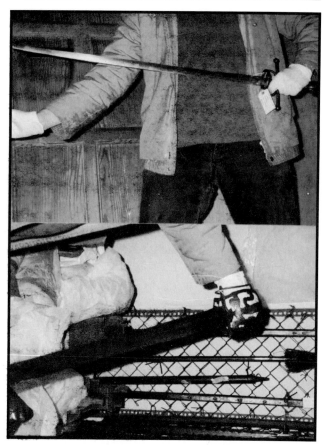

Figure 11. *Contrast between Italian and Highland swords [Author's collection]. a) A spada da lato or "side-sword", Italian, 16ᵗʰ century. Note the short, narrow, stiff blade, optimised for thrusting. b) A native Highland manufactured broadsword, mid-17ᵗʰ century. Note the long, wide, thin blade, optimised for cutting.*

Two figures are in the previously mentioned "St Andrews Ward", two are in what I.33 names "Underarm", and another has adopted an outside hanging ward with low hilt, which I.33 calls "The Crook."[54] One is in a "Low Ward" analogous to the medieval longsword "Fool's Ward" or "Guard of the Iron Door."[55] The right-foot-forward "Medium", "Inside" and "Outside" guards typical of contemporary English swordplay and the later military style of Highland broadsword are notable by their absence.

It should be noted that there are parallels between the depicted Highland wards and those for sword-and-buckler in some Renaissance Italian manuals. Marozzo has the Open Ward under the name Guardia Alta ("High Guard"), and the "St Andrews Ward" is similar to his Guardia di Testa ("Head Guard"). His Guardia di Coda longa and larga tends to have a drooping point like the "Low Ward", which Dall'Agocchie actually calls the Porta di ferro (Iron door) or Cinghiale (wild boar). Manciolino has an "Underarm Ward" as the Guardia di Sotto il Braccio, and several Italian manuals show an outside hanging ward, the Becha Cesa/Becha Possa in Marozzo and the Alicornio

("Unicorn") in Dall'Agocchie. Marozzo also has his buckler up by the left side of his face, in the manner of at least some of the depicted clansmen.[56]

However, there are also significant differences between the Italian material and the Highland sketches. The Guardia di Coda longa and larga or Porta di ferro is only shown by the Italians right leg forward, and with the blade angled down at no more than 30° it is still a thrusting ward; the Cinghiale is held left foot forward, but is held in quarta, also for thrusting. The Alicornio is angled up, and has more in common with the Prima rapier ward than the true hanging ward, and the Highland "St Andrews Ward" is not, as Marozzo's Guardia di Testa, designed primarily to guard the head, but rather is held pointing forward to threaten both cut and thrust, more like the Ochs of German longsword. The Guardia di Sotto il Braccio is held with the sword horizontal just under the shield, not angled down as with the Highland "Underarm", and, more significantly, is absent from Marozzo and Agocchie, and only appears in Manciolino, indicating it was not of great significance in the Italian style - in contrast, it is the single most important ward in I.33, and, appearing twice in the Sketches, would appear to be equally important to the Highland style. The Italians have an upright stance, rather than the low crouch of the Scots, and never hold their shields edge-on, which at least half the Highlanders do. This, combined with the fact that the Renaissance masters used the light cut-and-thrust spada da lato rather than a heavier military weapon like the Highland broadsword[57] (see Figure 11), should probably warn against using their style as the primary basis for reconstructing Highland sword-and-targe.

The Use of the Shield in Highland Swordplay

The Highland "targe" was a stout round shield of which the earliest surviving examples are from the 16th century, but are referred to in an Act of the Scottish Parliament in 1456[58]. The typical Highland targe was constructed of dense, strong wood, either oak or Scots pine, with two layers of 1/4 inch planks glued together at right-angles, forming a strong cross-ply. The front was covered with tough cow-hide and further strengthened with brass studs and metal plates on the front and sides, and the back was covered with cow, goat or deer skin, and stuffed to absorb blows. Some targes also had a 10 inch spike that could be screwed into the central boss.[59]

The 17th and 18th century Highland targes were a unique form of shield. Most were only 18- 21 inches in diameter, and thus significantly smaller than the large round targets described by Renaissance masters like di Grassi and Agrippa. However, they were also somewhat larger than the small buckler's used in I.33, and instead of being held with a "punch-grip", they were fitted with an arm loop and iron or leather hand grip, giving a sturdier hold against the impact of a thrusting pike, bayonet or heavy musket-butt, and also allowing a dirk to be held in the left hand and wielded offensively.

The targe positions shown in the "Penicuick Sketches" are more difficult to interpret than the

Figure 12. *Battle scene from the Penicuick Sketches [Author's collection]. A group of clansmen meet a charge of dragoons. From left to right the wards depicted are Underarm, Walpurgis' Ward, and the St Andrew's Ward. The dead would appear to be Redcoats, with drum and infantry hats. Note how the leftmost body has had his bayonet sliced off the end of his musket.*

sword wards. Some of the figures appear to have their targes held close to the left of their face, on at least a 45° angle if not flat-on. They would thus seem to be in danger of obscuring the swordsman's vision, despite MacBane's warning that "a Man that does not understand the Targe is better without it that with it, as it blinds his own Eyes."[60] In other sketches the targes are low and flat-on, protecting the body, or edge on, protecting the left side and closing the line to the swordarm.

This variety of postures might be explained by the different conditions of use the Highland soldiers had to face. For example, against a bayonet line, the shield might be expected to be held low to guard the belly. When duelling a single-sword armed British officer the shield might be best separated from the sword, but when duelling another shield-armed clansman it might be kept closer to the line of attack[61]. When coming under fire (one sketch shows the men facing a dragoon charge and being fired on by pistols - see Figure 12) they would be held up to cover the face, as often described in eyewitness accounts, such as at the Battle of Kilsyth in 1645;

> "with claymores and dirks and with heads down behind their targets they swept on with shrill hurrahs, high hoarse war cries, and the din of the pibroch in their ears...Furiously, with their keen claymores and long dirks they fell upon the Covenanters, hewing down horse and foot with equal facility, many of the former having their thighs shorn off close to the saddle-lap, and, in a few moments the foe became an inextricable mob."[62]

Figure 13. *Duelling Highlanders [Author's collection]. ressed in only their shirts and bonnets, two clansmen fencing, presumably in practice rather than in earnest. Note how the left-hand figure has his shield held edge-on as he lunges forward.*

Figure 14. *a) Holding his shield in an odd "flipped" position, MacBane engages a spear held in an equally odd grip [Author's collection]. b) MacBane demonstrates how to use a target against a Lochaber axe. Not that the shield is held edge-on, and is used to close the line to the swordarm as well as deflect the incoming attack, the basic concept behind the use of both I.33's small buckler and Talhoffer's great duelling shields [Author's collection]*

Apart from the aforementioned example of the dragoons, there is no indication which of these possibilities any of the Penicuick figures were engaged in or practicing for when sketched, except in one case. Here two clansmen are shown duelling with sword and shield in a very dramatic "action" shot. The left hand figure is shown with his shield edge-on by his side, launching an imbroccata or descending thrust at the right-hand figure, who is lurching backwards and covering his head with his shield (see Figure 13). This would seem to be an unlikely reaction to this thrust if that were all that was happening, and it would appear that the right-hand figure has struck first and is lifting his targe to defend the expected counterattack to the head as he passes out; instead, however, the defender has passed forward with a thrust aimed at the breast, underneath the shield. Although little in the way of concrete technique can be gained from this sketch, it does illustrate the use of passing footwork, movement in-and-out of distance, and the use of thrusts, cuts and feints as part of Highland swordplay.

One particularly curious aspect is that several of the targes are held "flipped" over, with the arm upside down so the face of the shield is on the inside. This position is also illustrated in, but sadly not explained by, MacBane (see Figure 14). MacBane says a little about the use of shields. He admires the targe, saying;

> "This Target is of great use to those who rightly understand it, but to unexperienced People is often very Fatal, by blinding themselves with it, for want or right

understanding it. Therefore who has a mind to use it must take care to have it upon an Edge, so as to Cover his Left side from which is a Defence against Ball or any Weapon."[63]

MacBane's advise as to how to defend yourself against a Highlander with broadsword and targe is not very hopeful; he essentially relies upon improvised armour and an old trick, suggesting that the odds were very much in the Highlander's favour;

> "take off the Right Slive of your Coat, and Roll it about your Arm, and that will Defend his Cut, put a wet Napkin under your hat and another about your Neck, then you may Attack with your Spadroon, either the Highland Man with his Targe, or a Horse Man and his Broad Sword; a Man with his Targe will certainly attack you, and your Left-side foremost, and Receiv-

ing his Cut on your Left Arm, your Arm being well Guarded with your Coat; Raise your Arm as high as your Head; for he can Cut neither Arm nor Head; then make a very quick Thrust to his Left Eye above his Targe, he will recover his Targe to save his Left Eye, which will blind his Sight, then you have a great Opportunity to Run him through the Body or Cut at his Legs."[64]

One of the most interesting aspects of this advice is MacBane's sure statement that "he will recover his Targe to save his Left Eye". Holding the targe in the position shown by MacBane and most of the Penicuick Sketch figures already guards the left side of the head, and the Highlander would seem to have no need to "recover" the targe to do so. It is clear, however, that MacBane deliberately allows the Highlander to make the first attack, and if it is correct that Highland sword-and-targe bore a strong resemblance to I.33's sword-and-buckler, then the reason for this becomes clear.

In the I.33 style, it would be expected that, as the cut is delivered, the Highlander would bring his targe forward as well to guard his swordarm against a countercut. This movement allows MacBane to raise his spadroon hilt "as high as your Head" and, with the point forward, thrust at the foe's left eye "above his Targe", which will necessarily have dropped during the Highlander's attack. The Highlander would then have to "recover" the targe to defend against this thrust, blocking his vision, and MacBane can complete his feint and thrust or cut underneath the rising shield. The situation is thus remarkably similar to that which appears to be illustrated in the duelling scene in the Penicuick Sketches, described above (see Figure 13). If another targe is substituted for MacBane's rolled coat, then the result may well be a genuine example of a Gaelic broadsword-and-targe fencing manoeuvre.

The Book of the Club of True Highlanders

One last source must be considered, and that is a remarkable book called "Clann man gaidheal an guaillibh a cheile" or "The Book Of The Club Of True Highlanders", a remarkable piece of work published in 1881. The Society of True Highlanders was a club of Victorian-era Highland enthusiasts who aimed to support the

"Dress, Language, Music and Characteristics of our illustrious and ancient race in the Highlands and Isles of Scotland,"[65] to which end they organised hunts, Gothic theatricals, balls, shinty matches and Highland Games at which cows were killed with a hammer, torn to pieces and barbecued. The book contains sometimes fascinating, sometimes completely spurious accounts of Gaelic culture, and although the excesses of Victorian antiquarianism can always be criticised, this volume also contains some extraordinary and beautiful sketches of Highland weapons and armour, and of Highland swordsmen.

Firstly are the four wards depicted for the two-handed Highland sword, commonly known as the "claymore" (see Figure 15). Two pairs of helmeted Highlanders are shown in Johannes Lecküchner's four basic positions of the Ochs, Alber, Pflug, and vom Tag.[66] The drawings in this case are credited to "La Noble Science de Jouers d'espee" ("The Noble Science of Swordplay"), a French manual from 1538 which is also mentioned by Logan,[67] and which Sydney Anglo has identified this as a French copy of Andre Pauernfeindt's fechtbuch from 1516.[68]

Figure 15. *Wards for the claymore from "The Book Of The Club Of True Highlanders", namely vom Tag, Pflug, Alber and Ochs.*

It is of course highly unlikely this manual was the sole source for Scottish swordsmanship - two handed swords are regularly depicted on West Highland graveslabs dating from a century earlier[69], indicating the weapon was widespread long before the arrival of Pauernfeindt's instructions on how to use it, and of course William Wallace was wielding his famous brand with considerable success before Lecküchner was even born.[70]

It must also be remembered that during the 15th century Scottish involvement in the wars in France reached it's peak; between 1419 and 1424 around 15,000 Scots fought in the French armies, from 1425 and 1440 the Scots represented between 10% and 20% of the total French forces, while the Lord of the Isles himself led a division of Islesmen at Poitiers.[71] It is therefore certain that Scottish swordsmen were fully familiar with the Continental traditions, and probably contributed to them as well as drawing from them.

"The Book Of The Club Of True Highlanders" also contains some equally exciting sword-and-buckler pictures. The similarity between the 13th century German sword-and-buckler manual "I.33" and the Jacobite-era Highland wards has been noted above, and this link is strengthened by the "True

Figure 16. *Sword-and-buckler figures from "The Book Of The Club Of True Highlanders'. Their relationship with actual Highlanders is unknown, but presumably they were chosen for inclusion for a reason.*

Highlanders", which contains several pictures copied from a manuscript "formerly belonging to Queen of Edward the 4th."[72] One scene shows two figures in stances very reminiscent of I.33, in Zornhut and Low Longpoint, with the swordhand covered by the buckler. Another purports to show a "sword dance", with a figure in I.33's Half-Shield facing one in Silver's True Gardant,[73] accompanied by a piper (see Figure 16). One can only presume the True Highlanders chose to use this particular manuscript because it had some Celtic or Scottish connection, a view which is supported by the presence of the piper.

The original manuscript is believed to be in the British Library, but at the time of writing it has not yet been located.[74] Edward IV, who reigned from 1461-71, was notable for the treaty of Wesminster-Ardtornish, in which he conspired with John of the Isles and the Lowland Douglas clan to divide Scotland between them[75], and it is entirely possible the original came from one of these sources, perhaps as a gift.

Conclusion

The Penicuick Sketches and other iconographic sources, although invaluable reference material, could not by any stretch be said to be enough to reconstruct the native fencing style of the Highland clansmen. They do, however, present several important facts which must be taken into account when choosing sources to work with. First of all, the medieval style of swordsmanship was certainly the basis of Gaelic technique, even in the mid-18th century. Secondly, the shields were used in different ways depending upon the enemy faced. Thirdly, the wards depicted would suggest that sources such as Silver[76] and earlier German manuals (Durer, Talhoffer, I.33, etc) should provide the basis for reconstructing native Highland swordsmanship, rather than Renaissance Italian (Marozzo, Manciolino, Agocchie) or later British military manuals (such as MacBane, Matthewson or Angelo).

A Note on the "Scottish Defence"

The author has been asked on many occasions about the so-called "Scottish defence". This phrase is supposed to have been coined by English soldiers to describe a tactic used by Highlanders during swordfights, where they would take a non-fatal hit in order to deliver a killing blow in return[77]. The author is unaware of any authentic references to this phrase, and such a practice would seem to go against the entire tradition of Western fencing, and thus appear extremely unlikely. However, the idea of the "Scottish defence" seems to be quite widespread, and there is another possible explanation for it's origin.

In the author's experience, a fencer trained in a style equivalent to that used by the 18th century British military, upon meeting "Open Ward" for the first time, is likely to misjudge the speed, distance and power of the attacks made from this ward. If the "English soldier" is standing right-foot-forward, sword held low with the point towards the enemy (Inside, Outside or Medium Guard), then as the left-foot-forward Open Ward "Highlander" passes forward with a "downright blow", the "English soldier" is quite likely to attempt one of two counters; the first is to attempt a direct stop-thrust or cut to the advancing foe before the sword falls, and the second is to extend their sword forward to parry the attack, and deliver a counterblow. The "Highlander", having committed their bodyweight into the forward pass, will in the first case either attempt to palm aside the stop-thrust or bring their descending sword down quickly onto the "English soldier's" extended sword-arm, and in the second case simply undercut the "English soldier's" forehand ward and strike his thigh. In both cases the "English soldier" is quite likely to land a hit, and the "Highlander" certainly will. In both cases, the "Highlander's" blow will be vastly more powerful.

In the situation described, the end result bears a striking resemblance to the "Scottish defence" - the Highlander goes home wounded, the Englishman goes home in a box. The regularity with which members of the Stoccata School of Defence, fighting from Open Ward, end up in such a situation when bouting with dissimilarly-trained swordsmen leads the author to believe that the "Scottish defence" may well have arisen due to the fundamental mismatch of fencing styles between the medieval-like Highlanders and post-Renaissance British soldiers.

Acknowledgements
The author would like to thank Stephen Hand for his valuable commentary and Saviolo references, Christopher Thompson for many lively and enlightening discussions, and Stuart Reid for supplying copies of the Penicuick Sketches, "out of the very goodness of his heart".

Notes

Note: *All illustrations have been redrawn from original sources by the author*

1. See for example James Michael Hill Celtic Warfare 1595-1763, 1986, Reid, Stuart, Highland Clansman 1689-1746, 1997, and David Stevenson Highland Warrior: Alasdair MacColla and the Civil Wars, 1985

2. John Clements, http://www.thehaca.com/bookreviews.htm

3. Christoph Amberger, http://www.swordhistory.com/reviews/cuttingedge.html

4. Quoted in Ken and Denise Guest, British Battles, 1996, p.190

5. Quoted in Ken and Denise Guest, British Battles, 1996, p.183

6. Thomas C Jack, History of the Highland Regiments, Highland Clans, etc, from Official and other Authentic Sources, 1887

7. Peter Berresford Ellis, The Druids, 1994

8. Stuart Reid, Highland Clansman 1689-1746, 1997

9. James Logan, The Scottish Gael, 1831

10. Thomas C Jack, History of the Highland Regiments, Highland Clans, etc, from Official and other Authentic Sources, 1887

11. Ibid.

12. Quoted in James Michael Hill Celtic Warfare 1595-1763, 1986

13. See James Logan The Scottish Gael, 1831 and John Laffin, Scotland the Brave, 1974

14. J. Wallace, Scottish Swords and Dirks: A reference guide to Scottish Edged Weapons, 1970

15. The one exception to this is the two-handed claymore, described below.

16. Thomas C Jack, History of the Highland Regiments, Highland Clans, etc, from Official and other Authentic Sources, 1887

17. Donald MacBane, The Expert Swordsman's Companion, 1728, p.77

18. Ibid.

19. Ibid

20. Quoted in Ken and Denise Guest, British Battles, 1996, p.179

21. Quoted in Ken and Denise Guest, British Battles, 1996, p.200

22. Quoted in F. Maclean, Bonnie Prince Charlie, 1988. p.137

23. J. Hill, Celtic Warfare 1595-1763, 1986

24. The Chevalier de Johnstone, A Memoir of the 'Forty-Five, 1858, p68

25. Quoted in P. Harrington, Culloden 1746: The Highland Clan's Last Charge, 1991, p.40

26. There is one possible source not yet analysed, that is Archibald MacGregor's MacGregor's Lecture on the Art of Defence, 1791. The only copy of this work the author is aware of is held in Kelvingrove Art Gallery And Museum in Glasgow, and, like the rest of their extensive fencing manual collection, has not yet been made available to researchers, despite numerous requests.

27. Sir William Hope, The Scots Fencing Master, 1687, p.159

28. Donald MacBane, The Expert Swordsman's Companion, 1728, p.77

29. Anon. Highland officer, Anti-Pugilism, or the science of defences. 1790

30. Quoted in Ken and Denise Guest, British Battles, 1996, p.179

31. Quoted in F. Maclean, Bonnie Prince Charlie, 1988. p.91

32. While a static cut with a sharp sword against a stationary target can certainly cause a considerable amount of damage (particularly if delivered with a moulinet), delivering the same cut on a forward pass, with the full body-weight behind it, will increase the power by several hundred percent. Anyone who does not believe this is invited to get a sharp sword and experiment for themselves.

33. Anon. Highland officer Anti-Pugilism, or the science of defences, 1790. LESSON VII

34. Anon. Highland officer Anti-Pugilism, or the science of defences, 1790. LESSON XVI. See also "Regimental Highland Broadsword" by the author, accompanying Anti-Pugilism through Chivalry Bookshelf (in press).

35. Donald MacBane, The Expert Swordsman's Companion, 1728, p.64

36. Quoted in Ken and Denise Guest, British Battles, 1996, p.200

37. T. Mathewson, Fencing Familiarized: or, a New Treatise on the Art of the Scotch Broadsword, 1805, p.x-xi

38. T. Mathewson, Fencing Familiarized: or, a New Treatise on the Art of the Scotch Broadsword, 1805, p.9-10. Although Mathewson does not use the word "pass", and attacks delivered in this manner would be "telegraphed" somewhat, this seems the correct interpretation. The next section reads "Doubling for the head is done in the same manner…The scholar doubles one, two, three, and guards the cut for the outside of the arm" - the "one, two, three" indicating three distinct fencing times of passing back, passing in to attack, and passing back out. It is likely that the "pass" here, especially for the initial attack, is done in the manner of the modern cross-over step, in that the feet do not change orientation during the movement - the right foot stays pointing at target (and the left remains at right angles) during the pass out and in, making it a relatively quick movement. Saviolo also does exactly this foot movement when coming up into Open Ward to cut (see page 9R of Vincentio Saviolo His Practise (1595). For a practical explanation of the passage see Stephen Hand The Practical Saviolo, Part 1, originally published in Hammerterz Forum Vol. 3, No.4 &Vol. 4, No.1 Spring/Summer 1997, although a heavily revised version is available from the author). The purpose of this movement becomes clear when comparing other British sword manuals of the same era. For example, the Highland Officer (1790) describes attacks such as;

"Your adversary being on a high inside guard, form a small half circle, turning the wrist on passing his blade, so that your hilt will be upward, and your swords edge to edge. Place your left hand on the swordarm to steady it, and drawing in your arm, bending the wrist, and raising your point, you will most likely hit the under part of his arm, and wrist"

and Godfrey (1797) claimed;

"Nothing can be safer in the Back-Sword, than lying firm to a low Inside, and waiting for the other's moving; the Moment he raises his Wrist is your Opportunity to go to it, and if you act according to that due Observation of Time, you cannot fail of meeting his Wrist."

Yet such moves are completely neutralised by Mathewson's tactic of passing back out of distance. The interpretation that the reason Mathewson slips merely as a precaution against a surprise strike to the leg cannot be correct for two reasons; firstly, a slip precedes the initial cut, and the only reason to slip at all in this case is to control distance, not to protect the leg. Secondly, the cut Mathewson then receives is not to the leg, but to the head, and again the purpose of the slip is to control distance, not to protect the leg. This is particularly clear in that the right leg is slipped "a full three feet" behind the left leg - this would be a bad thing to do against a leg cut, as it doesn't move the target area back any further (the left leg is stationary), but it does take the sword away from the target, making any parry or countercut to the opponent's sword arm impossible (the usual manner of dealing with cuts to the leg).

39. G. Silver, Brief Instructions upon my Paradoxes of Defence, (c.1605) ed. Matthey, Col. Cyril, 1898. "Strike and fly out" is Silver's oft-repeated mantra, and the cornerstone of his style eg Cap. 4 Point 14 "yf he com to encounter the Cloze & grype upon y'r bastard gardant ward, then yo Maye Crosse his blade w yo'rs unpo the lyke gardant ward also, & as he cometh in w't his feet & have gayned yo the place, yo may p'sently uncrosse & stryke him a sound blowe on y hed, & fly out instantly, wher in he cannot offend yo by reason of his lost tyme, nor defend him self upon yo uncrossing, because his space is too wyde wherby his tyme wilbe to longe in due tyme to prvent yo blowe, this may yo do safly."

40. In Saviolo's case the Master's rapier is extended directly at the Scholar's face, horizontal or near horizontal (essentially a Spanish ward). The Scholar steps forward and to the left with his right foot and then passes forward, thrusting an imbroccata in seconda inside the Master's blade, providing opposition, with the point below the Master's rapier hand, in an imbroccata "in manner of a stoccata" (See page 20 of Saviolo's His Practise, 1595. For a full explanation of the passage see Hand, S. The Practical Saviolo, Part 2, originally published in Hammerterz Forum Vol. 4, No.2 1998 although a heavily revised version is available from the author).

In comparison, in Mathewson's scenario the Infantryman has his bayonet extended at the Dragoon's belly horizontally or near horizontal. The Dragoon engages the bayonet on the outside line in a hanging ward, and as the bayonet thrusts "he will reverse his sword hand downwards" into an inside quarta, deflecting the thrust and providing opposition in the same way as Saviolo's Scholar's seconda does in the high line. Because the opposition is provided on the left of the Dragoon's blade, rather than the right, he finishes the move with a lunge rather than a pass. Otherwise, the technique is a mirror of Saviolo's, performed in the low line.

41. R. W. Chapman, (ed), "Johnson's Journey to the Western Isles of Scotland and Boswell's Journal of a Tour to the Hebrides with Samuel Johnson, LL.D." (1924), p.104

42. Ibid, p.313

43. Ibid, p.300

44. Ibid, p.313

45. The "Open Ward" is described in G. Silver, Brief Instructions upon my Paradoxes of Defence (C.1605), ed. Matthey, Col. Cyril, 1898, Cap. 3., Pt. 1. as;
"Open fyght is to Carrye yo'r hand & hylt a loft above yo'r hed, eyther w' yo'r poynt upright, or point backwards w'ch is best"

46. This ward seems unique to the Highlanders, and the author is unaware of it's appearance in any period manual. A vaguely similar ward is used by Talhoffer in conjunction with the large duelling shield, but this is more aggressive, with the sword held horizontally over the head or slightly dipped, with the point at target. There are also some similarities to the Ochs (Ox) stance of German longsword, but again the point is generally lower in this example. Some shadow of it might be seen in MacBane's "St George Guard", which he was particularly enthusiastic about, saying "it in my Opinion being the securest Guard of the Back Sword, for you do not only Defend your Face and Head, but ly in a Readiness to defende all other parts of your Body...it is the Guard that I shall Depend on" (p.62-3)

47. G. Silver, Brief Instructions upon my Paradoxes of Defence (C.1605), ed. Matthey, Col. Cyril, 1898, Cap.3 Pt. 4;
"Passata: is either to pass with the Stocata, or to carry your sword or rapier hilt by your right flank, with your point directly against your enemy's belly, with your left foot forward, extending forth your dagger forward as you do your sword, with narrow space between your sword & dagger blade, & so make your passage upon him."

48. J. Meyer, Kunst des Fechten c. 1570. This ward also appears in I.33, and is frequently illustrated in R.R. MacIan's The Clans of the Scottish Highlands (1845). MacIan's pictures, although not strictly contemporary with the Jacobite era, were painted under the careful eye of James Logan, and display a surprising great deal of detailed accuracy

49. J. L. Forgeng, (transl.) Fechtbuch I.33 draft manuscript, unpublished, F3/p.4

50. For a practical explanation of this maneuver see "Talhoffer's sword and duelling shield as a model for reconstructing Early Medieval sword and shield techniques" by Stephen Hand and the author elsewhere in this volume

51. Cheape, Hugh and Brown, "Witness to Rebellion; John

Maclean's Journal of the Forty-Five and the Penicuick Drawings" 1996

52. "Culloden: The Swords and the Sorrows", National Trust for Scotland, 1996

53. J. L. Forgeng, (transl.) "Fechtbuch I.33" draft manuscript, unpublished, p.63. Similar longsword wards appear in Germany as an early version of the vom tag/dach or oberhut ("from the roof") position (eg. see Ringeck, Sigmund, "Commentaries on Johann Liechtenauer's Fechtbuch", c.1440), and Vadi's posta di falcone and posta corona (see Philipi Vadi's "Book on the Art of Fighting with Swords" c.1487). However, in these cases the sword seems to be held to the side or the head merely to get it out of the way of the helmet, while Walpurgis' ward is cocked in order to give power to a deflective beat.

It is worth noting this is not a left-foot-forward version of the "Medium Ward"; although Angelo held his in a similar vertical position, Mathewson's variant was horizontal, and both are held with the arm fully extended, the purpose being too keep the opponent at a distance, as clearly stated by Godfrey (p.22), Wylde (p.23) and the anonymous Highland Officer (Lesson IV);

"The Medium is the Small-Sword Posture, and that alone may properly be called a Guard; which I define to be an absolute defensive Position, independent of your adversary's Motions"

"The Medium, Unicorn or Centre Guard is made thus, Extend your Arm Straight out at length, and your sword placed betwixt your Opposer's Eyes, lying true half-body, your Sword Hilt as high as your Chin, keeping it out at Arms end stiff; then if he charge you with a blow or stroke either to the in or outside, cross his Sword, which makes a perfect Guard: This Guard keeps your opposer from encroaching upon you"

"The Medium Guard Is between the inside and the outside; the thumb nail upward, so that the flat of the swords meet, both being on that guard. It is made use of when you oppose yourself in a posture of defense, before your antagonist, not knowing on what guard he means to join you. If he joins you on the outside, take care to oppose the outside; and vice versa, if he engages on the inside, oppose the inside"

54. Similar wards to these three for single sword also appear in German manuals, such as Albrecht Durer's fechtbuch c. 1520 and Paulus Hector Mair's "Opus amplissimum de arte athletica" c. 1530. The "Crook" is also illustrated in R.R. MacIan's "The Clans of the Scottish Highlands" (1845)

55. See S. Matthew Galas, "The Flower of Battle: An Introduction to Fiore dei Liberi's Sword Techniques", in Hammerterz Forum, vol. 2, #3 (1996), and Galas, S. Mat-

thew, "Kindred Spirits: The Art of the Sword in Germany and Japan", in Journal of Asian Martial Arts, vol. 6, #3, (1997). In practice this ward works very much like Silver's Passata Ward.

56. See Achille Marozzo, "Opera Nova", 1536, Antonio Manciolino, "Opera Nova", 1531, and Dall' Agocchie "Dell'Arte Di Scrimia", 1572

57. The spada da lato, literally "sword of the side" (Viggiani, 1575), was a thrust-oriented civilian sword used by the 16th century Italian masters. Although the average weight for such swords was comparable, at around 1.2kg each (although some side-swords were lighter, and some Highland broadswords exceeded this considerably - see "Wallace Collection Catalogues: European Arms and Armour: Volume II Arms", 1962) the blade profiles, balance and handling characteristics were very different. See Figure 7.

58. J. Bannerman and K Steer, "Late medieval monumental sculpture in the West Highlands", 1977

59. J. Wallace, "Scottish Swords and Dirks: A reference guide to Scottish Edged Weapons", 1970

60. D. MacBane, "The Expert Swordsman's Companion", 1728 p.60

61. For a practical explanation of the use of the shield, see "Talhoffer's sword and duelling shield as a model for reconstructing Early Medieval sword and shield techniques" by Stephen Hand and Paul Wagner and "Footwork in I.33" by Paul Wagner elsewhere in this volume

62. Quoted in P. Warner, "Famous Scottish Battles", p.118

63. D. MacBane, "The Expert Swordsman's Companion", 1728 p.66

64. D. MacBane, "The Expert Swordsman's Companion", 1728 p.60. This feint is also described in Joseph Swetnam's "The Schoole of the Noble and Worthy Science of Defence", 1617 (p.60);

"By false play a Rapier and Dagger may encounter against a Sword and Buckler, so that Rapier man be provident and carefull of making of his assault, that hee thrust not his Rapier into the others Buckler: but the false play to deceive the Buckler, is by offering a fained thrust at the face of him that hath the Buckler, and then presently put it home to his knee or thigh, as you see occasion; for he will put up his Buckler to save his face, but can not put him downe againe before you have hit him, as aforesaid"

65. C. N. MacIntyre-North, Leabhar Comunn nam Fior Ghael, (The Book of the Club of True Highlanders), Vol I, 1881

66. S. Matthew Galas, "Kindred Spirits: The Art of the Sword in Germany and Japan", in Journal of Asian Martial Arts, vol. 6, #3, (1997)

67. J. Logan, "The Scottish Gael", 1831

68. Sydney Anglo, "The Martial Arts of Renaissance Europe", 2000. The French original of "La Noble Science de Jouers d'espee" unfortunately does not contain pictures of claymore-wielding Highlanders.

69. J. Bannerman and K. Steer, "Late medieval monumental sculpture in the West Highlands", 1977

70. D. J. Gray, "William Wallace: The King's Enemy", 1991 and J. Mackay, "William Wallace", 1996

71. J. Laffin, "Scotland the Brave", 1974

72. C. N. MacIntyre-North, Leabhar Comunn nam Fior Ghael, (The Book of the Club of True Highlanders), Vol II, 1881

73. G. Silver, "Brief Instructions upon my Paradoxes of Defence" (C.1605), ed. Matthey, Col. Cyril, 1898, Cap. 3., Pt. 2.;

"Gardant fyght in gen'all is of ii sorts, y fyrst is true gardant fyght, w'ch is eyther prfyt or Imprfyt. The prfyt is to carry yo'r hand & hylt above yo'r hed w't yo'r poynt doune to wards yo'r left knee, w't yo'r sword blade somewhat neer yo'r bodye, not bearing out your poynt, but rather declynynge in a lyttle towards yo'r said knee, y't yo'r enemye crose not yo'r poynt & so hurt you, stand bolt upright in this fyght, & yf he offer to presse in then bere yo'r hed & body a lyttle backwarde."

74. The author himself has spent many hours in the British Library searching the Cotton Titus rolls for the original illustrations, without success, and would appreciate any additional information that might help track them down.

75. R. A. MacDonald, "The Kingdom of the Isles" 1996

76. It is the Author's belief that George Silver in particular is the most appropriate model, because Silver wrote specifically for the basket-hilted sword. Silver criticised the rapier's swept- hilt because it offered no protection ("such Rapiers be inconvenient and insufficient also for lack of hilt to defend the hand and head from the blow "; Silver, Paradoxes of Defence (1598), Ch.35) However, the "single hilt", as he called it, he esteemed greatly for the protection it gives the hand as well as it's offensive capability, and it's usefulness in battle conditions that sound very similar to those encountered by Highland warriors;

"The short Sword, and Sword and Dagger, are perfect good weapons, and especially in service of the Prince.

What a brave weapon is a short sharp light Sword, to carie, to draw, to be nimble withall, to strike, to cut, to thrust both strong and quicke. And what a goodly defence is a strong single hilt, when men are clustering and hurling together, especially where varietie of weapons be, in their motions to defend the hand, head, face, and bodies, from blowes, that shalbe given sometimes with Swordes, sometimes with two handed Swordes, battell Axe, Halbardes, or black Billes, and sometimes men shalbe so neare together, they shall have no space, scarce to use the blades of their Swordes belowe their wastes, then their hilts (their handes being aloft) defendeth from the blowes, their handes, armes, heads, faces and bodies: then they lay on, having the use of blowes and Gripes, by force of their armes with their hilts, strong blowes, at the head, face, armes, bodies, and shoulders, and manie times in hurling together, scope is given to turne downe their points, with violent thrusts at their faces, and bodies, by reason of the shortnesse of their blades, to the mightie annoyance, discomfort, and great destruction of their enemies. One valiant man with a Sword in his hand, will doe better service, then ten Italians, or Italianated with the Rapiers" (Silver, Paradoxes of Defence (1598), Ch.23).

The other direct connection with Silver is that Silver's "True Guardant" ward is found in only one other source, Anti-Pugilism by "a Highland Officer" (1790), where it seems to have been passed down through Scottish single-stick play from the pre-Culloden period. See "Regimental Highland Broadsword" by the author, accompanying Anti-Pugilism through Chivalry Bookshelf (in press).

77. see http://www.freedom2000net.com/userpages/bordenm/library/Articles/Non-asianfightingmethods.html, or http://www.etp.phys.tue.nl/bertus/schermen/types.htm

BIBLIOGRAPHY

Anglo, Sydney The martial arts of Renaissance Europe (Yale Univ. Pr. 2000)

Bannerman, J. and Steer, K. Late medieval monumental sculpture in the West Highlands (Edinburgh 1977)

Brown, I.A. and Cheape, H. Witness to Rebellion; John Maclean's Journal of the Forty-Five and the Penicuick Drawings (East Linton 1996)

Culloden: The Swords and the Sorrows, National Trust for Scotland, (Glasgow 1996)

Chapman, R. W. (ed), Johnson's Journey to the Western Isles of Scotland and Boswell's Journal of a Tour to the Hebrides with Samuel Johnson, LL.D (London, 1924)

Dall' Agocchie, Giovanni, Dell'Arte Di Scrimia (1572)

Durer, Albrecht Fechtbuch (c.1520)

Elcho, David, Lord, A Short Account of the Affairs of Scotland in the Years 1744, 1745, and 1746, (Edinburgh 1907)

Ellis, Peter Berresford, The Druids, (London 1994)

Forgeng, Jeffery L. (transl.) Fechtbuch I.33 draft manuscript, unpublished. (1998)

Galas, S. Matthew, The Flower of Battle: An Introduction

to Fiore dei Liberi's Sword Techniques, in Hammerterz Forum, vol. 2, #3 (1996)

Galas, S. Matthew, Kindred Spirits: The Art of the Sword in Germany and Japan, in Journal of Asian Martial Arts, vol. 6, #3, (1997)

Godfrey, John, A Treatise Upon the Useful Science of Defence, (London 1797)

Gray, D. J. William Wallace: The King's Enemy, (London 1991)

Guest, Ken and Denise, British Battles, (London 1996)

Hand, S. The Practical Saviolo, Part 2, in Hammerterz Forum Vol. 4, No.2 (1998)

Harrington, Peter, Culloden 1746: The Highland Clan's Last Charge, (Oxford 1991)

Hayes-McCoy, G. A. Scots Mercenary Forces in Ireland 1565-1603, (Dublin and London 1937)

Highland Officer, "Anti-Pugilism, or the science of defence exemplified in short and easy lessons, for the practice of the Broad Sword and Single Stick", (London 1790)

Hill, James Michael Celtic Warfare 1595-1763, (London 1986)

Hope, Sir William, The Scots Fencing Master (1687)

Jack, Thomas C, History of the Highland Regiments, Highland Clans, etc, from Official and other Authentic Sources, 1887

Johnstone, the Chevalier de, A Memoir of the 'Forty-Five, (London 1858)

Laffin, John, Scotland the Brave, (London 1974)

Logan, James The Scottish Gael, (London 1831)

MacBane, Donald, The Expert Swordsman's Companion, 1728

MacDonald, R Andrew The Kingdom of the Isles, (East Linton 1996)

MacIan, R.R. "The Clans of the Scottish Highlands", 1845

McIntyre North, C.N. "Clann man gaidheal an guaillibh a cheile" ("The Book Of The Club Of True Highlanders"), vol.1 and 2, 1881

Mackay, James, William Wallace, (Edinburgh 1996)

Maclean, Fitzroy, Bonnie Prince Charlie, (London 1988)

Mair, Paulus Hector, Opus amplissimum de arte athletica, (1510-1550)

Manciolino, Antonio Opera Nova, (1531)

Mathewson, Thomas, Fencing Familiarized: or, a New Treatise on the Art of the Scotch Broadsword, (London 1805).

Marozzo, Achille Opera Nova, (1536)

Meyer, Joachim Kunst des Fechten (c. 1570)

Reid, Stuart, Highland Clansman 1689-1746, (Oxford 1997)

Ringeck, Sigmund, Fechtbuch, Unpublished MS. Dresd. C487, State Library of Saxony, Dresden, Germany. (c.1440)

Saviolo, Vincentio His Practise, (1595)

Selby, John Over the Sea to Skye, (London 1973)

Silver, George, Paradoxes of Defence (London, 1599)

Silver, George, Brief Instructions upon my Paradoxes of Defence (C.1605), ed. Matthey, Col. Cyril, (London 1898)

Sloane MS. 376, (c.1600)

Stevenson, David Highland Warrior: Alasdair MacColla and the Civil Wars, (Edinburgh 1984)

Stewart, David, of Garth, Sketches of the Highlanders of Scotland, (Edinburgh 1822)

Swetnam, Joseph The Schoole of the Noble and Worthy Science of Defence, (1617)

Vadi, Filippo, De Arte Gladiatoria Dimicandi, Padua Italy (1482-1487) , codice 1324, fondo Vittorio Emanuele della Biblioteca Nazionale di Roma

Viggiani, Angelo Lo Schermo (Vinitia 1575)

"Wallace Collection Catalogues: European Arms and Armour: Volume II Arms", (London 1962)

Warner, Philip, Famous Scottish Battles, (Oxford 1995)

Wylde, Zachary The English Master of Defence, (1711)

AUTHOR BIOGRAPHIES

STEPHEN HAND

Stephen Hand was born in Tasmania, Australia in 1964 and graduated from the University of Tasmania in 1988 with first class honours in Geology. He became interested in historical fencing through his involvement in medieval and renaissance re-enactment between 1979 and 2000. Stephen also studied modern fencing between 1981 and 1987 and kendo in 1985. In 1998 Stephen and two colleagues founded the Stoccata School of Defence, a school of historical fencing in Sydney, Australia. In the last two years Stephen has been invited to attend most international western swordsmanship events, mainly teaching George Silver and Vincentio Saviolo. He is the SSI Deputy Director in charge of publications. Stephen is both an Acknowledged Instructor (in English sword and Elizabethan rapier) with the International Master at Arms Federation and a Master at Arms candidate. Stephen works as a computer game designer in Sydney, Australia where he lives with his wife and two children.

GREGORY MELE

Gregory Mele has been an ardent student of European swordsmanship for 15 years through a variety of venues, including reenactment, sport fencing, and historical fencing. In 1999, he co-founded the Chicago Swordplay Guild to create a formal salle d'armes to study historical European swordsmanship and its adjunct arts. In October of 1999, Greg organized and hosted the first Western Martial Arts Workshop as an attempt to promote these arts amongst practitioners throughout North America. Mr. Mele is the founder and Director of Swordplay Symposium International, an interdisciplinary colloquium of historical fencing instructors, arms and armor scholars, and researchers dedicated to promoting and advancing the study of Western swordsmanship and its adjunct disciplines, and with Luca Porzio is the co-author of *Arte Gladiatoria Dimicandi: The 15th Century Swordsmanship of Master Filippo Vadi.*

AUTHOR BIOGRAPHIES

JOHN CLEMENTS

John Clements has studied Medieval and Renaissance martial arts since 1980 and has researched and taught on the subject in six countries. John is director of ARMA,the Association for Renaissance Martial Arts. He is the author of the books,*Renaissance Swordsmanship: The Illustrated use of Rapiers and Cut &Thrust Swords*, and *Medieval Swordsmanship:Illustrated Techniques and Methods*, both from Paladin Press.His forthcoming work is *Historical Fencing*. He writes and teaches on the craft full time in Houston,Texas.

STEVE HICK

Stephen Hick has advanced degrees in computer science and lives near Washington DC and works as a Computer and Communications Engineer for a very large defense contractor. His serious research into the history and practice of European martial arts started in the mid 1980s.

RAMON MARTINEZ

Ramón Martínez is a teacher of classical and historical fencing. He studied classical fencing in New York City for ten years with the late Maître d'Armes Frederick Rohdes, becoming his protege. In late 1982, shortly before his death, Maître Rohdes conferred the rank of Fencing Master on Mr. Martínez. In all, Maestro Martínez has devoted over 29 years to the study and teaching of traditional fencing. He has spent years carefully and thoroughly researching historical fencing treatises in an effort to accurately reconstruct these varied styles. He is internationally known and recognized as the foremost expert on the Spanish school of rapier fencing, *La Verdadera Destreza*. Maestro Martínez is a member of the Council of Advisors of Swordplay Symposium International. He is associated with the *Federazione Italiana Scherma Antica e Storica*. He is the current president of the Association for Historical Fencing, founded to promote, preserve and revive classical and historical fencing. He is also one of the founders of the International Masters at Arms Federation and a research consultant for the American Society for Chivalric Research.

RUSSELL MITCHELL

Russ Mitchell was born in Newport, Rhode Island, USA, in 1971, and graduated from the University of Dallas with a major in History in 1994. Although always interested in martial arts, and especially historical arms and armour, he obtained his master's in History at the University of Texas at Arlington studying the relation of arms and armour to the battlefield during the campaigns of Emperor Sigismund of Luxembourg, which brought him to Central European University in Budapest, where he met his current wife, and had the good fortune to meet Prof. Csaba Hídan, who lives in Hungary afterbeing exiled from his native Transylvania by the Ceaucescu regime. Russstudied the military sabre under Professor Hídan, and teaches it on a private basis while studying Savate in north Texas.

EWART OAKESHOTT

Ewart Oakeshott was born in 1916 and graduated from the Central School of Art in London in 1936 with an Art Teachers Diploma. He served in the Royal Navy in WWII. In 1948 Mr Oakeshott founded the Arms and Armour Society. After illustrating Hilda Ellis Davidson's *The Sword in Anglo-Saxon England* and writing a number of influential papers, Mr Oakeshott wrote his first book, *The Archaeology of Weapons* in 1960. Since then Mr Oakeshott has written 13 books including *The Sword in the Age of Chivalry* in 1964, *European Weapons and Armour* in 1980, *Records of the Medieval Sword* in 1991 and *Sword in Hand* in 2001. In 1964 Mr Oakeshott was elected to a Fellowship of the Society of Antiquaries. Ewart Oakeshott lived with his wife Sybil in Cambridgeshire, England until his death on September 30th 2002.

WILLIAM E. WILSON

Mr. Wilson has been fencing for over twenty-five years, beginning under Maitre Bella in Hamilton, Ontario and continuing under Mr. Silverberg in Buffalo, New York, with additional further instruction from other masters and instructors, including Dr. Rita Ashcraft of Northern Arizona University. Mr. Wilson currently teaches classical foil, epee, and saber, and historical rapier, sidesword, longsword, and backsword to both beginning and advanced students. William Wilson is the President of the Tattershall School of Defence, a school of historical fencing, and is the advisor and coach of the fencing club at Northern Arizona University. At the AEMMA Workshop held in Toronto in October of 2000, Mr. Wilson was accepted as a master at arms candidate by the International Master at Arms Federation. In January 2002 the IMAF made Mr Wilson an Acknowledged Instructor in Italian Sidesword and Early Italian Rapier. He is also well-known as the owner of the Elizabethan fencing page, one of the oldest historical fencing Web sites on the Web and one of the first to offer online reproductions of period manuals, as well as the administrator of the rapier mailing list. He is also on the advisory board for Swordplay Symposium International and the Association of Historical Fencing. Mr. Wilson holds a Masters of the Arts from Northern Arizona University in Cultural Anthropology.

Chivalry Bookshelf

Publishers of New Works & Important Reprints

Western Martial Arts | Medieval History | Reenactment | Arms & Armour

 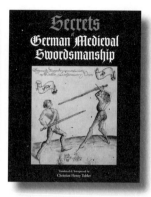  

   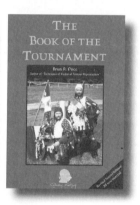

 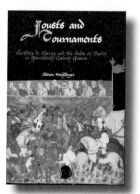 

Write for your free catalog or find us online:

http://www.chivalrybookshelf.com

3305 Mayfair Lane
Highland Village, TX 975077 USA
866.268.1495 toll free | 708.434.1251 worldwide | 978.418.4774 fax